Contents

Dedicated to all the bibliomaniacs, all of those who are never happier than when in a library or a bookshop and especially to my friend Katherine, formerly KP, who has always been the most kind and curious person and has led me to many wonderful books.

And always to Nicki.

And always to Archie.

Preface to the Paperback Edition

I am happy to say that my father really enjoyed *Bibliomaniac*. It was his favourite of the books I have written.

This book is about him because it was his passion for books that put a spell on me and led to my love of books too. It was a vital connection between us.

Sadly, he will not read my next book. He died a few months after *Bibliomaniac* was published.

The last time he left his house was to see me talking at the Chorleywood Bookshop. He sat in a comfy chair in the front row and when the owner introduced me, telling the audience that I had recently been awarded Author of the Year by the Booksellers Association, my father loudly remarked, 'I don't know why!' A typical move by him. He was proud of his children, but public displays made him embarrassed.

As my father became less mobile in his last years, I became his surrogate browser of the outside world. On tour, I'd always be seeking out books that I thought would delight him, which was always a good excuse for a phone call. The last book I delivered to him was a biography of the actor Robert Donat, whose films we watched together many times, in particular *The 39 Steps* and *Goodbye, Mr Chips*.

Returning from the Laugharne festival, another weekend of authors and book browsing with my bookseller friend Jeff, I went to stay over with my dad. The next morning, I was woken up by him calling for help. Entering his bedroom, I think he was worried he was having a heart attack. Actually, the pain in his chest was pneumonia, but we didn't know that then. I rubbed some cooling gel on his back and, when my sister returned, I popped into London for a book launch at John Sandoe Books. I am not very good at such social occasions, but this was for Sarah Bakewell, an author I admire greatly, and my dad always enjoyed stories of these literary events he could no longer take part in. Rather than return to his home after the wine and cheese straws, I went straight to Stoke Mandeville Hospital where he lay in a corridor.

In between my father's bouts of wakefulness, I read a copy of Raymond Chandler's *The Big Sleep* with a particularly vivid cover of a corpse in some orchids.* By dawn, my dad's hypnagogic dreams and his stretcher-bed reality had become confused. He told me, 'It was roast pheasant last night and I think it will be again today.' I suggested it was more likely to be an egg and cress sandwich and yoghurt.

Over the first three days, the prognosis was neither good nor bad, but he was 92 and a body at war in its tenth decade is often short of supplies. I popped down to Devon for a few days with my wife's family, but within twelve hours of arriving, I was summoned back.

For the last twenty-four hours, his consciousness had faded and so we sat around his hospital bed and read from his favourite book, *Tarka the Otter*. It was 1 April and we hoped that he might make it to the 2nd as Fool's Day as the day of death wouldn't suit him. He made it past midnight and on to lunchtime, and then the him-ness of him was gone.

The reading of books together, of *Tarka*, and *The Hobbit*,

* The cover was by Tom Adams, who also created some terrific illustrations for Agatha Christie books.

and the mid-1940s novelization of a favourite film, Powell and Pressburger's *A Matter of Life and Death*, created a sense of ritual over this last few hours. His birthday present arrived too late to be read, another 1940s novelization of a Powell and Pressburger film, *I Know Where I'm Going!*

In his last two years, he kept telling me that he had decided to stop ordering new books as he knew there just wasn't time to read the many he was surrounded by, but he was a bibliomaniac too. At least twice a week when I went to check the post, there would be a brown paper parcel for me with a new treat inside. His last purchase was *103 Not Out* from the lovely little independent publisher The Fleece Press; it's a book about the 103 Royal Mail stamps designed by David Gentleman, with an unfranked copy of every one of those stamps within its pages.

I am writing this while taking a break from sorting dad's books. It is taking time because every one must be scrutinized for things that may lie within. I pulled out a copy of a hefty historical romance in the Angélique series. I believe they were very popular in the 1950s and generally involved the eponymous young blonde woman ending up entangled with untrustworthy dukes. She was reaching higher this time – it was *Angélique and the King*. I thought it would make the charity donations pile, but when I opened it, handwritten on the first page was: 'Pam, for the best 365 days of my life so far, Nigel'. This was his first wedding anniversary, the paper anniversary, gift to my mum, and so it stays. Within two days, I had already collected 74 bookmarks and there will be many more to find, some leather ones with fading cathedrals embossed on them, occasional ones with tassels, and many cardboard page reminders from the charities he supported. There is a story in the bookmarks before we even start scanning our eyes across the books. The rituals of his death and the memories of his life are often bound, some paperback, some hardback.

When I was at Westwood Books recently, we talked of the things that fall from books. Once, they discovered that a long-forgotten bookmark inside a volume of botany was a cheque from Charles Darwin. They also received many books that had once been owned by Nicole, a young woman who died far too soon. In every book, she wrote where she bought it from, then on chapter one she wrote where she was when she began the story and on the final page where she was when it was finished, and sometimes a little precis of her experience between the pages too. How delightful that she left some of herself behind. Leave some of yourself in this book too. When you pass it on, I hope there is a bus ticket or four-leaf clover within. My friend Jeff told of how sometimes, when asked to sort through the books of avid collectors who have died, he is friends with them by the end of the process, even though he never knew the person in life.

Between the lines of *Bibliomaniac* is the story of how my father made me.

Robin Ince, July 2023

Tsundoku: An Introduction

Let's start with a battle cry, but quietly, just in case you are in the library.

I don't retreat into books, I advance out of them. I go into a bookshop with one fascination and come out with five more. I always need another book. I love their potential.

I love the moment of pulling an intriguing title from a shelf and exploring what's within, perhaps E. C. Cawte's *Ritual Animal Disguise* or Julian Symons's *The 31st of February* – 'an ugly vortex of horror at the limit of human tension'. On a perfect day I walk out of the bookshop with a canvas bag of known and unknown delights and find a tearoom, where I revel in each new purchase while tucking into a piece of Victoria sponge.

This is my holy time. Here is transcendence.

I have shaken off almost all of my other addictions, but never my insatiable desire for more and more books.

Books about William Blake.

Books about climate change.

Books about spider goats.

Books about the evolution of flight.

Books about avant-garde performance artists.

Books about Princess Margaret.*

Books about satanic transport cafés.

* Actually, I only have one book about Princess Margaret, but it is very good.

Those just happen to be the ones that have come home with me today.

In *The Nature of Happiness* Desmond Morris wrote, 'One of my great joys is going on a book-hunt. Finding a rare book I desperately want after a long search, acquiring it and carrying it home with me, is a symbolic equivalent of a hunt for prey.'

Being both a vegetarian and clumsy with a spear, I find this form of being a noble huntsman suits me. As a male who is far down the Greek alphabet when it comes to my masculinity, my delusions of warrior status when searching for a Shirley Jackson rarity ennoble me.

I have many gazelles mounted on my bookshelves. I do not buy books for their rarity or potential profit, I buy them because I want them, although there can be an extra frisson of excitement when you find you have purchased a rare bargain.

Browsing a thirty-pence bookstall, I once saw a 1921 hardback copy of *Relativity: The Special and the General Theory – A Popular Exposition* by Albert Einstein. I had a modern copy already, but I thought it would be nice to have an old edition, an artefact that enabled me to contemplate who had been in these pages before me. It was a sixth impression, so I imagined there were many copies out there and it would be worth only a couple of quid. Later I found out it could be worth more than £300. To make my thirty-pence purchase even better, inside was a 'bookmark', an old Methuen marketing ad for *The Warlord of Mars* by Edgar Rice Burroughs: 'Only the man who created TARZAN, the ape-man, could have written these amazing stories.' Book-hunting is big game.

My entire life and my career have been shaped by books and browsing. It was my delight in finding such oddities that led to me putting on a series of comedy shows where, with accordion accompaniment, I would read from gory pulp horrors, Mills & Boon classics of love with lighthouse-keepers, and lifestyle advice books such as *What Would Jesus Eat?* and *How to Marry the Man of Your Choice.*

This led on to a long-running podcast series about books and authors with my friend Josie Long, *Josie and Robin's Book Shambles*, and then to the science-book-based shows that in turn led to me making the long-running podcast series *The Infinite Monkey Cage* with Professor Brian Cox.

Books define me. They are even the reason I stopped drinking heavily. I realized that if I drank too much after a gig, the reading on the late train home was blurry and so became wasted time. In my finite existence I was missing out on comprehension due to intoxication, so I pretty much gave up.

Books are the reason that Brian Cox did not kill me when he first took me onto the moors for a harsh exercise regime together. He had already been training for three years; I hadn't swung a kettlebell in my life. On our first exercise session we took some heavy ropes and other weights. Brian looked as surprised as a physicist can, when I was still standing an hour later. I was even able to walk a little. It was as if I had compounded the physical laws of the universe and walked through two doors at once.

On the walk back I explained that, although I take no formal exercise, I walk miles on every tour I do and, as I stop in every bookshop I see, the weight that I carry increases on an hourly basis. Sometimes I have to buy books just to make sure the weight is equal on both sides. The Fyodor Dostoyevsky fitness regime.

My life is summed up by the Japanese word *Tsundoku* – allowing your home to become overrun by unread books (and still continuing to buy more).

Shelf space ran out long ago. However high and teetering the piles become, my bibliomania is unstoppable. I cannot buy only one book. It is no books or many books, though it is *never* no books. I can walk by a bookshop and my mind will tell me, 'Just keep on walking.' Then another corner of my mind says, 'Hang on, do you remember there is that one book you need for that project you are working on. Why not pop in and see if they have that *one* book and then pop straight out?' And I'm gone, like the addict I am.

Are these books useful? Perhaps most painfully, I have at least ten books about decluttering your life for a happier future, strewn around my house.

I want to know about everything, so I know about nothing.

At one stage my house became so swamped with books that I donated more than 1,000 of them to Leicester Prison* and got rid of a further 5,000 more to charities. And yet I know that my house is still overrun, always on the cusp of being justifiable grounds for a divorce.

I am sometimes asked how I read so much. I commit the cardinal sin among some bookish people: I leave books unfinished. I hop in and out of them, grabbing an anecdote, an idea or a philosophy and then putting them on the teetering 'to be continued' pile.

Whether they are useful or not, I am in love with books. I sleep with many piled on my bed and sometimes one that has gently fallen on my face, as exhaustion overcomes my ability to travel any further. In my dreams I run riot in a chaotic Borgesian library. Someone once told me that my lust for

* To any judge reading this: please show mercy on me and send me to the prison where I sent my books ahead of me.

books meant I had jumped from bibliophile to bibliosexual, but I think I prefer bibliomaniac.

I was lucky to grow up in a house filled with books. Books never meant boredom. If you think books are boring (and I presume you do not, or you wouldn't be reading this book about books, or be in a bookshop weighing up whether you want it or not), then it's my view that you simply haven't met the right book yet.

From an early age I would go with my dad to book fairs, where he would search for works by Henry Williamson, best known for *Tarka the Otter*, and Evelyn Waugh, who enjoyed depriving his children of bananas during wartime (I'll tell you more about that later). I remember seeing the Labour politician Michael Foot scouting for Byronic volumes, and once the Scottish eccentric and poet Ivor Cutler asking for rarities by Maurice Sendak, most famous for *Where the Wild Things Are* and *In the Night Kitchen.* On trips to central London with my dad I was usually the youngest child in the bookshops of Charing Cross Road and Cecil Court, looking intense in my NHS specs.

In the middle of 2021 I found myself at a loose end. I was meant to be going on tour with Professor Brian Cox, but the worries of playing arenas in a time of uncertain Covid variants meant that we decided to postpone it.

I had an idea. I had a new book coming out, *The Importance of Being Interested*, and it was a celebration of curiosity. It was a book that grew from my childhood immersion in *The How and Why Wonder Book of Time*, *The Big Activity Book of Prehistoric Mammals* and *Usborne World of the Future: Star Travel*, all of which eventually led to being able to read science books with hardly any pictures at all. I decided that I should go to where so many of my fascinations begin: the bookshop.

To fill the gap where the tour should have been, I would visit at least 100 bookshops across the United Kingdom. I swapped playing to 12,000 people in Manchester Arena for playing to twelve people in the Margate Bookshop.

Visiting all these independent shops highlighted to me exactly why the independent bookshop is such a vital part of the high street. These shops and the people who run them are the gatekeepers to stories we never knew we wanted to read; to ideas that might increase our happiness or help us deal with our sadness; to places that our mind never knew it might go. You can always have a proper conversation in a bookshop. You can skip 'Looks like the weather's on the turn' or 'Parking around here gets worse and worse' and skip straight to 'Have you read *Klara and the Sun* yet?' or 'There is a fascinating theory about self-driving cars and artificial intelligence – can you remember who's just written a book about it?'

The bookshops have found out something rather useful about me too, and that is that I am a very profitable person to have along for an event. Sure, it might mean that they sell a few more copies of *my* book, but even if they don't, they know their profits will go up because I'll go away with a caseload of other people's books. A simple afternoon-signing in Letchworth, England's first Garden City, led to me buying *The Last Cannibals* – 'she's a charmer, but she's a Cannibal'; *The Dharma Bums* – 'fighting, drinking, scorning convention, making wild love – zany antics of America's young Beats in their mad search for kicks'; and *The Furies* – 'now comes cosmic retribution – giant wasps'; as well as *Only Lovers Left Alive*, *I Can See You But You Can't See Me*, Lady Cynthia Asquith's *The Second Ghost Book* and *Devil's Peak* by Brian Ball – 'Stranded in a High Peak transport café during a freak snowstorm, Jerry Howard finds himself in a vortex of Satanism.'

I think I love books even more than I love reading. Their company means there is always the possibility of something to be discovered, waiting for me between the covers, which hasn't even entered my imagination yet. A small but pleasing change in my reality is waiting on every shelf.

I know that I have a predilection towards melancholy, social anxiety and self-loathing, and books form a great part of my prescription medication. When I say that books are my drugs, I don't mean that in a throwaway manner; they really do calm me, they really do shut off some of the voices for a while.

They really do take me out of time.

Books are not merely my escape, but an opportunity to explore the world – my chance to get the voices from the page to drown the voices in my head; the place to live in other people's dreamscapes. I am too anxious for some of the hallucinogens that my confident friends experiment with, so my trips are fuelled by turning pages.

Like most of my few friends, I am gregarious, but also antisocial, living in perpetual fear of judgement. I can spend time listening to the voices in books without worrying what those voices think of me.

This book is the story of an addiction and a romance – and of an occasional points failure, just outside Oxenholme Lake District station.

Footnote to explain any later narrative confusion

Shortly before this adventure began I had a lengthy conversation with an expert in neurodivergence who had followed my career and social-media accounts. After a three-hour conversation he told me, 'Basically, every answer you have given points very much to you being ADHD.'

This is something that audiences have been telling me for years. Regularly in the theatre bars after a show I am approached by a puzzled-looking person who says, 'My husband and I have made notes of the *seventeen stories* that you started but never finished, and we would like you to tell us the ending of at least five of them, to get some sense of closure before we leave.' Some of these stories I have no recall of at all.

I wondered what my wife would make of this diagnosis. Would it worry her? I once asked her and she said, 'That would be wonderful, because I've always thought you were bipolar.'

Anyway, the reason I tell you this is because this may be a more tangential book than you are used to. It is a story of many of the thoughts of books that crossed my mind as I crossed the UK on this rather hectic book tour. It may be chaotic, but it might make sense between the sentences.

CHAPTER 1

Out of Lockdown and into the Wicker Man

Wigtown to Laugharne

WIGTOWN
HORROR MOVIES
ALAN G FRANK
SECTION 28
children of the matrix
David Icke
LLAREGGUB
UNDER MILK WOOD
DYLAN THOMAS
LAUGHARNE
Practical Time Travel
The Famous Book Bus
Bus Llyfrau Dylans
Dylans Mobile Bookstore

I am unable to do things in moderation.

I thought it would be enjoyable to visit some independent bookshops when my book came out. 'Some' started out as half a dozen or so, then rose to twenty, was briefly fifty and then a gimlet-eyed lunatic swept his hand across the map and said with piratical glee, 'If it's gonna be fifty, it might as well be one hundred!'

After eighteen months of being rendered stationary by a virus, eighteen months in my attic, eighteen months in my head, I was now going to go *everywhere*.

I put the call out on social media: 'Are you, or do you know of, an independent bookshop that I should visit in the UK?'

I made a spreadsheet. By 'spreadsheet' I mean I grabbed a stack of Post-it notes any time I saw a reply and scribbled details haphazardly and illegibly. A lavish map of scraps and scrawls was soon a tour, and my spreadsheets were a Dadaist triumph – somehow both pointless and informative.

At 111 events, I ran out of days. I reached the point where I would have needed to manipulate spacetime to squeeze in any more destinations, and I've been warned to avoid doing that as it can have ramifications, in terms of changing the outcome of world wars and plagues.

I knew my wife would be happy to see the back of me. I have been a perpetually travelling performer, so it was perplexing for her to see me every morning during the pandemic. Eventually I grew a beard, so that at least she could think I was someone else.

If you travel, you probably know that the further you are from home, the more you are loved by those you've left behind. The distance erases your imperfections. I made a graph (in my head).

When I was in Wellington, New Zealand, I was longed for.

When I was in Boston, USA, I was missed.

When I was in Aberdeen, Scotland, I was asked how much longer I would be away.

When I was in Croydon, south London, I could hear the horror at my physical self returning. 'Oh my God, he'll be back in two hours, treading things into the carpet and moving the magazines!'

No one has been more loved than Neil Armstrong on 20 July 1969. 'Oh, Neil, you're so far away, I love you even further than to the Moon and back.' Two weeks later… 'I see that *someone* has left moondust all over the sofa.'

Before the bookshop tour, I had two festivals to warm up at.

First I would walk in the footsteps of Sergeant Howie, the doomed, virginal policeman sacrificed on a pagan island in hope of fruitfulness. I was off to Wigtown, Scotland's book town, situated in the countryside where the original 1973 *The Wicker Man* was filmed.

I became fascinated by this film when I was eight years old because of Alan Frank's *Horror Movies*. This was my first truly favourite book – a book of almost biblical importance to me. If there had been any 'favourite' book before then, it would have been Hamlyn's *Children's Bible in Colour*. I still fondly remember the violent illustrations of Abimelech being killed by a millstone dropped on his head and Absalom hanging in a tree branch.

The gore of horror-film books were only a small step forward from what The Bible had prepared me for. I used my birthday money to purchase *Horror Movies* and I would pore over the photographs and create feature films in my head from single shots of ravenous vampires – 'Christopher Lee begins to feed' – or cryogenically frozen Nazis – 'Nazis on ice!' *The Wicker Man* was represented by a single colour photograph of Edward Woodward horizontally viewing a hand of glory, the fingers fashioned into lit candles: 'Left: Edward Woodward surveys his "bedside lamp" with horror in *The Wicker Man* (British Lion 1973).'

This book was educational in many ways, as it was how I learnt my left from my right. I knew my monsters before I knew which hand was which, so when the pages said, 'Right: Karloff meets his mate in *Bride of Frankenstein*', and 'Left: Michael Hordern stakes a burning cross through Baron Zorn's heart', I began to get the hang of directional instructions.

Wigtown

Wigtown is Scotland's answer to Hay-on-Wye. Like Hay-on-Wye, it has many bookshops; also like Hay-on-Wye, it is some distance from a railway station. This means that you never know which author you might be sharing a lengthy car journey with. Last time I went it was with the former Conservative politician Kenneth Baker, one of Maggie Thatcher's Cabinet, and famously represented on *Spitting Image* by a rubbery puppet of a slimy slug. The journey was perfectly fine, but my head kept reminding me that this pleasant old man was someone I had once marched against on the streets of London. I recalled the despicable Clause 28 brought in by Baker's sneeringly homophobic government – a piece of legislation aimed at preventing the 'promotion of homosexuality in schools', which really meant the mentioning of homosexuality in schools. The propaganda would have been hilarious, had it not been so dehumanizing.

One of my most-prized second-hand book finds over the years is *Jenny Lives with Eric and Martin*. Kenneth Baker condemned it, perhaps as part of what he declared was 'grossly offensive homosexual propaganda' that was placed in libraries by 'left-wing authorities'.[1] *Jenny Lives with Eric and Martin* was centre-stage in the media's stirring-up in the 1980s of a homosexual panic that had been elevated by the AIDS crisis. It was ugly, brutal and degrading. It was also preposterous and infantile. *The Sun* bellowed, 'VILE BOOK IN SCHOOLS' of *Jenny Lives with Eric and Martin*. First, it wasn't available in schools – there was one copy in the Inner London Education Authority's library; and second, this was no Marquis de Sade. The book is about Jenny's dad, and his male partner, looking after her. Sordid pictures include a man with clothes pegs in his mouth hanging out the washing; the three of them licking ice-lollies; and Jenny sitting in a go-kart. At the back of the book is a charmingly simple cartoon with three stick-people.

In the book Fred tells Bill that he loves him. A woman with a handbag and hat overhears them talking about moving in together. She is all exclamation marks: 'Oh no! What is this! Two men cannot live together! It is very wrong!' She explains that her husband would never kiss another man. Fortuitously, at that moment her pipe-smoking partner appears.

'Now that is not quite right, dear. When I was young I was in love with a man and we lived together. But then I met you and it was you I loved most. And you loved me most. So we moved in together and got married.' He explains that it can never be wrong to live with someone you are fond of, and she agrees and they all happily wave bye-bye to each other.

If only it was always that easy.

To get to Wigtown, I first had to get from London to Dumfries. After months of solitude, a return to the rails was daunting. I decided I would spend most of the journeys-to-come in the vestibule, away from any mask-less hacking coughers. Even in plague-free days, I am a vestibule kind of guy.

The vestibule smelt far less of salt-and-vinegar crisps and broken wind than the main carriage. Standing for the three hours to Carlisle, I consoled myself by finding a very relevant article by an evolutionary biologist about how the invention of the chair was detrimental to our spines.* Somewhere north of Preston, the train cleaner came to empty the overflowing bin. He was a little older than me and looked like the kind of person who'd been in a post-punk band for a while, which it turns out he was, although they never got signed. As he grappled with the overstuffed bin, bruised grapes rolled out like a scabby victory from a fruit machine. He swore at each slippery juice-bauble and turned to me: 'Come the revolution...'

By this point I was reading *Getting the Joke* by Oliver Double and, by coincidence or synchronicity, I had reached a

* Apparently the chair promotes such an unnatural posture that not only do you end up with weak knees and inflexible legs, but also with a curved spine and other posture problems, such as lower-back pain, neck and shoulder pain and tight hips.

passage about Bertolt Brecht's 'Red Grape' theatre group. Here were grapes and revolutions on the page and in the air, and on the floor of the vestibule. I mentioned this to the cleaner and at first he looked understandably puzzled. This is a familiar reaction. I've come to realize, over many years, that my opening conversational gambits have a habit of being peculiar.

Then, however, rather than him running away screaming, the conversation broke into talk about bands like the Lotus Eaters, The Redskins and Billy Bragg as well as the joy of going to a record shop on Saturdays and hoping you had enough money to buy an album. The cleaner looked as if he was having a pretty shitty day, but after our five minutes of early 1980s nostalgia, taking himself back to his own post-punk band days, he went away whistling 'The First Picture of You' (the Lotus Eaters' number-fifteen hit of 1983). I was happier too. You get a better class of conversation in the vestibule. Thanks to my nose being in a book, we could talk.

There were no former Education Secretaries on the way to Wigtown this time. The journey would be with the chemist and author Kathryn Harkup. Fortunately I had recently given her publisher a positive quote for her book about the elements: 'Brimful of captivating stories and revelations'. I find giving quotes for books tricky. You need to be brief, but not trite. Sometimes you will smugly compose a two-line triumph of concise and informative wit, but when the book comes out, you'll see that you have been reduced to 'a triumph' or 'great read' or 'eloquent crab murders'.

I have attempted to dissuade people from asking for quotes, by explaining that if my name on a book sold lots of books, then the books written by me would sell a lot more, but then I realize they have already had dozens of knock-backs from reputable people and I am merely the last resort. (Who did I manage to persuade to blurb me on the back of this? Did it persuade you?)

Wigtown is quiet when we arrive, the day's bibliophiles having departed for the day. My evening reading is *Wicker Man*-related. When I can, I try to attach a local flavour to my reading events. *Ritual* was a novel written by David Pinner, published in 1967, and was supposedly the inspiration for the film, although there is some debate on how much of an influence *Ritual* truly was.

I open the book to a page where the policeman is being tempted by a naked woman in the room next door – a bit like the scene from the film where Britt Ekland (and her body-double for all the shots of her bottom) attempts to tempt Sergeant Howie. 'The left breast was fractionally larger than its sister. It was Anna's favourite. She flexed it towards the wall.'

There are definitely differences; for instance, Edward Woodward doesn't end up licking the wallpaper. 'With disgust, David realized he was licking faded dancer off the wallpaper. The dancer was painted yellow and purple. That is, before the licking began.'

Fortunately, there is only silence from the occupant of the room next door to me, and my flock wallpaper remains unlicked.

I am up early to browse. I don't want anyone getting first to a treat that I deserve.

In bookshops I suspiciously eye other customers, profiling them in case I think they may be after the same goodies as me, wondering if they have deliberately put the best books back in the shelves the wrong way round, so that I'll miss them. There are some shrewd movers among the browsers.

In every town I visit, I have the pointless mental talent of being able to remember all the books I have bought there before – a very niche mystery memory act.

Today I recall from Wigtown the annoyingly oversized book I once bought that didn't fit into any form of carrier bag, so I had to drag it around, like a book-lover with a Sisyphus curse. It was called *The Home Planet* and was full of beautiful images of Earth taken from space, with comments from astronauts. I had never seen it before, yet now I notice it in bookshops almost daily.

I also bought the considerably lighter *Reed All About Me*, the autobiography of the famously boozy, pugilistic actor Oliver Reed. On the front cover he simmers in a promotional shot from *The Three Musketeers*. On the back cover he stands in denim with his hand thrust down his trousers. I am not sure if the front and back are meant to be some kind of visual pun on him being a swordsman of two kinds, but I imagine I am putting more thought into it than the fast-buck publisher Hodder & Stoughton did in 1981. 'I was covered in custard and bleeding badly from a rather large cut in my mouth' gives you the broad gist of the style of his anecdotes, as does 'Some of the nuns got carried away.'

I start my morning on this trip in The Bookshop, Scotland's largest bookshop. It is a whole house turned into one. It reminds me of the sadly-no-more Cottage Bookshop in Penn, an inspiration for Terry Pratchett's 'L-space' in the *Discworld* series. The Cottage Bookshop was one of the bookshops that shaped my youth, with its tightly packed shelves placed closely together – a cricked neck guaranteed – and some irresistible prices. It was here that I bought vintage James Bond annuals (not so vintage then), books on the mysteries of the world by Colin Wilson, and many

Perry Rhodan science-fiction books, all of which remained unread, but looked lovely on my prepubescent science-fiction shelf.

The owner used to have an attic room where he kept his priciest books (not his mad first wife): £5 and over. I would sometimes accompany my dad into this fabled world and the door would be locked behind you. Eventually the owner stopped opening up the attic of his precious things, as apparently some browsers had been urinating in his vases when their cries for release were unheard.

The Bookshop of Wigtown is an even more dangerous place during the festival as it also doubles as the green room, where performers and their entourage hang out before and after events. You get drunk and then you are allowed to browse. The first time I visited the Wigtown Book Festival I woke up the next morning with far too many books by David Icke about the reptilian takeover of humanity.

Opening *Children of the Matrix*, I was fascinated to see the name Schopenhauer spelt incorrectly in three ways on the first page. A bad start; or a good one for readers who believe the Illuminati have controlled the spelling of philosophers' names for too long.

I also found a far more intriguing book on that drunken browse: *Lewd; The Inquisition of Seth and Carolyn* – 'Being a real and true account of the assertion of the people's ancient and just liberties in the trial of Seth Many and Carolyn Peck against the most arbitrary procedure of the court and its minions'. It is the story of a small commune in 1970 that was committed to the 'usness' of being. This 'usness' included naked events, and it was at this point that the authoritarians of America got involved. The book is a lengthy transcription of the court proceedings.

Q: What did you see about me? Would you describe the 'me' that you saw?'
A: You with no clothes on.
Q: Well, what parts of me did you see that made you feel that you should arrest me?
A: You with no clothes on.

Most of the proceedings move on in this way, describing the horror at witnessing the naked bodies of skinny hippies. This is typical of a certain kind of book that I buy, and of the alibis that I then make up for the necessity of having that book. First, I should make it clear that it is not the descriptions of nudity that draw me to such books, but rather that they describe something or someone so bizarre, unusual or unheard of that I imagine that one day it might be a loss-leader for a show I will put on, perhaps about odd trials, or the counter-culture, or men with beards in bad Y-fronts. My shelves are packed with books that could form the basis for a show, or at least part of one. Every arcane title is an event waiting to happen.

When I get to the cashier and I see the mounting sums I am about to pay, I tot up in my head how many minutes onstage the book will need to appear in order to make its money back. Say I am doing a gig for £500 for forty minutes. That's £12.50 a minute and so, technically, a book like *Lewd* (£6.50) has paid for itself if I read from it for thirty-two seconds. I would be rolling in it if I used it onstage for more than three minutes. Five years after buying it, it is still at zero minutes, but we'll see.

Another example of such a book might be *Dreams About HM The Queen (and Other Members of the Royal Family)* by Brian Masters. This was £18, but it turned a profit after just one gig in Trowbridge. Brian collected other people's dreams of the royal family, such as drinking sherry with the Queen when a man in a straw boater comes in with a bunch of bright new yellow pencils and declares himself the Keeper of the Queen's Pencils; Princess Margaret removing biscuits from a digestive-delivering bicycle; a member of the Royal Ballet deciding to go to Mars for the Queen, because the Americans and Russians are hogging all the limelight. My favourite is probably the Queen Mother showing off about all the jam she has made, but continually dropping the jars, much to her consternation.

No nudity, reptilian or human, at The Bookshop today. My favourite purchase is a collection of photographs of the actor, dancer and choreographer Robert Helpmann (including one of him posing as Margaret Rutherford). I am a great admirer of Helpmann. For my generation he is probably best known as the Child Catcher in *Chitty Chitty Bang Bang*, but he was the most dynamic human, laden with chutzpah. He toured solo ballet shows across the mining towns of Australia, starred in Powell and Pressburger's *The Red Shoes*, and was a fabulous wit. Famously, he played Oberon in a touring production of *A Midsummer Night's Dream* that performed at a sports arena one night. His dressing room was a cricket umpire's room. When Helpmann was given his half-hour call the stage manager heard no reply, so he entered the umpire's room to see Helpmann standing on a chair that was stood on a table, with him balancing atop, holding a mirror by the one naked light bulb in the room and applying his intricate black-and-gold eye make-up. The stage manager asked if he was all right. 'Yes, I'm fine,' Helpmann replied, 'but God knows how these umpires manage.'

I also bought Parker Tyler's *The Three Faces of the Film* because of its chapters on 'The Dream Amerika of Kafka and Chaplin' and 'Reality Into Dream Into Myth Into Charade Into Dollars', which contains the phrase 'a quasi-Pirandellian brand of illusionist realism', which I aim to prise into conversations on a twice-weekly basis.

To keep my browsing eyes sharp, I gave them a rest and took a walk under the sky in between rain showers, and found the graves of the Wigtown Martyrs – two women, Margaret Maclauchlan and Margaret Wilson, who were murdered by dragoons during a period known as 'the Killing Time', a conflict between Presbyterian Covenanters and King Charles II and James II. A bookshop with a proximity to an interesting graveyard is a fine combination.

Eyes restored, I bought *A Dictionary of Symptoms* from The Book Corner. This will be invaluable for identifying the differences between fistula and papillomata, water brash and dyspepsia. There is something for all my hypochondria needs, and the yellowing pages of a 1970s manual, with a vague aroma of roll-ups, seems so much more trustworthy than the internet. Every vague rash can now be my imminent Armageddon.

Having been almost parsimonious in my book purchases, it all collapsed at the last minute when I visited Well-Read Books of Wigtown. This was my downfall, my predestined sciatica. It is a beautifully curated shop, and the first hints of books on witchcraft created the sulphurous smell of trouble. The book of spell-casting cast its spell.

Before I knew it, I had found Stanislav Grof's *Books of the Dead: Manuals for Living and Dying*, and next to that was a book about *The Tree of Life*. The shop is run by a former QC. Unfortunately, when I got to the till I said, 'I don't suppose you have any more in this series?' and a vast pile thudded onto the counter.

I bought one on Robert Fludd and *Earth Magic* by John Michell (author of *The View Over Atlantis*). I decided I didn't need any more and had a cup of tea and a cake. But that gave me time to think and made me realize that I did need some more, goddammit! What do they put in those cakes? Or was it the tea?

For my book event that evening I was interviewed by Lee Randall, an expert inquisitor. The last time she interviewed me in Wigtown something peculiar happened. In my book *I'm a Joke and So Are You* I had written about a car crash that I was in shortly before my third birthday. My mother was severely injured. Being nearly three, I thought I must have caused it. Lee asked me about the accident, and some long-hidden emotion – muffled and kept under wraps for decades by an intense Englishness – suddenly made itself known and I burst into tears live onstage. I don't think Lee had ever experienced such a spectacle before. I regained my composure quite quickly, but my mind, with a maturity that was rare for it, said to me, 'Don't get out of this with a joke. Don't make fun of this. It was real, and turning it into shtick belittles what just happened.' Then we moved on.

This time, though, we talked about spaceflight and the block universe, and there were no deeply hidden emotions to take me, or Lee, by surprise. At the signing table I sat behind Perspex while people in masks told me their names and I said, 'Sorry, Corinna?... Colin?... Coriolanus?... Ah, Kenny... NO! Kerry.' The dedications with the most crossing-outs are worth the most: honest.

Laugharne

I sneak my Wigtown book bags back into the house while my wife is at work – nothing to see here. In the past I have nipped home with some bags of books, only to find that she'd come back early and so I had to secrete them under the shed. I'd come in empty-handed and whistling, a jaunty tune being the clear signifier of a terrible 'five hardbacks, a large-format art book and seven Penguin Modern Classics' guilt.

I am out of the door again for the journey to Laugharne before my presence is noted. She'll simply think the books have been breeding again.

Laugharne is one of my favourite festival destinations. If you have read *Under Milk Wood* you'll know that this is where Dylan Thomas built Llareggub. It is a festival of fascinating people, just far enough away from London that the more pompous elements of media society cannot be bothered or don't know it exists. Its isolation serves to weed out the incurious who, at the first mention of changing trains at Swansea, remember they are doing something terribly exciting in the Cotswolds that weekend.

It's the Brigadoon of arts festivals. Guests have included Patti Smith, Ray Davies, Peggy Seeger, Linton Kwesi Johnson and Jackie Morris. On one visit I spent the night having a fireside chat with the artist Peter Blake about our shared love of masked wrestlers. The air smelt of toasted marshmallows as he told me stories about Kendo Nagasaki. Memories like these can jolt me out any melancholia.

When I contemplate the mercurial rise of some with whom I have shared stages, and who now spend their days wondering which helicopter will go best with their loafers,

I remind myself that my strange career has led to moments when I've talked to world-famous artists about piledrivers.*

Laugharne is also temporary home to one of my favourite bookshops, Dylans, a mobile library turned into a mobile bookshop by Jeff Towns, passionate bookseller and collector for more than fifty years. He is a man full of tales and knowledge, and what he doesn't know about Kendo Nagasaki, he makes up for with stories about Ted Hughes and Oliver Sacks.

The day before the festival some of us gather together for a meal. I am seated opposite the poet and hugely successful TV producer, Henry Normal. I have recently taken to performing poetry, and Henry has recently returned to being a full-time poet. It seems that we were both struck by the same poet in our youth: not Keats or Yeats or Rossetti, but Spike Milligan, particularly his *Small Dreams of a Scorpion*, a thin volume of his more serious thoughts on human folly.

The forecast for the weekend is perpetual rain. This is a perfect location for couples in lovingly maintained Citroën 2CVs to pull over in the hope of a walk, but then get no further than looking at the view through the windscreen wipers. They will sip from a Thermos of oxtail soup, brushing fallen pickle off their sou'westers. This morning, though, it is sunny and I take the opportunity to go on the Dylan Thomas birthday walk. As I walk up the hill, I meet Henry coming down. We are both walking with pencils in hand. Further up, I divert from the birthday walk and take an overgrown path where the blackberry-pickers don't go. The berries are many

* The piledriver is the move where a wrestler grabs their opponent, swings them upside down, then rapidly sits down, pummelling their head into the canvas.

and are either dried up or mushy and mouldy, so I think of Seamus Heaney and his blackberry-picking.

But when the bath was filled we found a fur,
A rat-grey fungus, glutting on our cache.
The juice was stinking too. Once off the bush
The fruit fermented, the sweet flesh would turn sour.

By the time I had finished mourning the blackberries, Jeff had set up his bookstall. Sadly, Dylans book bus is no more. It had been barely clinging on to its MOT for some years, and 2020 saw it fail for the final time. It should be buried like an elephant, and all of the book buses should make pilgrimages to see the final lending graveyard.

I walk away from his shelves with a handful of good, hard science – *Flying Saucers and Commonsense* and a 1936 volume from the Occult Book Society on *Practical Time Travel*. Hopefully I will tell you more about practical time travel last week. My Ufologist friend Dallas Campbell is particularly envious of my copy of *Flying Saucers and Commonsense*, as all subsequent reprints became *Flying Saucers and Common Sense* (you see, you thought it was *my* typo, not theirs). I rarely read the UFO books I buy, but I can never resist them. I am still connected to them by ethereal ectoplasm, due to my love of *Arthur C. Clarke's Mysterious World* and *The Unexplained* magazines of my childhood. *Our Mysterious Spaceship Moon* is yet another madeleine-cake in my life.

The Saturday is a five-gig day: three interviews with authors, one solo show about my latest book, and a comedy set above a pub to finish it all.

The day begins in church. There are many vicars on my family tree, but godlessness means that I missed the ecclesiastical calling. Today I get the opportunity to lean on a font and proselytize. What I do not know at the time is that Julie Christie is in the audience – to some people, a religious icon in herself, as well as the star of a movie with the most grotesque church murder I can think of, *Don't Look Now.**

Today's church service was with Christie Watson, nurse, novelist and professor. It was an interview that had been thrown at me at the last minute. I hurriedly read her book, *The Language of Kindness: A Nurse's Story,* but when I met her she said, 'Oh, let's not talk about that, let's just start talking and see what happens', and we did.

Julie Christie enjoyed it and that's the main thing.

After my solo talk that evening, I saw Richard, the festival promoter, standing with a smile broader than any I have ever seen on his face previously. I bounded up to him, only to discover that his wide smile was for the benefit of a camera – he was being photographed next to Julie Christie. It was the first time I had ever seen him star-struck, but that was a pity, because in the photo from the evening, of him and Julie Christie, Julie was obscured by an ebullient man in a duffel coat. If only my coat had been red.

Facing the end of the working day, I thought, 'What would Dylan Thomas do?', so I went to the pub. At 1.30 a.m. I still had the vague hint of sobriety, or at least the delusion

* During lockdown I spent a few months living with my dad and I discovered that age does not matter when it comes to embarrassment. He might be ninety-one and I might be fifty-two, but sitting with a parent watching the lengthy sex scene between Julie Christie and Donald Sutherland remains as excruciating as it was when I was fourteen years old. Fortunately, I had to deal with some urgent emails. I am sure this would have not been an issue, had I been born French.

of sobriety, and I walked under the clear sky, staring at the stars. The longer I stared at the stars, the more of them came into view, but long though I stared, I saw no hints of UFOs – only of photons of light that had travelled vast distances, unimpeded until I got in their way, and that was good enough for me.

CHAPTER 2

It All Began at the End of the World

Chorleywood to Bristol

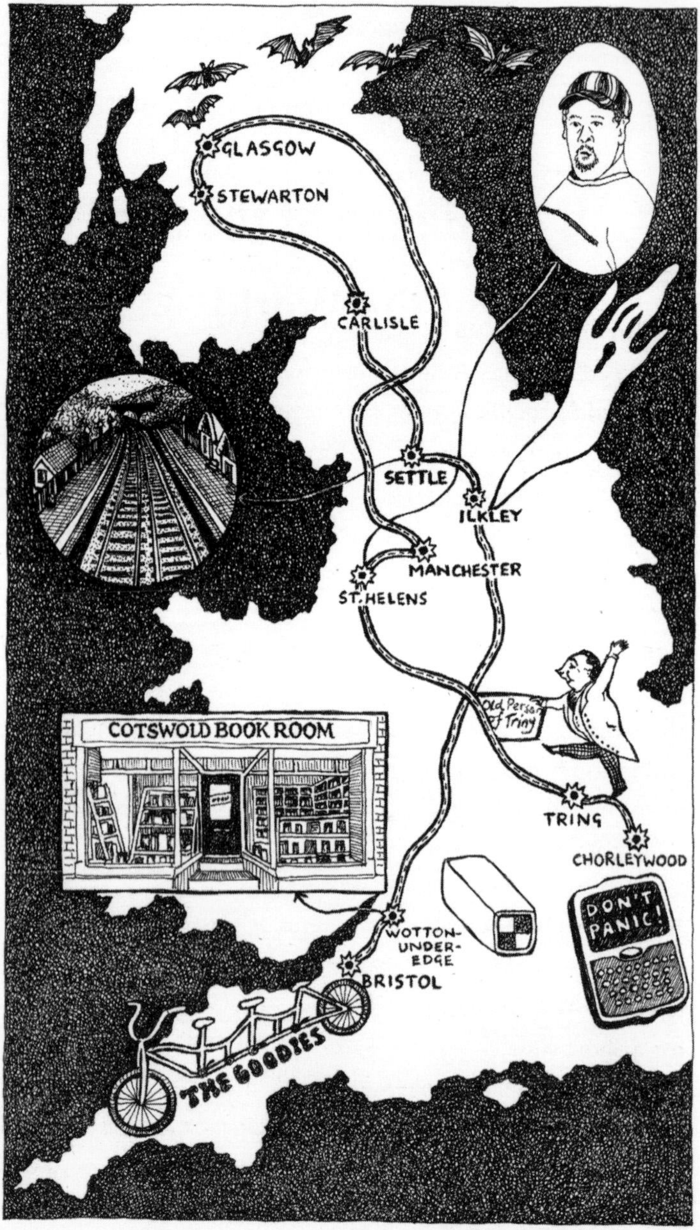

GLASGOW
STEWARTON
CARLISLE
SETTLE
ILKLEY
MANCHESTER
ST. HELENS
Old Person of Tring
COTSWOLD BOOK ROOM
TRING
CHORLEYWOOD
WOTTON-UNDER-EDGE
BRISTOL
DON'T PANIC!
THE GOODIES

For an eleven-year-old it would have been thrilling to read Douglas Adams's novelization of *The Hitchhiker's Guide to the Galaxy* whatever the circumstances, but the excitement was doubled when Rickmansworth, the next-door town to where I lived, appeared in the first paragraph. I was one step closer to being on the science-fiction map, and all because of a girl in a café in Rickmansworth who, 'nearly two thousand years after one man had been nailed to a tree for saying how great it would be to be nice to people for a change', realizes where it has all gone wrong and how the world could be blissful for all; but, sadly, she times this revelation moments before the Earth is demolished to make way for cosmic progress.

Rickmansworth was the place where I went to buy Blondie singles at WHSmith and see *Watership Down* in the arts centre, and now here it was, *in a brilliant book*. It probably remains the greatest claim to fame for the town, closely followed by Wham!'s Andrew Ridgeley owning a wine bar there for a short time.

The first official bookshop visit on my tour is just one short Tube stop from Rickmansworth. Chorleywood Bookshop is the bookshop of my childhood. It was here that I pored over the *Star Trek* fotonovels, but never had the £1.25 needed to make one my own. It was here that I leafed through Target Books' *Doctor Who* novelizations. I still have *Doctor Who: The Deadly Assassin* in the bookshelf by my bed: 'The Master's bloodless lips drew back in a smile of hatred. The body, as well as the mind, could be attacked. If The Master's plan worked, the struggle within the Matrix would soon be ended – by the Doctor's death.'

The importance of *Doctor Who* in the 1970s and 1980s for lonely children like myself cannot be underestimated. The Doctor's heroics were something to cling on to as you walked with fear across the school hall with your lunch tray, wondering where you could sit without torment.

Later, this was the bookshop where I would bring money that I had 'borrowed' from my mother's purse to feed my *Mayflower Book of Black Magic Stories* habit, each cover decorated with a skull in stages of decomposition or reanimation – a skull that would sometimes cry out to me at night: 'GUILTY!' I have only ever stolen money to feed my hunger for books.

There were *Pan Books of Horror Stories* too, the covers with silhouettes of rotting ghouls, dozy-looking bats, sneaky wolfmen and snail- or worm-infested mouths. '"Help!" He swallowed a snail. Choking, he widened his mouth for air and felt a snail crawl over his lips and onto his tongue. He was in hell!' There's not much horror in bookshops these days; you need to find specialist shops for snail death and cannibalism today.

Chorleywood is the ceremonial starting line. I am returning to do a proper event, but it feels right to make my first bookshop the first bookshop. It is not an auspicious start: plenty of pre-orders to sign, but no in-shop visitors. My paranoid mind is reminded by my rarely heard rational mind that the main event is sold out and it is all fine.

An altruistic browser pops in, sees my despair and, after some light interrogation, decides she will buy my book for a friend, although she is not sure which friend yet.

I walk back to my dad's house through the woods where, when I was young, you could find pornographic magazines hidden in tree trunks. I ponder how the World Wide Web has long replaced the woodwide web when it comes to the distribution of erotica and readers' wives.

Tring

There was an Old Person of Tring,
Who embellished his nose with a ring;
He gazed at the moon every evening in June,
That ecstatic Old Person of Tring.

Edward Lear, *A Book of Nonsense*

The limericks of Edward Lear always seem a terrible cheat: Tring – ring – Tring again? Mind you, he was a teenage prodigy when it came to capturing the colours and form of a parakeet, so who am I to grumble.

Our Bookshop in Tring is a very recent addition to Tring high street. It seems that many people in 2019 had the thought, 'You know what – now is the time to live out my dream. I am going to open that bookshop I've always wanted, before the end of the year.' Then, six months into trading, nature's inventive mind created a new, highly effective virus, and all browsing was shut down. No one starts their dream of running a high-street bookshop thinking, 'Aha, at last, a plan that will make me a millionaire and then I shall crush the puny humans like ants, thanks to the enormous sales of poetry anthologies and beautifully designed books about fungus', but this was a vicious jab of misfortune and bad timing for so many people.

And yet it may also have worked to many independent bookshops' advantage. Our Bookshop put a basket on a bicycle and started pedalling around town, delivering books to the housebound population. Many other bookshops did this too, and some did not stop at books – also delivering prescriptions and groceries to those with health risks.

Over time, people also began to realize how much better it is to be in a bookshop than to be online. The tangible joy of leafing through unexpected books, the visual delight of seeing covers glinting under the lights, the friendly and exuberant advice on new books... as lockdowns ended all such things have made people feel the true worth of the physical bookshop.

Tonight the bookshop is full. As the audience drink their complimentary glass of Prosecco, I browse the shelves, looking for other people's books that I can recommend during my talk. At this early stage, I am determined to deliver a different talk at every shop. Just as I think I am settled on starting the evening by talking about the Apollo 8 mission, I see the spine of Ursula K. Le Guin's *The Lathe of Heaven*, and so instead I begin the talk discussing research into the benefit of dreams, and the visitations that come with sleep paralysis. I keep on this new tangent until I think the audience look more confused than I am.

I also follow the three-cough rule. If one person coughs, then I think, 'Ah! Someone has a bit of a cough – these things happen.'

If a second person coughs within thirty seconds of the first cough, my mind starts to prepare for a possible fast change of subject, but still says to me, 'Hey! It's October, people do get coughs, but there is now the possibility that the first cough alerted this person to the tickle in their throat, which would have gone unnoticed if I was more fascinating.'

A third cough within a minute seals it. They are all noticing the tickle in their throats, so go straight into the impersonation of Brian Blessed landing on Mars.

St Helens

After thirty years of touring the UK, there are still towns and cities I have not played in, so this tour is helping me complete the list of *everywhere*. Despite frequent gigging in Liverpool and Manchester, I never played the town in between them, St Helens.

When I think of St Helens I always associate it now with children being forced to eat their cooked pets. This is because I have read Michael Pennington's memoir, *Becoming Johnny Vegas*. Included in his list of memories of his St Helens childhood is:

> Volunteering my pet Blacky when I thought Dad was joking about whose rabbit was going into the pot, until I came home and found him skinned and strung up –
>
> 'I saved you these.'
>
> 'What are they?''
>
> 'His ears, tail and feet. They're meant to be bring you good luck.'

As the old joke goes, they didn't bring Blacky very much good luck.

Other memories that Michael shares of his St Helens childhood, which I'm sure will not be used in any St Helens Tourist

Board brochures, include watching a child wipe his bottom on some corner brickwork to examine his worms.

I am speaking at a brand-new community bookshop, The Book Stop.

Too new. It is not actually open yet. It had hoped to be open, but Brexit has created a shelf shortage. The books have nowhere to sit, so I am at the community cinema instead. I never like a big 'Ladies and gentlemen, please welcome...' and, as usual, I just start talking as people wander in. At the end of the talk the chairman of the community group says hello to the audience and tells them that he has learnt a great deal from this, his first bookshop talk: 'Always tell the author that you are going to introduce them *after* you have told the audience the safety rules; anyway, in the event of emergency, the fire exits are *here* and *here*.' Shortly afterwards the audience depart from the cinema in the happy knowledge that they would have survived a conflagration in hindsight.

Manchester

I take the train to Manchester Victoria and then wheel my suitcase the mile and a half to the International Anthony Burgess Foundation, where Blackwell's have set up an event. I have not read enough Anthony Burgess. Perhaps, like many of us, I have only read *A Clockwork Orange*, but I have *The End of the World News* on a shelf at home, poised to be read one day.

I am still unsure about my book talk. The audience all sit quietly, listening to what I am saying. When performing, I have an unease around silence, with the club-comedian critic who lives in my head shouting for more jokes, more laughter. A saner voice says, 'This is fine. No one's coughing.'

I prefer staying with friends to a hotel, as the transition from gregarious, feted performer to solitary man wondering if anyone has boiled his pants in the hotel kettle can feel whiplashingly abrupt. (I was first told of the dirty pants being boiled in hotel kettles when signing books on my last tour, so now the tea- and coffee-making facilities often remain untouched by me.)

Whenever I am in Manchester I stay in Levenshulme with my friend Carl. He has a lilo with a built-in pump, so it's all mod cons for sleepovers. Carl is an Anthony Burgess fan, so I take his advice on where to begin. His favourite is *Earthly Powers*, which is rather long and I have a tediously brief attention span. At around the 209th page my mind starts deleting all memories of characters from the first 150 pages and I forget why Larry shot the horse, and who Bernadette's long-lost mother is. Carl recommends his second favourite, *The Pianoplayers*, which at 208 pages is exactly right.

Glasgow

I keep a pile of published diaries by my bed. When I am bleary-eyed, I find that a good way of warming up my reading eyes is to scan across the diary entries of Derek Jarman, Joe Orton or Vere Hodgson, whose *Few Eggs and No Oranges* is subtitled 'A Diary showing how Unimportant People in London and Birmingham lived through the war years'. For this leg of the tour, I've brought along the diary that I have reread most often, that of Kenneth Williams. He never fails to fascinate me. When I was a teenager working in a department store, I once heard a very loud man doing an over-the-top impersonation of Kenneth Williams. Unsurprisingly, it turned out to be Kenneth Williams himself.

Today is 10 October. On this day in 1952, Williams 'went over to Croydon with John but didn't like Croydon, so returned straight away'. In 1969, on the day I was born, Williams wrote, 'I had a dream last night that I was making love to a Lothario – a foreman like 40ish working class – even in the dream I was rejected. I wonder how much significance dreams have.'

Last night in Levenshulme I dreamt of nothing. The lilo absorbed all my night thoughts.

I am going to Glasgow to talk twice at Mount Florida Books. The shop is just around the corner from Hampden Park football stadium and I have managed to choose a day when there is an international game on. Katia, the owner, and I have carefully worked out the timing. The first talk will start at 5.30 p.m., allowing the bookish crowd to sneak in thirty minutes after kick-off while the streets are quiet. I will be under strict time restrictions to ensure that they can all sneak out before the final whistle. There will be an hour-long break between talks that should allow the streets to flood with football fans and then subside.

I love Glasgow. It is one of my favourite places to perform. As with Liverpool and Belfast, I used to be nervous of the city and the people. They are tough and I am a milksop. Over time, I realized they can sniff out the disingenuous. They've been through too much to put up with bullshitters. So the less disingenuous I was, the more fun I had. Also, they talk fast and so do I. I get to southern England and people say, 'Please slow down, take a breath – we can't take it all on board', but there are no such problems here.

I time my arrival in Glasgow Central station very, very badly – one hour before kick-off.

The taxi queue is vast.

The excited choruses of the fans are echoing off the clouds.

It is drizzly.

I am wearing new shoes.

My suitcase has a whining wheel.

My rucksack is book-heavy.

I start walking. For once, I follow the chanting mob rather than run away from them. I know they are going my way. As long as someone is draped in a flag and singing, ahead of me, I am heading in the right direction.

I almost walk past the bookshop, but I am spied by Dan, who is standing in the Mount Florida Books doorway and his shout brings me to a halt. Dan is a pal with a narrowboat, who roams the north-east of England and Scotland. He often gives me intriguing presents, such as late-nineteenth-century microscopic slides of cell samples of diseases.* I have quite a collection now of small pieces of hearts, lungs and spleens from the long dead.

I nearly missed Mount Florida Books as its shop sign says, 'Art by Zaz Tattoo'. Before it sold words on paper, this shop sold words on skin, as a tattoo parlour. Katia crowdfunded her purchase of the parlour and aims to use the profits to fund literacy projects in Glasgow. Like so many of the booksellers I meet, this is a calling and not simply employment. She has worked in bookshops for many years and now plans to use all that experience for her vision of building 'a different type of bookshop'.**

The space is beginning to take shape. It reminds me of the bookshops in contemporary art galleries, where you feel the

* The first time Dan gave me a box of disease slides, I was flying on a plane the next day. I was a little worried that they might not be acceptable hand luggage, but was relieved to discover they were fine for the overhead lockers. Apparently a cell-thick strip of dropsy from 1897 is not considered a potential terrorist threat.

** Katia spent eight years managing the Review Bookshop in Peckham.

urge to buy everything that you see because it will make you a more fascinating and civilized person.

For these talks I am joined by Josie Long, with whom I have co-presented a book podcast for many years. We are united by our love of Kurt Vonnegut and Jean Rhys and a fascination with the Glasgow trade unionist Jimmy Reid, despite the fact that he once showed up Kenneth Williams terribly, but deservedly, in a discussion about trade unionism on the *Parkinson* chat show. You don't get so many trade unionists on Saturday night primetime any more.

By 5 p.m. the advance on the stadium is just a pavement peppering of weaving, tardy drunks and fathers shooing on their children.

At 5.10 p.m. the audience start tiptoeing in.

At 5.30 p.m. we promptly start talking.

At 6.30 p.m. Katia warns us it might be a draw.

At 6.40 p.m. I am given the hasty signal to wrap up fast, and I sign books and chat while Katia checks how the football is going, so that we will have some idea of the mood of the imminent exodus. At the last minute Scotland wins and, seconds before the gates open, the final audience member departs. Exit, pursued by a joyous mob.

Katia decides she should treat us all to chips and fizzy pop. We worry for her safety, but Katia is bold. She salutes us and departs, locking us into the shop. It is the dream we have always had: being locked in a well-organized bookshop with the promise of imminent chips.

We feel like strange exhibits in another land, as the supporters good-naturedly and boisterously parade by, some banging on the windows like bad children trying to goad the lazy library-monkeys in the zoo.

I was determined to get through the first week without

buying any books, but at day three I can feel my resolve weakening. It is a small bookshop, but perfectly curated. The books all look so delicious. My fingers start to run across spines.

Katia survived. We ate chips and browsed.

As the last football supporters went over the horizon, our next audience began to arrive. The evening audience included two men who run one of Glasgow's leading sex-toy shops, and a nurse whose patients are pipistrelle bats.

After the second signing, we were asked if we would like to see a bat or two. Would we ever.

The bat-nurse brought in two live bats for us to marvel at. This was beginning to turn into a perfect day. The thrill of seeing the bats, looking at the delicacy of their wings, surviving the football crowd and the joy of chips, tipped me over the edge. I needed books.

Katia gave me a copy of *The Disordered Cosmos* by Chanda Prescod-Weinstein, a book that explores the magnificent ideas of what we know about the universe, but also the problems of social injustice within science. With that gift, the dam was broken. It is an oddity that you can be in a bookshop of many floors and find nothing, but in a space where the books are fewer but arranged with such passion and intention, you can find many.

Every shelf had something that I needed.

I was aware that there were many bookshops still to go and, should I be rabid here, I would find myself with no space for any prizes to be found in Penarth or Exeter, Sidmouth or Swansea. So I chose based on weight.

Ursula K. Le Guin's *The Carrier Bag Theory of Fiction* is a short essay that could fit in a pocket, a sneaky book with an eleven-page essay bulked up with a twenty-page introduction, and pleasingly purple in its design. Some books are worth owning for a paragraph, and some slight books may have few paragraphs, but each one has punch and vigour. Donna Haraway writes in her introduction, 'A brave student of dragons, Le Guin's stories are capacious bags for collecting, carrying, and telling the stuff of living. A leaf a gourd a shell a net a bag a sling a sack a bottle a pot a box a container. A holder. A recipient.'

That would do.

Another book that could fit in the other pocket of my duffel coat was *A Nazi Word for a Nazi Thing* by So Mayer, a book inspired by the 1937 exhibition of degenerate art staged by the Third Reich.

Audre Lorde is someone I feel I should know more about, describing herself as 'black, lesbian, mother, warrior, poet'. I reckon she will give me perspectives unavailable from my metroland childhood, and her collection of poetry and essays, *Your Silence Will Not Protect You*, looks beautiful:

Love is a word another kind of open
As a diamond comes into a knot of flame
I am black because I come from the earth's inside
Take my word for jewel in your open light.

And what goes best with a lesbian warrior poet? A history of Scottish music hall, of course. I will pass it on to my pal Andre Vincent, a pantomime dame, so that he has something to read while he is having his girdle tightened at Worthing Pavilion.

Stewarton

Sunday morning and I am off to The Book Nook in Stewarton. As Sunday trains are enigmatic and elusive, the proprietor,

Sarah, kindly collects me from Josie's Glasgow flat. Each bookseller has a story to tell. Of all the new bookshop owners I have met, Sarah had the shortest distance to travel from grand opening to pandemic lockdown – eight days. She tells me of her life, her family and the loss of her son, Gordon. There is a warm honesty to her and an infectious excitement to what she is doing. I am the first bookshop event she has put on.

Before I met Sarah, I had been planning on talking about trying to find consolations from science when we deal with the death of those we love. I ask her if she would mind if I talked about a friend who lost his son. She encourages me, and we talk about how the stories we tell give permission for others to share theirs.

I have a Sunday congregation that would please an optimistic vicar, and it seems as if the good people of Stewarton have come out to celebrate having their own bookshop. I have to scarper fast to get to Carlisle for a late-afternoon event, so I do not have time to see the bookshop itself, the one upside being that I will not come across a new temptation.

Carlisle

Arriving in Carlisle, I find myself on the horns of a dilemma. It is getting close to charity-shop closing time, but my luggage has become unwieldy enough that I would not be able to navigate around any of the shops without creating a scene, or being the recipient of furious huffing from people brushed by my canvas bag as they pore over monarchistic mugs and costume jewellery.

To hell with it: what if I miss a treat? Let me create a scene and get caught in a revolving clothes-display stand.

The Oxfam bookshop is closed already, but this has rarely been a successful browse for me. The best find I can remember in this Oxfam shop was a book about The Stuckists, a movement founded in 1999 to promote figurative art, when conceptual art was hogging the limelight. The Stuckists' manifesto stated:

> The ego-artist's constant striving for public recognition results in a constant fear of failure. The Stuckist risks failure wilfully and mindfully by daring to transmute his/her ideas through the realms of painting. Whereas the ego-artist's fear of failure inevitably brings about an underlying self-loathing, the failures that the Stuckist encounters engage him/her in a deepening process which leads to the understanding of the futility of all striving. The Stuckist doesn't strive – which is to avoid who and where you are – the Stuckist engages with the moment.

The manifesto also declared that Stuckists embraced all that they denounced.

Carlisle's British Heart Foundation shop is still open. For a small shop, it has an indecently large religious section, suggesting the frequent deaths of Anglican hoarders.

My favourite recent religious book acquisition was *Ronnie and the Sacraments* by Mrs A. C. Osborn Hann. It's from the action-and-education *Ronnie* series, which also includes *Ronnie and the Creed*, *Ronnie and the Commandments* and *Ronnie and the Lord's Prayer*.

> They saw Gay kneel down at the Altar rail, and presently they saw the priest come to her with the Holy Bread and Wine.

'That's Jesus coming to her,' Margaret whispered to Ronnie.

They watched while all the people knelt at the Altar rails.

Gay's face was very serious when she came back. It was just as if something wonderful had happened to her. And so it had.

It's another exciting adventure in the world of transubstantiation, although I have recently discovered that there is also a *Ronnie and the Catechism* adventure, which I think is top of my *Ronnie* list.

Osborn Hann, the wife of a vicar, also wrote the *Peg* series of books, *The Pluck of the Coward* and *A Brownie from the Caravans*. The last is the story of 'nine-year-old Carlotta', who is 'from a traveller family and has recently come to live locally. She has got into scrapes at school, so Brown Owl suggests the Brownies try to secure her as a recruit.'[1]

There are no copies of *Ronnie and the Catechism* today.

The last time I was here I bought *Poptastic!*, the autobiography of the relentlessly cheery radio DJ Tony Blackburn. I don't know why I did this.

Browsing can put me in a manic frame of mind, and I frequently look along my shelves and try to work out the thought processes that led to my purchases. I have realized that reason is rarely part of the equation.

Maybe I opened Blackburn's book on this paragraph.

Because I was usually portrayed as Mr Goody-Goody in the press, I'd sometimes receive a bit of a ribbing from the more drunken elements in the Radio One

Roadshow crowd. It wasn't particularly pleasant to hear the occasional chorus of 'Tony Blackburn's a wanker!' from a few blokes at the back, but one of the first rules of partying and having fun is that there'll always be someone wanting to spoil it.

There's nothing quite so alluring as *Poptastic!* today.

There's a large book on 'True Life' mysteries, but my collection of books on Bigfoot, lake monsters and shadowy Cornish cats is large enough for the moment. I leave the shop and realize I am too late for another Carlisle favourite, Bookends, the labyrinthine bookshop combining old and new books where you can expect to find browsers who got lost in the basement in 1987 and have been living off diced sheet music ever since.

I am being interviewed by Lee Randall again today and fail to burst into tears for a second time in a row, so hopefully she'll put Wigtown 2019 down as an aberration.

Among the people queuing for me to sign books afterwards are two sisters I've met before at an event, and they remind me that their mother once asked one of my favourite ever post-talk questions at a book festival. I had been talking about my book on why we become who we become, and how we deal with it – a topic examined using stories and myths about comedians. In the Q&A afterwards I would usually get questions on Laurel and Hardy, anxiety, impostor syndrome and what it was like working with Ricky Gervais.

When hands went up on this particular night, there was one that seemed more eager than any other, with some kerfuffle attached.

'I have a question!'

'Don't take my mum's question.'

'I want to ask it.'

'It's a stupid question.'

I said that any questions were acceptable, and the daughter sank into her seat, hiding herself from the world.

In a clear and loud voice, the mother asked, 'When I was in the queue, there was a woman behind me talking about "the thinking man's crumpet" and I can't remember who that is, can you?'

'Yes, it's Joan Bakewell.'

The mother smiled like a victorious Oliver Hardy and I looked out at the audience, hoping that all the other hands weren't immediately going to pop down as people mumbled, 'Oh, that's what I was going to ask too.'

On this night the daughters asked that both books they were buying were dedicated 'To Joan Bakewell'.

Finished by 7 p.m., I had an evening to kill or be killed in.

I sat alone with some books in a pizza restaurant. I like reading alone, with garlic bread within easy reach. I imagine people look on this side-dish and solitude and see an enigmatic loner, a travelling man with a story to tell. Actually they probably think, 'Is that the guy who used to teach me sociology and got kicked out of the college for drunkenly spraying aggressive graffiti about Baudelaire all over the modern-languages block?'

Settle

Every day I wake up unsure whether anyone will turn up at the bookshops. At the very start of the tour I had a dark belief that I would be standing in solitude in ninety-eight of the 100 bookshops, being laughed at by the life-size cardboard cutouts of TV stars with their large advances and ghostwritten books.

Every author has a story of travelling 400 miles to a book talk because 'everyone on our remote island loves your work'. They end up standing in front of three people, having now discovered that the population of the island has been greatly exaggerated by their publicist. Two of the audience leave as soon as they find out the author is not Len Deighton, and the remaining one knits and mumbles throughout.

Due to stormy weather and the ship captain's indifference, the author remains trapped on the island for some time, drinking so much shoe-polish wine that he eventually believes he *is* Len Deighton. It's the literary festival as Heart of Darkness. So goes my mind.

The trick, when doing poorly attended signings, is to create the illusion that you are there for something else: hang near the table, don't sit behind it, so that no passers-by see the spectacle of disinterest. Maybe hold a duster or some furniture polish, so that at least you seem to have a purpose. Look as if it is mere coincidence that you happen to be near a table with your book on it, and a big sign with your face on it and the words 'book signing 2 p.m.'.

I am on the way to Limestone Books in Settle. I try to blend in with the shelves when I arrive. I am never so arrogant as to presume that people are there for me, even if they are staring right at me while saying, 'Hello, I am looking forward to your talk. Can you sign my book?'

Eventually I check with Tanya that her bookshop does not normally suddenly fill up like this at 12.58 on a Monday, and she assures me that they definitely are there for me, and so I begin. Afterwards I chat to a seventeen-year-old in cosmological dungarees decorated with planets and stars. She tells me that she is the only girl at her school in the last five years to study A-level physics. I file that story away, realizing it is a fact worth repeating when talking about the battle against a sex divide in science.

Departing from Settle, I experience my first almost-transcendent moment of the tour.

I have a fifty-minute wait for the train, but I'm fine with that. It is not like being delayed at Birmingham New Street. I have a proper cheese sandwich from the local bakery, a bottle of ginger beer, and a bench in the sunshine with a geologically majestic view. I am a singular incarnation of the Famous Five at the beginning of an adventure with smugglers.

The station recalls an England created by a 1940s Hollywood set designer, for a movie starring Ronald Colman and Greer Garson about a romance involving a man who has lost his memory after being gassed in the trenches.* I am detached from the twenty-first century.

The next destination is Ilkley and its literature festival. The pub I am staying in is a mile and a half from the venue – the first church venue of the tour – and I make the most of the autumn evening light to walk across the town.

The older I get, the bigger the sky has become and I do not know why this should be. Why did it take so long for me to notice how wide the sky is, and why does it seem to keep expanding once I have noticed that? Touring becomes far more ominous in winter, so I make the most of the embers of autumn and walk towards the dusk and into Ilkley.

The church is full, but socially distanced, so it looks like a classroom of naughty children, all of whom have been separated for pulling plaits and propelling spit-balls. Book-festival audiences can be a little different from bookshop audiences, as they have not come for you specifically, but instead have

* Obviously I am referring to *Random Harvest*, but you knew that.

come because they attend *everyone* who comes to the festival. You may be sandwiched between a talk on how olive oil changed the outcome of the Peloponnesian War and an epic poem about the prevalence of chlamydia in koala bears. At the end, you hope you have persuaded enough people of your worth that you have at least some semblance of a queue to sign books. At book festivals there is also the danger of bumping into grumpy historians who have monetized the more appalling splinters of their personality, and who look at you through their monocle as their tongue slides across the red wine on their teeth. This does not happen today.

I return to the pub in the company of Jeremy Dyson, writer of one of my favourite television series, *The League of Gentlemen*, as well as *Ghost Stories*, a terrifying play based around three haunting stories.

Books united us when we first met. We were on a radio show. Jeremy was promoting the play, and I just happened to have in my hand a copy of Guy N. Smith's giant killer-crab novel *Crabs on the Rampage*, so we began a lengthy discussion on the pulp horror and paperback carnage of our childhood.

Today the evening ends with Jeremy explaining to me Jungian archetypes, after a brief diversion into the work of the disgruntled male's philosophical pin-up, lobster celebrant Jordan Peterson.

Wotton-under-Edge

If you judge a bookshop by the quality of its Battenberg cake, then today is the day I will visit the finest bookshop in the land. I will be disembarking at Cam & Dursley railway station for the first time.

It is a three-train journey. The longest stretch is Leeds to Cheltenham Spa. I am hoping to read, but I find it very hard to switch off exterior noise and there are three extremely chatty chefs from Leeds to Birmingham New Street. Actually it is just one very, very opinionated chef and two others, who occasionally nod. With the exception of a brief mention of béchamel sauce, the conversation focuses on complaining loudly about people who have not given him what he deserves, which is generally free beer.

When not complaining about the many who have wronged him, it is a monologue on all the times the chef has got 'battered' and 'leathered' – 'fifteen pints on the way to the station', 'necked one in every pub that day' – and then on how pathetic the alcoholics in Wetherspoons are, who want a drink at 8.30 a.m. For him, it seems alcoholism is not about quantity, but about when to drink your fifteen pints a day.

Cam & Dursley is a skeleton of a station, the antithesis of the solid brick stations between Carlisle and Settle. It is what you would make with the leftover plastic when you have finished an Airfix model.

Seventy years ago the Cotswold Book Room in Wotton-under-Edge was merely the front room of someone's house. It is now owned by Cathy and Gideon York, a nurse and a nuclear engineer who did not want to imagine the high street without an independent bookshop.

This is the seventh day, and the twelfth event so far. I have covered about 1,100 miles. I don't want to slow down but, with a home-made Battenberg in front of me, I sit for a while. This is the rural-idyll independent bookshop tour location that will be an early scene in the film adaptation. Gideon and Cathy will be played by Hugh Bonneville and Olivia Colman, and I will be played by Bill Nighy. The cake will be played by Javier Bardem.

Wotton-under-Edge is all pretty houses and thin, sloping streets ready to have a little straw strewn on them for a Sunday-night Jane Austen adaptation. Strolling about, I find an intriguing-looking side-street cinema, and then I find Chris, a regular at my West Country shows. I invite him to join me on my charity-shop browse. I spy a copy of Keith Emerson's autobiography, *Pictures of an Exhibitionist.* The back cover tells me, 'This is one of the most remarkable music memoirs ever written, from one of rock's greatest exponents.' Knowing that Chris likes his prog rock, I point him in its direction. This is a noble gesture, as instinct tells me it is probably worth far more than the £2 it is going for.

I check later on and discover you'd be hard pressed to find it for less than £100. I saw the gazelle, but I let Chris bag it. Today I was a noble and selfless huntsman.

Back at the Cotswold Book Room, the event is totally sold out, with all fourteen tickets gone. I sign books before I start talking, as some of the audience may have to run off before the end because they have children to collect from the school gates. The intimacy of small rooms means that you have to fight against the affectation of performance. You can't simply put on the same old show afternoon after afternoon, when people can see hints of artifice in the eye. Fortunately I have practised this for a long time and the older I have become, the more informal I am.

My pal Laura* kindly comes to collect me and take me to her home town of Bristol for my next event. She agrees about

* Laura came with me on my last tour before the pandemic, when she was known as 'She Makes War'. Now she is known as 'Penfriend'. She is a brilliant musician and is hugely underrated. With tenacity and talent, without a record label, she managed to get her last album into the Top Twenty.

the quality of the Battenberg cake and tells me about her afternoon of cold-water swimming.

Bristol

Today is my first time back in Bristol since its Slapstick Festival 20 months ago. I was lucky to be hosting an event then with The Goodies and, after a forty-year wait, I got them to sign my favourite childhood books. I had read their books over and over again, huddled in the corner of my bedroom, the silliness of them never seeming to fade. I had worked with individual Goodies, but this was the first time working with all three. I have rejected my fear of being ashamed of declaring my admiration for people I was working with some years ago. We are so good at sharing our negative thoughts without a blush, and yet so quickly redden when expressing admiration.

How could I not admire the authors of books that contained poems such as:

William Gladstone
What a squirt
He wears lipstick
And a skirt

And

Show me a home
Where the buffalo roam
And I will show you a house with a very messy carpet.

I am glad that I took that moment before we walked onstage to ask all The Goodies for their autographs and express my love for their work because, sadly, Tim Brooke-Taylor would die a few months later from Covid complications.

The TV tie-in comedy book was one of the hottest items in the playgrounds of the 1970s, whether it was *Monty Python's Big Red Book* or *The Goodies' Book of Criminal Records*. It was frowned upon by the more conservative corners of the staffroom, considered too rude for gentlefolk and young children. In my teens I went to the school bookshop that would open at lunchtimes and ordered *The Rutland Dirty Weekend Book*, inspired by the BBC's *Rutland Weekend Television*, along with Billy Connolly's *Gullible's Travels*. I waited and waited and heard nothing. Many weeks later I asked their whereabouts and was told that no one had any idea or any record of such an order. Digging around like Woodward and Bernstein, I found out that the books had arrived and their vulgarity had turned that day's bookshop volunteer's hair grey with shock, and they had been returned to the gutter from which they had risen.

This was not the first time that my childhood tastes were deemed too extreme for polite society. One Christmas I excitedly opened some parcels of books and found two big hardback anthologies, both adorned with images of hooded skeletons bidding the foolhardy, and sometimes barely clad, to their doom. On Boxing Day they were gone, never to return.

Nothing was said, but I was told later that my grandmother had taken it upon herself to become Lord Chamberlain and read enough of both books to decide that they were too sordid for my frail mind. I have no idea if this subconsciously played such a large part in my thoughts that the next Christmas I pulled so forcefully on the cracker I was sharing with her that she flew from her chair, broke her wrist and had to go to hospital. I, devil child, with paper crown and crumpled joke.

She remained silent when I received the richly illustrated *Encyclopaedia of Witchcraft and Demonology** the next year, despite the very first page being home to a staggeringly unarousing image of some pale, bony-arsed men encircling a naked woman, arms skywards in celebration of some devilry.

Further female toplessness can be found on page 63, a mural of a nude witch with her toad and kitten familiars from the Basque Museum. On page 65 there is Hans Baldung Grien's painting of two witches with a goat and a 'dwarfish' child. On page 171 there's a photograph of a modern witch in an overly cumbersome goat-mask. On page 220 there's a witch submitting to the tongue of a dragon. And page 135 has a photograph of a naked man who seems to be penetrating his lawn while lying in the middle of a pentagram.

I think by the time I was receiving these books, it had been decided there was no hope left for me. I was destined for satanic rampages.

Yet again, good fortune has meant that I am too late to browse in another of my regular Bristol bookshop haunts, The Last Bookshop on Park Street, where all books are £3. The stock comprises remaindered books, and I rarely leave with fewer than ten. The moment you have one in your hand, you know it cannot end there.

* The encyclopaedia has an introduction by Hans Holzer, author of *The Psychic World of Plants*, the most expensive second-hand paperback I bought in 2021. It promises to answer questions such as 'Does a carrot scream when uprooted?' and 'How do plants feel about being eaten?' It also has my favourite second-hand book delight: a cutting placed in the book by a previous owner. As well as discovering the emotional range of a carrot, I will now know how to 'Stop a toothache – by black magic'. All you've got to do is carry the paw of a mole with you.

Do you know anyone who can buy just one book? Do you know anyone who leaves a bookshop only with what they walked in to buy?

On my last visit to the shop I reacquainted myself with Angela Carter and then scolded myself for having left it so long. She is one of those authors I've decided there must always still be one book of hers left to read. With Kurt Vonnegut, I have kept *Bluebeard* unopened, but ready on the shelf. I tried it with Jean Rhys too, but she wrote so little and such spartan novels that I accidentally read them all. Angela Carter's final work, *Wise Children*, is the novel of hers that I always have waiting for me until the diagnosis of impending doom.

The Last Bookshop is also where I found one of my favourite science-fiction novels of all time, *Roadside Picnic* by Boris and Arkady Strugatsky. It was while they were writing another novel, *The Doomed City*, that the Strugatskys started to formulate the story of *Roadside Picnic*. According to Boris, the first plotting notes in their journal began: '... a monkey and a tin can'.[2]

I chose *Roadside Picnic* for a BBC radio show where each guest had to bring a book to the table to discuss. I could still feel then that sense of science fiction being disreputable, pulpy nonsense for smelly boys estranged from life.

Like books on factual science, this remains a genre that rarely bothers the literary salons, apart from on specialist freak-show nights. *Roadside Picnic* was famously adapted for a movie by Andrei Tarkovsky, *Stalker*, which is definitely deemed worthy of the attention of those in high-culture hammocks.

The film *Stalker* became Geoff Dyer's *Zona*, where he dissects the film scene by scene – it is the book of the film of the book. Dyer describes exactly what he sees as he watches the film.

> The barman comes in from the back – he is wearing a white barman's jacket – lights a cigarette and turns on the lights, two fluorescent tubes, one of which doesn't work properly: it flickers. He looks at the flickering light. You can see him thinking, 'that needs fixing', which is not the same at all as 'I'll fix that today', but which is very nearly the same as 'it'll never be fixed'.

Geoff followed up *Zona* with another scene-by-scene narration of a film, but rather than writing about something intellectual like Ingmar Bergman's *Winter Light* or Alain Robbe-Grillet's *Last Year at Marienbad*, he chose the alpine Nazi war thriller *Where Eagles Dare* for his book '*Broadsword Calling Danny Boy*':* 'Checking in at the Nazi-themed ski lodge, the fräuleins are given a frosty welcome by the S-and-M-looking receptionist.'

Bookhaus in Bristol is another recently opened shop. It began selling books in July 2021 and is owned by Jayne Pascoe and Kevin Ramage who previously set up the Grove Bookshop in Ilkley. It is a roomy, light bookshop, inspired by Bristol's history of radicalism, and is situated in the rapidly developing wharf area of Bristol, where you can eat food from all around the world in a converted shipping container of your choice.

I am interviewed by Dr Hannah Little, who is writing a book about extraterrestrial language. Frankly, I don't want to

* At this point in writing, my mind has gone into an endless game of tag where each book leads to another book, and the only way to break this is with a footnote. As I have mentioned *Where Eagles Dare* I feel that I must tell you to read Ingrid Pitt's autobiography, *Life's a Scream*. This is far more than an actor remembering her horror-movie past; it is about being a child imprisoned in a concentration camp, and her incredible resilience in the face of rejection and misogyny.

talk about my book – I want to talk about hers. Laura and I eat veggie-burgers outside a cargo crate and I drink my two-beer maximum.

A statue of Thomas Chatterton sits in Millennium Square, a short walk from Bookhaus. Wordsworth wrote of him:

The marvellous boy,
The sleepless Soul that perished in his pride.

I sit next to Chatterton, dead at seventeen, never knowing he would be revered as the first Romantic poet:

Poor superstitious Mortals! wreak your hate
Upon my cold remains.

Two hundred and fifty years later the superstitious mortals made him solid and something to be revered. He has the Rowley papers on his lap and at his feet.

Farewell, Bristolia's dingy pile of brick,
Lovers of Mammon, worshippers of trick!

Bidding farewell to Bristol's 'Aldermanic fools', I imagine this statue would have been among the crowd that pushed Edward Colston's statue into Bristol Harbour. More history was learnt that day by toppling a statue into the water than from all those times it sat above sea level, I imagine.

Chatterton is joined in Millennium Square by William Tyndale, William Penn and Cary Grant – on his way to Hitchcock's *To Catch a Thief*, by the look of him. Ideologically safer, they are sculpted without inflatable armbands.

My budget hotel is quiet and sterile, which is just what I want. I have no need for film-flam and minibars; after all, I still have one final slice of Battenberg to keep me going. I risk boiling the kettle and then psychosomatically (hopefully) get the vague tang of pants when I drink my tea.

I turn on the television, expecting nothing except the possibility of experiencing some bland umbrage at seeing a comedian with a television job that I envy, and am therefore delighted to find a documentary by KT Tunstall about the Scottish poet, musician, artist and performer Ivor Cutler. As well as spotting Cutler at the book fairs of my youth, I saw one of his final gigs. The audience was instructed to applaud at half the usual volume, as he said he didn't like too much noise. We all dutifully attempted this, though Cutler remarked that our effort was slightly spoiled by the man who said, 'Yay!' when he reached centre-stage. For the majority of the performance he moved back and forth between his notebooks and his harmonium, and when he reached one or the other we were rewarded with a song or a poem. There was a beautiful anti-dynamic to the occasion. The first Ivor Cutler book I bought was *Gruts*, a collection of his radio stories first broadcast on the Home Service between 1959 and 1962. I have a particular fondness for 'How to Make a Friend', in which he explains how to build up your social circle using a bucket of whitewash, some cobbler's thread and a nice red silk dressing gown with dragons on it.

I go to sleep with Cutler's song 'Women of the World' playing in my mental jukebox:

Women of the world take over,
If you don't the world will come to an end...
It won't take long.

CHAPTER 3

I Only Play in the Finest Freezer Cabinets

Sidmouth to Birmingham

griffinbooks
BIRMINGHAM
cover to cover
Crickhollow
CRICKHOWELL
SWANSEA
PONTYPRIDD
CARDIFF
PENARTH
POWERED BY KINDNESS
SIDMOUTH
EXETER
SHELF LIFE
BOOKS AND ZINES
LITTLE TOLLER
BOOKS

The waiter shows me a coin trick at breakfast. He is a French prestidigitator, when he isn't asking if you would like your eggs fried or scrambled and your toast preference.

With the coin still hidden in thin air, two of the other breakfast guests ask if it is possible to get a vodka. It is 9.30 a.m. 'What is it with you English? You are always drinking,' he says emphatically.

I hastily change my order from absinthe over easy to beans on toast.

I am reading a book about general relativity. Unfortunately the waiter confuses someone reading about relativity with someone understanding relativity. I muddle through his astute comments on Einstein and spacetime, each answer further underlining my ignorance. This is *why* the English drink all day, just in case social embarrassment involving theoretical physics suddenly crops up. Inebriation breeds cosmological confidence.

This dummy-run conversation may be useful, as the first event of the day is at a science festival in Sidmouth.

You'll know Sidmouth if you've read *The Tale of Little Pig Robinson* by Beatrix Potter. It is disguised as Stymouth, which is also built out of bits of Lyme Regis and Teignmouth: '"Now take care of yourself in Stymouth, Nephew Robinson. Beware of gunpowder, and ships' cooks, and pantechnicons, and sausages, and shoes, and ships, and sealing-wax. Remember the blue bag, the soap, the darning-wool – what was the other thing?" said Aunt Dorcas.'

Sidmouth is full of the sort of seaside charity shops where you might get lucky with a hidden classic. The closer you are to the sea, the more the charity shops resemble the way they used to be, with the mustier, dustier, well-thumbed paperbacks of the 1970s, pulp classics like *The Drums of Dracula* or *Dragon Skins*, about the collision of skinhead culture and the kung-fu craze. One of my finest finds was at the Red Cross shop in Deal, where I found *Hawk the Slayer* by Terry Marcel and Harry Robertson: 'In a time when the dark clouds of chaos covered the land and the roads were filled with death, Voltan the Dark One rode out...'

It was a mere £1. At the time this title was changing hands for £60 plus, but nowadays the market in *Hawk the Slayer* books is not as bullish, and a shrewd investor might pick one up for £35 – a warning that investors in the second-hand book market must realize that the value of swords and sorcery may go down as well as up. I am hoping that one day I will find the novelization of George A. Romero's *Martin* for £1 in a British Heart Foundation shop in Hastings, in between games of crazy golf. It sells online for as much as £60, but I've had no luck so far. And there are no such essentials in Sidmouth today.

My talk is in another church. I wander in the graveyard beforehand, in search of an interesting name or the start of a story.

Carl from Winstone's bookshop had put an enormous amount of effort into ensuring that the science festival could fit me in, but at the last minute he got the two-striped lateral-flow test that would place him in his attic for ten days, eating processed-cheese slices and After Eight mints slipped under the door by his cautious family.

Afternoon shows, unsurprisingly, have an older crowd, and the extra delight is that many of them were put off science at school sixty years before, so they have decades of questions that have been fermenting and there is rarely an awkward silence when it is thrown up to the floor. Today we plunge into the Sun, before attempting to reach the edge of the universe, and then wonder about the language we need to talk to extraterrestrials. If only Hannah Little were here now.

Running out of copies of books to sign in the church, I pop over to Winstone's to sign some more. I ask to use their toilet and, as with all bookshops (apart from one, which you will read about later), there follows an apology for the pokiness and navigation that will be required. Most bookshop loos are also a further storeroom, often for old publicity material and cardboard cutouts. Sometimes it can be quite distracting attempting to urinate while being watched by a smiling, cake-holding Mary Berry, although for some, this might be a beautiful dream. I dance a short Heath Robinson tango as my coat catches on an Usborne book carousel.

I then make my way to Exeter, where I pick up a very reasonably priced film tie-in of *Logan's Run* at the British Heart Foundation – 'a terrifying novel of the 23rd Century'.

Exeter is only my second-ever event in an Oxfam bookshop – a last-minute replacement for Beaminster's Little Toller Bookshop after the bookshop discovered that they had an event in Liverpool on the night I was coming to visit. Fortunately, being promiscuous in my conversations with bookshops, I had recently complimented Exeter's Oxfam online, and in return they told me they had now doubled in size and if I ever fancied doing an event with them, they would promise me an audience and a lectern.

I like charity bookshops, because I can delude myself into believing that I am committing an altruistic act by purchasing too many books. I am not satisfying my consumer lust – I am digging a well in Uganda.

The most I have ever paid for a single book in an Oxfam bookshop is £150 for a first edition of Philip Larkin's *The Whitsun Weddings*, a book that I had the good fortune to study for A-level and which, despite the worst words he shared with Kingsley Amis, I am still inordinately fond of. It will be an expensive night for me in this Oxfam too.

Another Exeter favourite is Book Cycle, a shop that supports the charity of the same name that seeks 'to empower children worldwide through the provision of free books and educational resources'. The bookshop has a 'three book purchases per day' limit and you donate what you want for them. Don't be stingy!

Last time I was there I picked up yet another Colin Wilson book. He is an author who has become a habit of mine. At times I have owned seven different editions of his first book, *The Outsider*. I picked up yet another copy of *Beyond the Outsider*. It had a scrawled message in it, which I thought might be from Wilson himself: 'To Rich' (or 'Dick' or maybe 'Nick') 'with affection and admiration. Colin Feb 65.'

The three-book rule can be agonizing, though. I also bought *The Dangerous Sex: The Myth of Feminine Evil* by H. R. Hays: 'In this enquiry into misogyny, H. R. Hays suggests men must face their own compulsions before a true and balanced relation between the sexes is achieved.' Although the book is without pictures, what I did find within was that it had been used to press four-leafed clovers, one of which was found between pages 174 and 175, the chapter on 'The Bosom Snake'. But my copy of *Foucault for Beginners* came without such ephemera.

Sitting in the nearby teashop later with a lemon sponge, I came to the conclusion that it was Colin's signature in the edition, and then started to wonder who Rich (or Dick or Nick) might be. Nick or Dick or Rich had definitely read it all, as the paragraphs deemed most pertinent were marked with pencil and occasional marginalia such as 'Poetry', 'presupposition?' and 'sex fantasy'.

Before the Oxfam talk, Jez from the Oxfam music shop next door shows me some intriguing CDs. I realize that Jez is the author of a wonderful book about George A. Romero's *Martin* from the *Midnight Movie Monograph* series. The series also includes a book on *Death Line*, my favourite cannibal horror-atrocity movie, set on London's Piccadilly Line.

Later I see Jez both selling and defiling a musical instrument. Someone is keen to buy a stylophone, a 'miniature analog stylus-operated keyboard' created in 1967 – a portable sound of the future from the past. Unfortunately the 1970s advertising campaign was fronted by Rolf Harris, the beloved TV and recording star who was then convicted on twelve counts of indecent assault. Jez succeeds in removing his face from the packaging, and a stylophone is sold.

It's nice to have a lectern to lean on. I imagine that it gives me a certain gravitas that is only dispelled by opening my mouth.

On a high after the gig, I return to the glass cabinet of Oxfam's most treasured items. I loiter, I turn away, but I keep returning.

There is a *Metro-Land* Betjeman box, but at £300 I don't even dare ask what's in it. Later, I discover it is a beautifully made book of artwork by Glynn Boyd Harte, limited to a print run of 220 copies, each page illustrating the Metro-Land that Betjeman visited in his TV documentary about the Metropolitan Line (which has far fewer cannibals on it than the Piccadilly Line).

Even books that I leave behind can educate me. Artist and writer Glynn Boyd Harte and his artist wife, Caroline Bullock, were described as young fogeys. 'Like all British thinkers, they run for months on ginger nuts and tea,' wrote the writer of the *New Georgian Handbook* in 1985. Hart's first book, *Murderers' Cottages*, was made up of images depicting Staffordshire china souvenirs of notorious murderers' cottages. These included Miniver Place, Bermondsey:

> House of Frederic George Manning and his wife Maria (née de Roux). Together they were involved in cruel murder upon the person of Maria's former lover, Patrick O'Connor. He was invited for supper; Manning stabbed him repeatedly and his wife buried him under the kitchen floor. Their joint execution took place on the roof of Horsemonger Lane Gaol on November 13th 1849.
>
> Charles Dickens later wrote a letter to *The Times* protesting to execution in public, having paid ten guineas for five tickets to view this one.

You could also find out about the hovel of William Collier; about the Red Barn where Maria Marten was murdered; and about William Palmer, the Rugeley Poisoner.

The advantage of my perpetual ignorance is that, had I known all this as I looked in the cabinet, *Metro-Land* would have been irresistible and I would live in even more cluttered poverty, awaiting the few payments I would receive when the documentary crews came in every few years to make another series about crazy hoarders constantly on the precipice of being crushed.

The book that does make it out of the cupboard has the hourglass nebula staring at me from the cover: *Glimpses of Other Realities, Volume 2: High Strangeness* by Linda Moulton Howe. I love that nebula and I love the term 'High Strangeness'. Colin Wilson has written the introduction. After reading this book he was in 'an almost permanent state of excitement'.

I flip through it, aware that as I have made them open the cabinet door, I must take something away from it. I start the normal arguments in the trial scene that go on in my head at such moments: 'But, Your Honour, this is not purchasing a book so much as making a donation. Think how much deeper they will be able to make that well with these sixty pounds.'

I look at the poor-quality sketches of abductions, alien faces and tools used to cut and penetrate. The aliens usually look like goths in a Tokyo nightclub.

> 'Rose said the incomplete female bodies were coated with gold dust like the woman in the Hollywood film *Goldfinger*...'
>
> 'The controller resembled a praying mantis being that wore some kind of headgear...'
>
> 'Linda Porter's depiction of "grey scientist" lifting her diseased heart out of her "old body" while she watched in a newly activated cloned body...'

You know the rest. Reader, I bought it.

Crickhowell

Crickhowell is place of contention for enthusiasts of Middle Earth. Wales was an inspiration for J. R. R. Tolkien and the Welsh Tourist Board is keen to use Hobbits as a honeytrap to lure visitors. Living just outside Birmingham, Tolkien wrote of the Welsh language, 'I heard it coming out of the west, it struck me in the names on coal trucks and drawing nearer it flickered past on station-signs, a flash of strange spelling and a hint of a language old and yet alive. It pierced my linguistic heart.'

According to the Tourist Board website, he named the Hobbit settlement of Crickhollow after Crickhowell, but those more fluent in Elvish are less impressed by this claim. Some question whether Crickhollow is a settlement or merely the name of Frodo Baggins's new house. Others are perplexed as to why Frodo did not return there after 'the war', and about what happened to all his furniture. The more I dig into this on the many forums, the more removed I become on any further thoughts on this Crickhowell/Crickhollow issue. Much like *Doctor Who* or Jack the Ripper, there seem to be articles of faith, should you make these your obsessions, so I decide to leave the Orcs, Ents and Trolls to their own devices.

This is my second visit to the Crickhowell Literary Festival, which is run by the Book-ish Bookshop, winner of Independent Bookshop of the Year Award in 2020. Like so many independent bookshops, it is marked by its perpetual activity. It offers what online purchasing cannot. It is a place of events and cakes and interaction. Its shop sign states: 'Books, conversation and more'. The judges said of it, 'The scope of what Emma and the team have achieved is extraordinary. It's a great bookshop that does everything right, but it's so much more besides – a true community hub that has a spirit of huge commitment to both the Crickhowell community and to indie bookselling.'

When I arrive it is too dark to read the tilting gravestones in the grounds of nearby St Edmund's Church, so I go and sit on a bench by a fire station, waiting for showtime. I have hit one of those points on tour where the isolation, the perpetual feeling of being an alien in so many locations, can bring on a little anxious melancholy.

During the show I am allowed to overrun and, as stage-time is a break from solitude, I do so. I discount the first twenty minutes because I didn't feel connected to the audience (my fault, not theirs), but somewhere during a story about connecting with the Standing Stones of Callanish I think we are beginning to go places.

I sign busily in the foyer. The audience includes Anne Goldsworthy, a teacher with whom I had previously had a very useful conversation, for my book's chapter on education and imagination. She told me of the excitement that primary-school children experience when trying to understand the digestion process by squeezing damp food through old tights. Try it, but ask permission to use the tights first and don't put them back in the drawer still full of sodden Jaffa Cakes.

Also in the queue, ten-year-old Finlay had a question for me and I couldn't answer it. It involved the Stones of Callanish. Just in case you are reading this, Finlay: the answer was Lewisian gneiss.

There was time for a pint of tropical IPA in Treebeards Bar. Now I had context – now I was 'that author' rather than 'that weirdo who is not from around here' – and I could drink happily in public. I had reached that part of the day where I belonged, but I would go back to being a stranger again by around midday the next day in Pontypridd.

Alone in my hotel room, I spread goat's cheese on an oatcake while watching a documentary about Cliff Richard.

Pontypridd

Emma's husband, Drew, kindly offers to drive me to Pontypridd, delaying by one more hour my return to being the alien.

We drive through the hills and talk about consciousness, which is a relief, as I can't talk about football. It has always made going to the barber's difficult. Little knowledge of FA Cup ties and million-pound transfers, as well as what Manchester City should do in midfield, has often left me mute whilst being shaved around the neck and asked if I want a candle in my ears (*no!*). What I have found is that if you dare to move away from the presumed requirements of male banter, you can get to go to many other places too, from the Mars Rover to painkiller addiction. I think men can be fearful, on both sides of the scissors, concerning what we are meant to talk about. It requires a conversational risk.

Books often give me paths into conversations – more often with a question than an answer. Books have made me happier to say, 'I don't know', and books have made me more eager to listen. When books are not my 'social' life, they enhance my social life.

Drew and I talk about what we have learnt about consciousness so far, happy to admit our uncertainty and our confusion rather than to impress each other with our knowledge and false expertise. For years I was a master of false expertise. I knew how to look like I knew what I was talking about, while paddling wildly under the surface.

It took a long time, but now I can say, 'I don't know.' For instance, I don't know about the aquatic ape hypothesis, but I know some people get quite cross about it, and other people, including Sir David Attenborough, are quite interested in it.

Although evolutionary anthropologist Elaine Morgan may be a specialist subject to some people – and despite the fact that Storyville Books in Pontypridd is smaller than the minimum size a bookshop should be to make it viable (according to the Booksellers Association) – you'll find her work on the shelves there. One of the delights of visiting so many bookshops is that you'll always find a local-author section. Sometimes that section will mainly concern traction engines or novels about a forgotten local revolutionary quilt-maker, and at other times – as here in Pontypridd – it will have a book about human evolution going through an aquatic phase during a primitive ape phase.

From the local section I also find out about William Price, a Welsh doctor with a neo-Druidic bent.

Not only is Storyville Books small, it is without plumbing, so I have to go over to the covered market to spend twenty pence to spend a penny. The loos are pristine, so the money is clearly going back into the porcelain and fixtures. On the way out, I hear rumours of a urinary-tract infection and a sigh of 'unsurprising', as the regulars discuss the October ailments roster.

I have enough time to visit three charity shops and all of them are also taking part in competitive illness, both from behind the counter and with the browsers. Gout, neuralgia and 'something I can't put my finger on, but it always starts to throb about 3 a.m. and that's the night done for me' all make appearances, as well as 'Sometimes she doesn't go for four days – agony.' From my limited research, there is an outbreak of ailments in Pontypridd that are 'beyond the realms of science'.

I think competitive ailments should be televised, preferably broadcast straight after *The World's Strongest Man*. After seeing Nordic males lifting trees over their heads and pulling articulated lorries through swampland, we'd go behind the counter of a Pets in Crisis charity shop. Those behind the till have been specially chosen for their predominantly undiagnosed agonies and trials, and then they must see if they can outdo the poorly who enter the shop. I imagine the winner will be the one without arms, legs or a head, merely a small ear at the base of their neck, not dissimilar to the lead character in Dalton Trumbo's haunting, tragic anti-war novel, *Johnny Got His Gun*.*

It is a nice, chatty group that pops in for the signing, and everyone offers me some new morsel of information or gossip about Pontypridd, but there's not even the slightest hint of an anecdote about a fungal toenail or inflamed ear canal, so it seems that at least the bookish here are well. I am also a happy surprise, which is an encouraging thing to be on a Friday. A couple who were due to see the now-postponed Brian Cox show in Cardiff passed by and were shocked to spot me in the window of their local bookshop. They have a young lad called Orion, so they are, unsurprisingly, keen on astronomy. They had been expecting to see me in an arena in Cardiff, and now they are finding me in a bookshop that is technically too small to be a bookshop. I leave with an invitation to play a gig in a forest, one of my favourite kinds of gig.

* My favourite anarchist historian, Howard Zinn, wrote that *Johnny Got His Gun* 'had a shattering effect on me when I read it. It left me with a bone-deep hatred of war'.

Swansea

> And if you're lucky you might still see boys from the hill riding wild horses down into the city centre, trotting bare-chested past the big McDonald's. Though that's a detail you could never include in a short story. No one would believe it.
>
> Joe Dunthorne on Swansea[1]

Jeff Towns picks me up from Swansea station and wants to know if I would rather go back to his house to relax or go straight to the many rooms where he keeps the vast collection of books and memorabilia he has collected as a book dealer over the last fifty years...

What do you think?

I am soon book-blind. It takes a few minutes for my eyes to adjust to all the spines and all the glory of these possible acquisitions. Shelf after shelf after shelf.

Jeff's whole life has been bookselling and books. He has a deep love of poetry, and a fascination with Surrealism, the Beats and under-appreciated women authors. During lockdown, he inspired me to start selling books too.

Each day at midday he would put up ten books or leaflets on Instagram, at £5 or £10, including postage. It was my daily catnip – my chance to browse while quarantined. I was waiting outside his virtual shop door at midday on the dot. Monday was Marxist Monday; Friday was Feminist Friday; and Saturday was often solely for books, essays and pamphlets about Dylan Thomas.

Looking back, I have no idea why I didn't buy Bernard Shaw's *The Sanity of Art: An Exposure of the Current Nonsense about*

Artists Being Degenerate, or the *History of Croydon Airport*; and I was sadly too late to get the limited-edition signed copy of Tom Baker's children's book *The Boy Who Kicked Pigs*: 'One day, it was in the summer, Robert was alone in the front room watching *Postman Pat* again and suddenly he was struck with the desire to kick a pig. His toes tingled and itched and his calf muscles fluttered. Robert was possessed.'

My multiple purchases from Jeff stretched from *Witchcraft: A Warning* by Aloysius Mullins to Karl von Frisch's book on the vision of bees.

Once I started selling books too, it meant that no money passed between Jeff and me. He would buy books from me and I would buy from him, and our tally between each other would gently meander between profit and loss. When I was putting the day's books online, I would earmark those that I thought Jeff would want; and I knew that when he was putting his online, he would be playing the same mental game with me. He knew that pamphlets on voodoo ceremonies and 1950s lecture notes on neuroscience by a long-forgotten professor would probably go in my direction.

Also, while I was unable to see my dad due to the pandemic, I would buy him books from Jeff too, so that he had some interesting post to open: a pocketbook of Rupert Brooke's poems bound in moleskin; a couple of Ronald Searle cartoon collections; magazines of 1940s film stars; and a letter-writing kit for soldiers in the trenches in the First World War. These gave our daily phone conversations somewhere interesting to go.

Jeff is the first person I share my excited and excitable news with, when I pick up a rarity or peculiarity in a charity shop or jumble sale; and it is Jeff that I ask for advice from, when I am unsure about the rarity of a book.

When he still had a bricks-and-mortar shop in Swansea a post-lavish-lunch Kingsley Amis would occasionally teeter in. One day he asked Jeff, 'Do my books still sell?'

Jeff replied, 'Yes, but not as well as your son's.'

And that was Kingsley's last visit.

Jeff often finds himself called upon when an elderly book-lover has died. Rummaging through the shelves, he pieces together the mind of the departed. He sent me photographs of some of the books from a recently departed ninety-two-year-old autodidact's collection: books on the control and prevention of swarming by bees, on Sylvia Plath and on suicide, on the craft of comedy and the art of neurotics.

He would also buy up books from miners' libraries. These were community libraries filled with great works of science, literature and philosophy, and the books were frequently well-thumbed and digested. *Do Miners Read Dickens?* is a history of the South Wales Miners' Library. The title comes from a question asked by an academic, who was quite bemused by the idea that a coalminer might spend his free time reading *Little Dorrit* or *The Pickwick Papers*.[2]

Looking through the books of one miners' library, Jeff noticed that Marx's *Das Kapital* rarely spent a second on the shelf, and that the date-stamps had become a blur of ink. Winston Churchill's volumes on the life of the Duke of Marlborough were unbroken, unstamped and untouched. Churchill sent the army in to support local mine bosses in 1910 and this had not been forgotten by library card-holders.

This is why I love ex-library books. Ex-library books are considered inadequate in the second-hand book-dealing world, a lumpen, smudgy cousin to the pristine and, preferably, unread. A first edition plummets in price if it has been around the municipal library. But I prefer the ex-library book;

the untainted first edition has no history. When I look around stately homes and find myself in the library, I see the leather books behind caged doors and wonder how many of them were ever read. How many of those printed words came off the page and spun around someone's mind? Did any of those books move or change anyone?

My library edition of Douglas Adams's *The Restaurant at the End of the Universe* was withdrawn from the shelves of West Sussex Libraries on 2 October 1989 after eight years of service. It started taking the people of Shoreham-by-Sea, Worthing and Littlehampton through space and time on 10 April 1981. When I look at the first lines on the yellowed, vaguely tea-splashed first page – 'The story so far: In the beginning the Universe was created. This has made a lot of people very angry and been widely regarded as a bad move' – I can feel extra momentum from the people who have read it before me. There is a memory on those pages of all those people excitedly getting hold of part two of the *Hitchhikers* series: the story they've been waiting for, queued for, put in a request for at Arundel Library.

My first edition of Ursula Le Guin's *Earthsea* trilogy also has a rich history of lending from Ewell Library between 1977 and 1982. I think of the train from Ewell East to London Bridge: while others were bored by Nigel Dempster's diary in the *Evening Standard* as the train stalled at Mitcham Junction again, the Le Guin reader was on a journey with wizards and dragon lords across the Sea of Ea.

My favourite ex-library book is Chelmsford Public Library's edition of the *Penguin Modern Painters* series on Frances Hodgkins. Although its lending history has been torn from the page, the rules of the library remain pasted on the inside cover. These include the fines: 2d for the first overdue week,

3d for each week from then on. And the library's opening hours: 10 a.m. to 8 p.m., but with early closing on Thursday.

And there are rules concerning infection: 'Books which have been exposed to infection or have been in premises where there is infection must *not* be returned to the library but handed at once to the Borough Sanitary Inspector, Coval Lane, Chelmsford.'

My book on John Cage from Caerphilly Library appears never to have been loaned out, but I am sure Cage would have appreciated this silence and would have made something of it.

The most fascinating find from Jeff's storeroom was placed before me by Jeff himself, who clearly knew I would find it irresistible: *Through Darkest Pondelayo* by Serena Livingstone-Stanley, edited by the Rev. Barnaby Whitecorn, DD. The authors though are a ruse, and this is actually the first published work of Joan Lindsay, best known as the author of the uncanny classic *Picnic at Hanging Rock*.

Through Darkest Pondelayo is a spoof travel journal lampooning the adventures of two female colonial explorers, with the subtitle 'An account of the adventures of two English ladies on a cannibal island'. It contains mocked-up photographs that veer somewhere between Surrealist and Dadaist collages, from our pith-helmeted explorers sitting passively on a crocodile – 'A peaceful interlude at the swamp of the blue lily' – to a picture of an Edwardian maid in a wasteland, looking at a witch doctor whose head is growing out of his body like an ambitious marrow.

July 19th Swamp of the Blue Lily

I wish the Pondelayans would drop the ridiculous habit of naming their places after something that is not there

> at all like Dead Mother-In-Law's Cove and now the Swamp of the Blue Lily. I mean Frances and I have been looking for the blue lily for the last hour and the only flower we can see runs along the ground bright yellow and smells of dogs...[3]

I never knew this book existed until Jeff placed it before me, and it was instantaneously necessary.

Tonight I play in a storage freezer, or at least a former storage freezer. My venue in Swansea was once filled with king-prawn party rings, Arctic Rolls and budget pavlovas, all waiting to be distributed across south Wales. It is now the Volcano Theatre, the venue chosen by this evening's bookshop, Cover to Cover, recently shortlisted for Independent Bookshop of the Year Award.

I can only hope that I brought as much joy to the people of Swansea as the fish fingers and crispy pancakes and king-prawn party rings once brought to the christenings and wakes of the people of Port Talbot, Tenby and Kidwelly. Tim, who runs Cover to Cover, was once one of Jeff's pupils in bookselling and has inherited all his mentor's delight in the printed word. My talk is particularly chaotic as I am still coasting on the delirium from peak browsing. Fortunately the audience understand that it is a benign insanity and happily accompany me into some of the more obscure and absurd corners of scientific discovery.

It is hard to perform poetry in Wales, especially when there are aficionados of Beat poets and of Dylan Thomas in the audience, but I tap into my spirit of chutzpah and carry on. Afterwards the crowd is almost as garrulous as I am, and the signing takes even longer than usual. Everyone has an anecdote or the story of an observed star. Some share memories of those they stargazed with, now gone, and the connection still felt when looking at Mars or the constellation of Camelopardalis.

I drink myself down later on with a large glass of red and then retire to Jeff's, where he tells me about booksellers of the past, some shrewd, some kind, and some criminal.

Cardiff

The number of books I have acquired in the last seven days is now preposterous, and Jeff suggests that he could send them back to me at home, but I want them close to me now. They are mine. I now have one whole rucksack packed with books, a wheelie suitcase (with a squeaky wheel) containing clothes and toiletries (and some more books), and two large misshapen carrier bags full of books of many sizes. I am the busker version of the mobile library.

I am a magnificent sight.

I am a piteous sight.

I am a sight to behold.

Today is the smallest bookshop of the 100: I am going to Shelf Life Books and Zines. It is in an arcade in Cardiff of interesting stalls, near a pub where a very drunken man once asked me if I was The Fonz. In Cardiff on a Friday night it is hard to know what the correct answer to such a question is, to avoid being punched. I was not punched, but I believe I found an answer that made me Schrödinger's Fonz. To the boozy man, I was both the Fonz and not the Fonz.

On my way to the bookshop I pass the new statue of Betty Campbell, Wales's first black head teacher. It is a beautiful and inspirational statue; she grows out of a tree trunk and shades the children below her, who are engrossed in reading, playing and conversation. We need more statues of teachers and librarians, this is a good start.

Shelf Life is a not-for-profit radical bookshop run by Rosie, who is a mean guitar player as well as a very generous soul. The shop is more of a corner than a room, and the audience – should they come – will be on the benches of the coffee bar and on any stool, cushion or in any stairwell that can offer space to lean or squat.

Unfortunately there were a few shelves of second-hand books in one of the arcade's clothing stores and it turned out that I needed three of them: *The Death of Cinema: History, Cultural Memory and the Digital Dark Age*; *Words Without Pictures*, an anthology of prose pieces from comic-book writers; and Dr Eustace Chesser's *Woman and Love* from 1962, in which a doctor informs readers about the meaning of orgasm, takes them through fears of abnormality and tells them what they should tell their daughter. Certain lines rise off the page, such as 'A more experienced man would not have found it so exciting to make love to Vera.'

Five minutes before the talk, I knew there would be at least two people attending. In the final minute, everyone turns up. I decide I need a badge from the badge-bucket by the till, so I buy a nice pink badge that says 'powered by kindness'.

This talk is in the open arcade that Shelf Life sits in the corner of, with no shop walls to protect me. It can be a battle to get over the self-consciousness that comes from appearing to be so arrogant that you can stand in the open and demand to be heard by whoever is passing.

Behind the crowd of official attendees, young people with dazzling hair and elegant piercings peer in and seem bemused to see an old man talking loudly about the curvature of spacetime and astronauts, and then reciting poems about anxiety and star systems. Some are even bemused enough to stay.

I try to make sure that the bookshops I approach might attract different audiences, considering that those who come to an Oxfam bookshop may be different from the ones who come to a feminist bookshop, who in turn may be very different from the ones drawn to a comic shop, though all are curious and interesting, however many holes they have in their nose or tattoos they do, or don't, have peeking out from their neckline.

I am relieved that we sell all the copies of my book – not merely for my ego, but for Rosie, as her shop is so tiny that I feel success is even more important on this occasion. I live my life in constant fear of letting people down. A presumption of imminent failure surrounds me like a force-field that knocks over a favourite mug or vase. My awareness of exactly how much work everyone involved in independent bookshops puts in, to keep surviving in high streets so full of chain-stores, means that I have never viewed this tour as a personal frippery. From the first excited reply back in July, I worried about the clash between expectation and reality – that bookshop owners would be apologizing at the surprisingly low turnout and I would be apologizing for failing to be either an attraction or Len Deighton.

During the signing at Rosie's I receive a mixture of book recommendations and archaeological advice. I'm told I must read Brian Catling's *The Vorrh* and that I should find time to visit Tinkinswood Burial Chamber – that it is Neolithic and megalithic. In his *The Modern Antiquarian*, Julian Cope writes that locals believed faeries lived in the stones at Tinkinswood and 'if you sleep there on the nights preceding

May Day, St John's Day or Midwinter's Day, you will either die, go insane or become a poet!'[4]

Penarth

> Piers are examples of engineering excellence, of architectural frivolity and of novel response to social needs.
>
> Simon H. Adamson, *Seaside Piers*

The last time I did an event with Griffin Books, they booked me for a church. This was obviously a lesson learnt, because this time they have realized that my true home is at the end of the pier. Actually, it's the beginning of the pier, as Penarth pier has its theatre by its entrance.

Griffin Books was winner of the Welsh Independent Bookshop of the Year Award at the British Book Awards in 2021. Its website declares that 'a town without a bookshop is a town without a soul'. I thought this derived from Neil Gaiman in *American Gods*: 'What I say is, a town isn't a town without a bookstore. It may call itself a town, but unless it's got a bookstore, it knows it's not foolin' a soul.' But I'm told it is actually from Lucy Dillon's *The Secret of Happy Ever After*, the story of a hard-headed businesswoman who takes over a neglected bookstore and then lots of things are learnt, and people grow and change as they usually do in such scenarios.

Mel from Griffin Books has told me it doesn't matter if I overrun a bit, which is always a mistake, as 'a bit' must be defined or I will interpret it as 'so it can be twice as long as it says on the ticket'. Eventually the signal from her that stopping really is a necessity becomes flamboyant enough that

I know I must shut up and get my pen out, although I keep nattering as I sign. I am sure some people are thinking, 'Just sign the book and let me go!'

Name-spelling is an issue. There are five Nikkis tonight, but they could be Nicki or Nicky, or Nikki or Niki or Nikky, not to mention Nicci. I also learn about ekistics, from a woman in the queue who is almost as overly enthusiastic about her subject as I am about mine.

Birmingham

I am very fond of Birmingham.

It is the main setting in Kit de Waal's *The Trick to Time* and Jonathan Coe's *The Rotters' Club,* both favourites of mine. It is the birthplace of one of my first favourite authors, John Wyndham, who felt like the bridge from childish things to adult books. I have felt like a Chrysalid ever since I first read him.

I am fond of Birmingham too because I am fond of places that are all too easily dismissed. I always cheer on whoever is losing in a game of darts or snooker, which means that I am never satisfied with the outcome.

I am fond of the sense of humour that comes from people who know that others may ignore them or consider them laughable. I am fond of the fact that Birmingham Art Gallery has a great winged statue of Lucifer, penis out and one foot moving from the plinth, as if he is about to walk among us, as the first thing you see when you enter. Some municipal art galleries are tamer with their welcomes, more pastoral or heavenly, while Birmingham Art Gallery is wrestling with your soul from the moment you cross the threshold.

What I do not like about Birmingham is how I always end up in one of Dante's circles of hell – Limbo, Midlands branch – when I try to get from the station to anywhere. If I have ever managed to get to my destination without giving up all hope, without screaming at the sky, without weeping near bollards, without finding that I have walked a mile to return to where I was, then that has been quite wiped from my memory.

The ultimate test of artificial intelligence will be when satnav is able to get you where you want to go in Birmingham rather than suffering a nervous breakdown and singing 'Daisy, Daisy, give me your answer do'.

Day 12 was the first day that I thought the 100-bookshop tour might kill me.

I am aware of what I look like to passers-by. I have gone from hobo to madman – Don Quixote in a duffel coat. I am swearing at puddles, I am screaming at wasteland. I manage to get in contact with Alex, a regular at my Midlands gigs who I know is attending this event. I imagine, when he hears me, he presumes I have rabies. I am the dog Cujo.

He manages to lead me to where I need to go. It was there all the time, but not when I was alone; when I was alone the building was invisible. It is the Thinktank science museum. Sadly, I tried to find an independent bookshop in Birmingham city centre, but could not. I don't like missing out Birmingham on any tour, because the citizens will think I was deliberately avoiding them.

There is a bookshop inside Thinktank, so that counts. There is also a mummified green sea turtle (if not mummified, then at least dried out), a human skeleton and a triceratops head. I have no time for any of this. I am exhausted. I am sodden with my own sweat and self-loathing. I try to dry my hair and face with paper towels, but become flecked with towel fluff, as if trying to stem death by a thousand tiny shaving cuts.

I sit in the middle of the lecture theatre ten minutes before start time and wonder: 'Am I a man or an exhibit?' I am looked at with intrigued eyes by the audience as they walk in. This afternoon's questions include 'Are you taller than Princess Margaret?' It is the first time I am asked this during this tour, but perhaps it will not be the last. By the time I finish, I am salty, but dry. I imagine this is how Lot's wife felt.

Alex gives me a lift to New Street station, which makes everything much simpler. He is off to see Bruce Dickinson, leader singer of Iron Maiden and the author of the *Lord Iffy Boatrace* books. Trains are delayed and cancelled. Being overburdened with bags means that I cannot merely slide into the train – I am my own scrapyard. Many people lunge and elbow to find a seat, so I am satisfied to have a corner of the vestibule again, shared with five others. Nobody seems to possess the necessary aggression that those who are seated have displayed. We shrug at each other with vague smiles, all aware of the absurdities of Sunday travel, and of humanity too.

I have come to the end of the first leg of the 100-bookshop tour.

Returning home, I leave my bags at the door, hoping to sneak them in surreptitiously when my wife is distracted, but the carrier bags reveal themselves audibly as I put them down on the tiles. I walk into the light and see my wife's face. I have an inkling that she is wondering if she might be happier as a melancholy widow.

As I fall asleep I realize that, like me, Birmingham city planners had never heard of ekistics. I know about it now. Do they? Ekistics is the science of human settlements. Its aim is to achieve harmony between the inhabitants of a settlement and their physical and socio-cultural environments. Now you know.

CHAPTER 4

Pity the Llama

Oxford to Norwich

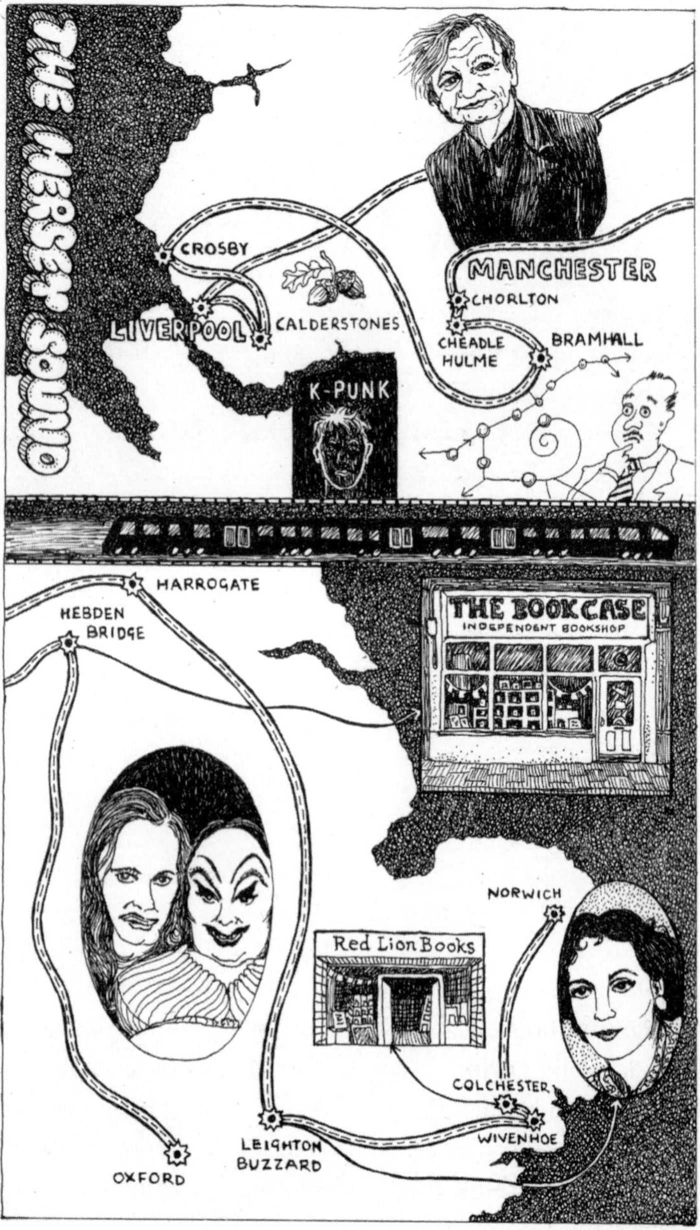
THE MERSEY SOUND
CROSBY
LIVERPOOL
CALDERSTONES
MANCHESTER
CHORLTON
CHEADLE HULME
BRAMHALL
K-PUNK
HARROGATE
HEBDEN BRIDGE
THE BOOKCASE
INDEPENDENT BOOKSHOP
NORWICH
Red Lion Books
COLCHESTER
WIVENHOE
LEIGHTON BUZZARD
OXFORD

I've been browsing the bookshops of Oxford since I was eight. Oxford was always my mother's favourite day-trip. There are so many past browses to recall.

The most important Oxford book for me was Danny Peary's *Cult Movies*. It opened me up to weird movies beyond the horror genre; now it wasn't just Karloff and Lugosi, Cushing and Carradine, it was Divine and David Lynch, Kubrick and Cocteau. As usual, I judged this book by its cover and I was right to do so. It had on it the famous monochrome image of a cinema audience, all in their cardboard glasses, but this had the lenses all coloured red and green. The audience are watching *Bwana Devil*: 'The World's First Feature Length Motion Picture in Natural Vision 3-Dimension' – 'A LION in your lap! A LOVER in your arms!'

I obsessed about the films within the book, many of them totally unwatchable in 1970s and 1980s Britain, so I had to make them up in my head. *Pink Flamingos* was a prime fascination: 'Divine, Crackers and Cotton enthusiastically decide to move to Boise, Idaho. Spotting a small dog defecating on the sidewalk, Divine scoops up the feces with her hand and puts them in her mouth – proving … that Divine is "not only the filthiest person in the world, but is also the world's filthiest actress".' I think that is one of my favourite Wikipedia entries, succinct and to the point.

I still buy any book written by John Waters, a civilized and urbane man who created atrocities on celluloid for a peer group that he described as 'the hate generation'. Of all the books I lost when my basement flat flooded with sewage (and I lost many), my copy of *Shock Value* by John Waters, with its pink leopardskin cover, is probably the book I mourn most.

Cult Movies also introduced me to Werner Herzog. How could I not be intrigued by him, with this summary in the book about the end of his film *Aguirre, Wrath of God*: 'Almost everyone is either dead or dying. Gaspar is shot by an arrow but thinks it is an illusion. Flores is killed. Aguirre decides he will conquer Mexico, marry Flores, and found a pure dynasty. His only live companions, now, are the monkeys which overrun the spinning raft.'

This fascination, respect and awe for Herzog expanded incrementally when I read *Conquest of the Useless*, his account of making *Fitzcarraldo*, and even more so when I read his leading man Klaus Kinski's insane autobiography, *Kinski Uncut*.

Kinski's description of the time he strangled a fly that had maddened him, with the thread from a tablecloth, and then incinerated it should be the maddest story in any autobiography, but it is one of the sanest stories in this one. When I am truly mad, I will one day arrange my books in order of their connections with each other. Every book, it seems to me, has tentacles that spread. Alan Frank's *Horror Movies* will be at one end of the house and Octavia Butler's *Wild Seed* will be at the other, and in between I will work out how one led to the other over forty-five years.

Oxford's Blackwell's is a deceptive bookshop – the bookshop as wizard's cave. I miss the front door on every visit, presuming that it must be a much bigger entrance. From small beginnings, the shop seems to keep unfolding as you walk through it, like some kind of trick of spacetime. It is on many levels. Just when you think it can't be any more subterranean, it goes down another level. Small corners turn into vast worlds. Discreet corners suddenly sprawl.

I am talking in the philosophy section – the section of any bookshop where the time spent browsing is in inverse proportion to the time spent reading what I have bought there. I have such good intentions with those books about Kant and Hegel, by Jean Baudrillard and Mary Midgley, but really I need someone to sum up what they have said and then I can go back to reading about *The Curse of the Living Corpse* and the *Perils from Planet Mongo*. It has been highly advantageous to the tills of bookshops that I am a man unaware of his limitations.

Hebden Bridge

Whether you're on a train approaching Hebden Bridge from Leeds or from Manchester, as you approach the town you can play the game 'Who's getting off at Hebden Bridge?'

Hebden Bridge is the centre of an alternative-culture heartland of the north-west. There is a sartorial style, and a certain choice of paperback to identify, that ups the odds of it being a passenger's destination. I correctly predict that the woman with the pierced lip reading the Rebel Inc. edition of Barry Gifford's *Southern Nights* will disembark there. Too easy!

Tonight was nearly a night off. I was meant to be on the Wirral at Linghams booksellers in Heswall, a store with a shop front as delicious as any ice-cream parlour. Sadly, the owner, Sue, found that some of her events were not selling as they usually did in pre-Covid times and I was among the author casualties. By chance, as the cancellation came through, Nicola on Facebook told me it was a pity that I was not coming to Hebden Bridge. Immediately I emailed The Book Case there, and Kate replied with an immediate 'yes please'. They had presumed that they weren't 'on the list'. I explained that I had never been so organized as to have a list; that this was more a frantic explosion of an idea rather than a military operation.

I looked up the shop on their website – slate floor, Penguin tote bags and a range of *Little People, Big Dreams* picture books that introduce children to Simone de Beauvoir, Ada Lovelace, Georgia O'Keeffe. How could I have missed this bookshop? I can also make out a Leonard Cohen poetry collection and Christie Watson's *The Language of Kindness: A Nurse's Story*. I decide this is a shop displaying exemplary taste.

I arrive in Hebden Bridge just before the Oxfam shop shuts. I'm that annoying final customer coming in when the volunteers thought the shutters could come down. This is good for their coffers. Hasty browsing means that I make snap decisions. This afternoon, at one minute to five, I need Olivia Laing's *To the River* about the River Ouse, the river that Virginia Woolf drowned in. Dipping in, I find a paragraph that reads: 'I am haunted by waters. It may be that I'm too dry in myself, too English, or it may be simply that I'm susceptible to beauty, but I do not feel truly at ease on this earth unless there's a river nearby', and that is enough to persuade me.

Opening books at random is often a good method of making a decision as to whether or not to buy, especially when time is limited. I open another book at random and find myself in the middle of a chapter about the Goddess of the Witches, 'the Queen of Heaven, the pure Huntress of the Moon'. Furthermore, she 'rides the clouds, very cool, untouched by man, filling the night with psychic brilliance'. It turns out that I need such goddess religion and I keep to one side *The Great Cosmic Mother: Rediscovering the Religion of the Earth* by Monica Sjöö.

I am drawn to some 1940s children's picture books by Henry B. Kane. They are illustrated with photographs rather than paintings, and *The Tale of the Promethea Moth* is particularly attractive. There seems to be a whole set and I would have had them all but, with the sweaty mad book-burden around Birmingham still fresh in my mind from forty-eight hours before, I only take a moth and a crow with me. I am no Noah.

You can still get tea and cake in Hebden Bridge after 5 p.m., being a civilized sort of place. England still suffers from the presumption that after 4 p.m. everyone has to start drinking alcohol or the underpasses will go short of piss.

I find out what I can about Henry B. Kane as I toy with my lemon sponge. He sounds like a human being after my own heart: 'While Kane's personal and professional lives were rooted in the Boston area, his artistic abilities and book projects allowed him to travel in his mind's eye, by immersing himself in the variety of habitats and settings that his collaborating authors explored.'[1] The 'B' stood for Bugbee.

The Book Case is full, the crowds are warm and Nicola from Facebook – the reason I have this last-minute gig here – is in attendance too.

It is dark walking back to the station. It is an impressive station, solidly made of stone in 1840 and with heavy iron signs directing me, and others telling me to stay off the line. I am initially alone and the air is damp, and the signals and lamps give off a misty glow. I feel there might be ghosts in the air. I prepare myself to hear 'Halloa! Below there!' and get ready to find myself standing in the middle of Charles Dickens's *The Signalman*.

As I start walking into an imaginary ghost story in my head, I step in some real sick. Caught in my dream of elegant hauntings, I failed to notice that vomit is puddled about the platform. Someone has not stuck to tea and cake. I have shifted from a Victorian ghost story to Dylan Thomas's bathroom.

Chorlton

I feel at home in Manchester and its suburbs. I am a southerner with northern sensibilities. It was always *Coronation Street* for me rather than *EastEnders*. My grandfather fought in the Manchester Regiment during the First World War. A few branches further back on the family tree, my ancestors crossed the border to be Yorkshire vicars.

Much of my cultural education comes from Manchester – The Smiths, Caroline Aherne, The Buzzcocks, Lemn Sissay, Carol Morley, Jeanette Winterson, Jack Rosenthal, Joy Division, Shelagh Delaney, John Cooper Clarke and Mark E. Smith, the sneering autodidact with gums full of speed, whose fecund career created thirty studio albums, which is considerably fewer albums than band members. Being a member of The Fall offered no security. In 2008 Dave Simpson wrote *The Fallen: Life In and Out of Britain's Most Insane Group*, which includes Mark E. Smith's review: 'I just f***ing burned it.'

Smith's autobiography, *Renegade*, feels like sitting down in the pub with him and being told a load of stories, but without the same level of threat. It can seem that Mark E. Smith not only didn't suffer fools gladly, but didn't suffer anyone gladly. You could power a mission to Mars with the hostility created if you placed him and Lou Reed in a wardrobe for an hour.

The bands of Manchester were a literary-minded bunch. Richard Boon,* former manager of The Buzzcocks, who eventually became a librarian in Stoke Newington,** told me that every musician in those post-punk days had a book in their pocket – and not merely for show or an *NME* photoshoot. And there was a time when fans were interested in the books their idols read.

New Musical Express, the inky bible for teenagers when music and the library were our escapes – before screens could dominate and divide – ran a feature called 'Portrait of the Artist as Consumer'. The artists would name the musicians, icons and books kept on the shelf nearest to them. Mark E. Smith listed Kurt Vonnegut, Friedrich Nietzsche, John le Carré and two novels by Colin Wilson. Lydia Lunch cited *Justine* by the Marquis de Sade, the short stories of Charles Bukowski and the Book of Revelation. Not everyone chose books and music. Blixa Bargeld, from Einstürzende Neubauten and Nick Cave and the Bad Seeds, chose mottos, food, dreams, martyrs, disease, syphilis, scurvy and Hildegard von Bingen.

I have three Manchester destinations today, starting at Chorlton-cum-Hardy, once the location of a much-loved

* Richard also appeared on the page on which I first opened Morrissey's autobiography, 'and then Richard Boon said something very unhelpful'. Compared to many others, he survived Morrissey's book unscathed.

** My favourite librarian story comes from Stoke Newington. A ninety-two-year-old book-lover whose eyesight meant she relied on talking books decided she should hear *Fifty Shades of Grey*. The librarian warned her it was a bit racy, but she was having none of it. Two weeks later she rang the librarian: 'Disc four is filthy.' 'I did warn you.' 'No, it's filthy, it looks like it's got jam or marmalade on it. It won't play at all.'

comedy club, The Buzz, which was run by Agraman, the human anagram. Chorlton was also the final resting place of Quentin Crisp, 'the stately homo of England', whose books *How to Become a Virgin*, *Resident Alien* and *The Naked Civil Servant* I devoured as a teenager – an education into another world and a very individual mind. Whenever I approach Chorlton he comes to mind and I hear him say, 'blinded by mascara and dumbstruck by lipstick'.

On the way to Chorlton I pass the Southern Cemetery, inspiration for The Smiths' 'Cemetry Gates', in which Morrissey recalled the 'dreaded sunny day' when he would walk around the memorials and slabs with his friend, the artist Linder Sterling, quoting Keats and Yeats and Oscar Wilde.

Chorlton Bookshop could be an Edward Gorey illustration. It is both mysteriously inviting and funereal. Its windows are fenced in by iron, and it feels both dark and illuminated. Its signage is utilitarian: black paint, neat font, big letters – 'Chorlton Bookshop'. It has survived the pandemic serving customers with their orders through a hatch. It fought another battle in 2014 when it was proposed that there would be a bar over two floors in the premises next door. The booksellers live above the shop and a late-licence bar would have made living and reading very difficult. Locals banded together, protested outside with signs reading 'Books not Bars' and the council listened. There are many bars in Chorlton and this is the only independent bookshop. It proves that we need to fight for what we love while it still breathes, and in Chorlton they did.

Usually I sneak into shops where my events are being staged and browse my way to the counter. I think some of the bookshops expect an entourage, rather than a man and his rucksack peering over his fogged spectacles at the Virago section.

Once spotted, though, I am greeted with tea and biscuits. Drinking coffee seems surly in a bookshop, unless entirely necessary. I hesitate over the biscuits. This is the first of three shops today and I ponder, 'What if the next one has cake, and the one after has gateau?' I risk it.

Midweek daytime book signings are usually quieter, which gives more time to talk. I never like being hurried. I have a long chat with a retired hospital psychiatrist, and discuss the nature of insanity from an R. D. Laing perspective; and I then talk about the demise of *New Musical Express* with a twenty-two-year-old, who also gives me band recommendations. I advise her to read Mark E. Smith's *Renegade* and the memoir of loss by Mark Everett (of Eels), *Things the Grandchildren Should Know*.

I lose confidence in my ability to work out the bus and tram connections to get me to Cheadle and splash out on a cab. Cheadle is my favourite Manchester suburb name, with Timperley a close second; they have the rhythm of town names in children's fiction.

Browsing in the Oxfam bookshop, I find a copy of a book that I wrote with local physicist Brian Cox. I ask them if they would like me to sign it and they say yes, so today is a four-bookshop event day, even if this is only one book.

Turns out I needed a poetry anthology edited by John Arlott, a book on fashion and image in twenty-first-century New York and an updated edition of George Gamow's *Mr Tompkins* stories. Gamow was a brilliant physicist and a pioneering voice in understanding the Big Bang theory of the universe. He wrote the *Mr Tompkins* books to help people gain an understanding of revolutionary ideas in cosmology. Mr Tompkins goes on adventures in his dreams, where the laws of the universe are different from our own. For instance, falling asleep in a lecture about relativity, he finds himself in a world where the speed of light is ten miles per hour.

I need stories like this if I am ever going to start understanding the universe. What I probably don't need is Heidegger's *Being and Time* AGAIN. Nigel behind the counter tells me that, despite reading it a few times, he still knows no more of Heidegger than Monty Python has taught him, and he asks me to come back with a precis. I say that I expect to get two pages in before surrendering. Bertrand Russell wrote of Heidegger's *Being and Time*, 'Highly eccentric in its terminology, his philosophy is extremely obscure. One cannot help suspecting that language is here running riot.'[2] Philosopher Roger Scruton wrote that it was 'formidably difficult – unless it is utter nonsense, in which case it is laughably easy'.[3] I am not smart enough to be able to tell which from which.

Greenhouse Books in Cheadle is mainly a second-hand bookshop as well as a vegan café. The cake looks great, but I've only just eaten biscuits. Janet runs it with her son, Jonathan. He is also a poet. I buy a local magazine with some of his work in it.

My Greenhouse Books talk is in the derelict shop next door, a white space that feels like a launderette that has forgotten to install washing machines. I will be the tumbling clothes that they stare at today.

I get lots of thorough questions and, after the talk, the other people who work in the shopping arcade pop in. They all buy books too. For a small arcade in Cheadle, it turns out that I am 'an event' and I am very happy to be one. Dr Eve from the Chinese Medical Centre is followed by Anna, who is a nail technician with an interest in biotechnology. I almost make it out of Greenhouse Books without a purchase, but then I spy a postcard of James Baldwin and a book about Maria Marten's murder in the Red Barn: 'Why did a squalid village murder become the most famous murder of the nineteenth century?' I suppose I should find out.

The biscuits seem so long ago now that cake appears necessary and delicious. Fortunately, I am offered no cake when I get to Simply Books in Bramhall. Their café is closed while the pandemic still seems so uncertain – gateau could be a super-spreader. I have a few minutes alone on the first floor of the bookshop, so I use that time to put the books of my friends facing outwards on the shelves, and the books of my enemies into darker corners.

Simply Books is run by former teachers Sue and Andrew, and is home to a knitters' group as well as numerous readers' groups. Sue says, 'If we just focused on money, it wouldn't work. By engaging with the community we are letting people know we are here.' They also run a cinema group. Impressively, the artist and author Oliver Jeffers chose it as the only UK bookshop that he would do an event in, when he launched the book he illustrated, *The Day the Crayons Quit*. Jeffers's *The Incredible Book Eating Boy* is a true engineering feat of a pop-up book and comes in my top three favourite pop-up books. Number one will always be the M. C. Escher pop-up book, simply for its chutzpah – attempting to make 3D versions of images that portray scenes that cannot possibly exist in a 3D world.

I return to Levenshulme and the self-inflating lilo. Carl has a chihuahua with attitude visiting him. Its bark is definitely bigger than its bite. It is relentlessly noisy and has bulging eyes like angry bubble gum on the verge of bursting.

I used to know a woman with two far more amiable chihuahuas. She was a large rural woman and they were small, even by the standards of miniature Mexican dogs. Not wishing to leave them at home when shopping or outside the supermarket, she would place them inside her bra and then wear over them a voluminous tweed coat. Fortunately, in the warmth they fell asleep and didn't wriggle too much.

Liverpool

Poetry began for me in Liverpool. The first book of poetry I bought was *Mersey Sound* by Brian Patten, Adrian Henri and Roger McGough.

When I went for my university interview to do an English degree I am pretty sure I remember saying that McGough meant more to me than Browning. I'd seen Roger McGough at the Edinburgh Fringe Festival, but Robert Browning was never there.

It is three bookshops around Liverpool today. The journey from Levenshulme takes me through Bootle. Bootle sounded fictitious to me when I was young – a perfect name for comedy routines. It might be because I came to know it from Kenny Everett's autobiography *The Custard Stops at Hatfield*:

> I'm sure my Mother hasn't forgiven me for being born at that unearthly time of day. She used to take it out on me by showing me postcards of a place called Bootle which was near where we lived and was where you were sent if you were a naughty boy. Bootle was full of holes, due to the bombs and Hitler and all that.

It's a fifteen-minute walk from the station to the centre of Crosby. The streets are quiet, or were until I started dragging my suitcase through them – the wheel squeals like Beatlemania.

Pritchards Bookshop has been on the high street for more than forty-five years. It is the perfect neighbourhood bookshop and was named one of the highlights of the town, along with Antony Gormley's statues on the beach, when Crosby was listed as one of the best places to live by the *Sunday Times*.

Today people are mainly buying my book for daughters and sons who are off to study at university. I am told that I am intended to be the cheerleader for their first year of theoretical physics or forensic botany. A geologist also comes in and explains to me why it is scientifically necessary to chew rocks.

As usual, I am drawn to the local-interest books and see one by Joan Boyce about being a Littlewoods Pools Girl. Processing Littlewoods Pools coupons was at one time one of the largest job providers for women in Liverpool.* This book is the voice of those women. The author's son is Frank Cottrell-Boyce, author of prize-winning screenplays and children's books. He was the writer of the 2012 London Olympics opening ceremony – the one that people excitedly anticipated would be awful and were then frustrated by it being rather wonderful.

After Crosby, I go to talk to Liverpool's oldest oak in its largest Druid park, Calderstones. The Calder Stones are six megaliths that are the remains of a Neolithic burial site. The Allerton Oak is more than 1,000 years old and won a Tree of the Year competition in 2019. It has such a central place in the imagination of local people that during the Second World

* A social-media pal told me what it was like, when she was thirteen and went for job experience from school to a week at Littlewoods. She told me of the sense of empowerment and independence these women oozed and of the 'no shits given' attitude that 'just screamed out'.

War, Liverpool soldiers were sent acorns from it, as tokens from home.

The afternoon's shop event is at The Reader. Not just a shop, it is the base for a reading charity celebrating and encouraging social reading where people sit together and read aloud – sometimes children, sometimes old people with dementia, and sometimes visiting prisons too.

I once took part in a group reading of Alistair Fruish's *The Sentence*. Alistair works in prisons, bringing in as much art and inspiration as various governors and Home Secretaries will allow. He found that many of the inmates he worked with had minimal reading skills as they had been deprived of a great deal of education. One of the problems they had was with punctuation, so Alistair wrote *The Sentence* – a story with only one very, very long sentence and where all the words are of one syllable.

At the public reading eight of us readers sat on stools on the stage, and we were conducted by Daisy Campbell. It required intense concentration. There was no preordained order of who would read at any given time. Someone began and we all had to follow their words carefully, never knowing when we would be chosen to step in and read ourselves. When a reader had read around three pages, Daisy would suddenly point at another reader to step in. If any of the audience went to the toilet, the bar or to have a cigarette, then a reader from the stage was chosen by Daisy to follow that audience member and continue reading. Sometimes we were reduced to only four people onstage, with four people off somewhere following different audience members. Sometimes two of us would be standing with two smoking people, creating a stereophonic experience. On one occasion I almost walked into the toilet cubicle with the woman I was reading to. It was reading as an act of shamanism. We all left feeling dazed and elated.

The final talk of the day is for the Merseyside Skeptics, in conjunction with News From Nowhere, a not-for-profit radical and community bookshop. It is a member of the Alliance of Radical Booksellers and, having been a few times previously, I know that every visit is an education in itself, such is the unusual quality of its stock. I always find books I didn't know existed. Last time it was Patti Smith's *Devotion: Why I Write* and *K-Punk: The Collected and Unpublished Writings of Mark Fisher*, a highly readable cultural theorist who, sadly, took his own life before he was fifty.

Fisher's last book was *The Weird and The Eerie*, a study of the disturbing and uncanny: 'The perspective of the eerie can give us access to the forces which govern mundane reality but which are ordinarily obscured, just as it can give us access to spaces beyond mundane reality altogether.'[4] My selfish reaction to his death was, 'Didn't you realize how much more I wanted to read from you?'

His work is typical of much that I find on the shelves of News From Nowhere – books that make you feel that reality has changed a little, and that new corners have been illuminated.

The Skeptics couldn't use their usual venue, so we found ourselves in the back room of a swanky cocktail bar. Most modern bars are swanky to me, so I admit that it might seem quite humdrum to you, but it was spacious, geometrically sharp and there were many pierced olives and spirals of lemon rind. While those near the neon drank Manhattans, they were unaware that just yards away there was an enthusiastic discussion about chimpanzee language and event horizons.

When I finally stopped talking, we all knew we were too dowdy for such an environment and retired to the Philharmonic Dining Rooms, the first purpose-built Victorian pub to be a Grade 1-listed building. They serve a good pint, but it is when the pint has almost passed through you that you truly find out why it is Grade 1. It has some of the finest urinals you will ever wee into. They are so renowned for their design that it is one of the rare male toilets that women actually want to visit. I once had to escort a historian to the Philharmonic Dining Rooms toilets after last orders, as she was desperate to view the wonder of the marble washbasins and mosaic floors.

I return to the budget-chain hotel of my choice: sterile, friendly, usually quiet. I'm aware that sleep may be harder to come by, as I need to leave early to get to the Harrogate Literary Festival for an interview at 11.30 a.m. When the opportunity to sleep is limited, my anxious brain decides to nudge me awake like an antsy child on Christmas Eve.

Initially there's a possibility of seven and half hours' potential sleep. Then the couple next door return. It is a Thursday and they have had a good night. The hubbub of noise suggests that they are going to make the most of their night away from the family. They put on the Stereophonics' 'Have a Nice Day' and that gets them in the mood. The combination of loud sighs and moans and pub rock-music is like pine air-freshener being used after someone has been excessive in the bathroom; the attempt to conceal it makes it far worse on all fronts. Fortunately, they are spent by half-past midnight, but now that time has closed in on me, my brain decides that anxiety should replace sleep. Eventually I surrender, prop myself up and turn to an emergency insomnia book. These are books that I love and know well, so I can saunter through their landscape without worrying that I am missing something. For this journey, it's Edna O'Brien's *The Country Girls*: 'You're a right-looking eejit.'

Harrogate

On Friday there is an awkward public-transport double. First a trip from Liverpool Lime Street to Harrogate, then Harrogate to Leighton Buzzard: 380 miles in all.

I am very early for the Harrogate Literature Festival. The event is in a hotel ballroom that has a hint of the out-of-season Overlook Hotel. Will I be playing to the living or to the ghosts of those who tangoed there?

On my way I accidentally pass by the Oxfam bookshop. I have had a whole day of not buying a book, so I wonder whether maybe my habit has waned or is at an end. Maybe I can make it two days.

No. First, I need *Bigfoot: The Yeti and Sasquatch in Myth and Reality*. This is a Readers Union' Book Club edition and includes details of other exciting book-club choices, such as the science-fiction book club's choice of the month, *Killer Pine*, and *Guns Covered with Flowers* from the crime-fiction club.

Second, I need a copy of Jack Finney's *The Body Snatchers*, a book that went on to be adapted at least three times as a movie. It is a good story for our paranoid, untrusting times.

The final question is: do I need the hardback first edition of Colin Wilson's *The Occult* or Keith Thomas's *Religion and the Decline of Magic*? The answer to both must be *No*. I own both of these in paperback and, if I am honest, though I am fond of *The Occult* as it was my first Colin Wilson, it frequently makes no sense at all, though in a pleasingly nonsensical way to me – unlike Deepak Chopra, say. On the fiftieth anniversary of *The Occult*, the *Fortean Times* wrote, 'Wilson whizzes all over the place. No sooner does a thought pop into his head than it clatters out of his typewriter...'[5] This might explain my fondness for him.

At the festival itself I end up having rather a tangential discussion with the interviewer, Matt. I am either a very easy interviewee or very difficult, depending on what you can run with. The one thing you will rarely get is an awkward silence, though there might be some awkward hectic noise. My mind always hurries and makes connections very rapidly, so within seconds we can be many miles from what the question was actually about. I like to be surprised by what I say – it makes me work harder to find out what I mean.

The train to London is delayed and full, so the vestibule is mine again.

I am too tired to read, so I hypnotize myself with passing cooling-towers, although I am occasionally interrupted by a sound loop of the Stereophonics spliced with approaching orgasms. Exhaustion can bring out the worst from my memory.

Leighton Buzzard

Leighton Buzzard was home to Mary Norton, creator of *The Borrowers* series, the children's version of Jean Genet's *The Thief's Journal*.

Leighton Buzzard's bookshop means business – it is called simply Book. It is a small and bright shop in a pretty brick-lined arcade. There is cake and tea, but by the time I arrive the audience are arriving too. The cake is cut, and I place it in my eyeline. It will be my reward and incentive to keep to time. I eye the sponge drying out as I talk about the death of the universe via a big rip.

I talk a little about dreams, and during the Q&A I am asked what I dreamt recently. They may regret this. Having had no dreams the night before, I have to go back to a Wednesday dream, when I was in the house of the chihuahua. The late Paul Newman and I had to give a lecture at a college campus. It was badly laid out and, to make it worse, although Newman was alive, he was also dead and had to be held up by bits of string, like a clumsy marionette. Being both dead and alive made Newman very grumpy.

I don't expect any payment for doing events, whether the bookshop is charging for seats or not, but I do like it when I am paid with a book. Tonight the book is *The Quiet Zone* by Stephen Kurczy. It is about Green Bank in West Virginia, the location of the US National Radio Astronomy Observatory. The sensitivity of the telescopes there is such that it is illegal to operate any electrical device emitting radio-frequency interference within a ten-mile radius – no Wi-Fi or mobile phones. While I read about the silence I can hear a stag-night working out the route to the next round of Jägerbombs.

Wivenhoe

> Those who spend the greater part of their time in reading or writing books are, of course, apt to take rather particular notice of accumulations of books when they come across them.
>
> M. R. James, 'A Neighbour's Landmark'

East Anglia seems a popular destination this Saturday morning. The carriages are packed, and many people are still breathing out last night's excess. Is everyone on my train going in search of one of the lost crowns of the kings of Albion? No, it appears they are going to the Lion Walk Shopping Centre in Colchester.

This is fortunate, because finding a lost crown of a king of Albion rarely turns out well, as readers of M. R. James's 'A Warning to the Curious' know. His uncanny tales always play in my mind as I travel through East Anglia.

I am changing trains first at Colchester for Wivenhoe, an idyllic village that feels like it could be a suitable location for an academic to unearth something uncanny and strange. It is also where Francis Bacon came when he wanted to export the cacophony of Soho life to rural Essex. He would come to visit the artist couple Denis Wirth-Miller and his partner Richard Chopping, known as Dicky. The legends of their antics can still be heard about in the Rose and Crown pub in the village. At that time Dicky was designing the covers of the James Bond books. These iconic hardback covers are more about decay than sex and glamour – a little bit Mexican Day of the Dead, with skulls and roses, and flies on gun handles or infesting dead fish and conch shells.

Wivenhoe Bookshop is white-painted and timbered. It has the look of both Olde England and New England. Autumn is being swept out of the shop when I arrive. I am pleased to see *Why Marianne Faithful Matters* displayed prominently on the shelves.

It's a small bookshop, however, so my event is in the church opposite. A well-dressed elderly gentleman is in the churchyard and asks if he can get tickets for 'this talk'. I tell him that I think it is sold out, but I am the one delivering the talk and will happily give him a precis while we are standing around the tombs. He looks at me like a madman, so I point him in the direction of people who know what they are talking about. I notice that he has hearing aids. I was once told, by the author and editor Diana Athill, that I spoke too fast for her hearing aids, so maybe that was the issue.

I browse the graves. One is for a man called Philip Sainty, a yacht-builder who lived for ninety years and died in 1844. I have not seen the name Sainty before. Next to the Sainty grave is a much smaller stone in memory of a man who died with Nelson at the Battle of Trafalgar. I am later informed that Sainty's yachts were sometimes built for altruism and sometimes for smuggling.

The talk is in the church's newly built function room, which has a beautiful view over the churchyard, and a serving hatch with a tea urn and a wide selection of biscuits on plates that would work as the perfect proscenium arch for Victoria Wood.

The crowd is predominantly of retirement age or beyond, and they all seem to have a warm, investigative glint in their eyes. They look eager to be challenged and to be challenging. The audience make voluble gasps when I talk about the size of the universe and the number of stars within it. I want to be expansive about the expansion of the universe, but I am also aware that I need to be at Red Lion Books in Colchester by 3 p.m. I keep talking and signing until I am told the train is approaching.

After the peacefulness and birdsong of Wivenhoe, the Saturday franticness of Colchester winds me. The town centre is hectic with buoyant goths, bickering couples and people who have started their Saturday night a few hours before sundown.

My path is littered with charity shops, but I have no time to spare – well, maybe a little bit. It seems that I need a six-DVD set of The Three Stooges with a book attached.

Red Lion Books has a bland shop front concealing many fabulous worlds within. It was started by Sarah and Peter in 1978 and focused particularly on science fiction and fantasy. It is now run by Colchester's self-declared 'Book Club Queen', Jo. It is busy with browsers, and questions on Philip K. Dick, children's ghost stories and the Hairy Bikers are flying about in all directions.

I am talking in some disused office space above the shop. Jo has kindly bought me a vegan sandwich and some ring doughnuts, but there is no time, so I will rely on the energizing effect of my churchyard shortbread two hours before.

This is a much younger audience, which includes two eleven-year-old girls in the front row, back from their Saturday-morning drama club. A mug of tea is covertly positioned by my feet after I begin my talk. The shortbread in my system has begun to fade and, twenty minutes in, I feel dizzy and start to lose my balance. I don't tell anyone, but decide to do the rest of the talk sitting down. I feel this now gives me the posture of a storyteller and the gravitas that comes with it, though the light-headedness continues.

I end up reading one more poem than usual. I like reading my poetry, although I am quite aware that I am not a proper poet and will usually dismiss my work as 'just some words in a shape'.

After the book signing I talk to Alex, who tells me he bought a copy of Freud's *Totem and Taboo* from me when I was selling some of my book collection online. Alex is now going to study anthropology. In so many books there is the possibility of something we can be that we had never known existed until we turned the first page.

My third bookshop of the day was going to be the

Woodbridge Emporium, but they had to cancel due to ill health. I sign some books to be sent on to them. I must apologize to purchasers in Suffolk, as you might have found some doughnut sugar in between the pages. The doughnuts make me feel that I am alive again, and I manage to walk in a straight line all the way to the station.

Norwich

The bookseller for my event at the Norwich Science Festival is The Book Hive, which achieved some notoriety when the author Susan Hill cancelled an event there, apparently because they chose not to stock pro-Donald Trump books. She cancelled the event without telling the shop why, but then wrote a piece explaining her reasons, without naming the shop, for the *Spectator*. The owner, Henry Layte, disagreed with many of Hill's accusations, but wrote in an open letter on the bookshop's website, 'The point of an independent bookshop is that it creates an identity, fostered by and for the community which it serves, the authors who live near by, the landscape that surrounds it, the trades and professions that flourish there, its history, its future, and so, yes, very much, its political persuasion.'

Various people took sides online. This sort of feud is now stoked so often, with the ease of attracting a speedy mob via social media. If a contentious book is not stocked, it is soon spun into a tale of censorship rather than taste. What I love about many independent bookshops is that the character of those within the shop can be displayed on the shelves. In that ugly capitalist judgement, the market will decide, but as long as a bookshop – however quirky its tastes – sells enough books to remain solvent, then it's up to the owners what they wish to put on their shelves, and for me that's that.

I am introduced to the stage by Ben, a man who had been elbow-deep in a dead llama some hours before: a first for me. He'd been running a 'for all the family' llama autopsy. The cupcake-eating kids had to be reminded to step away from the 'splash zone' when munching on their icing. I rarely find llama pancreas an enticing accompaniment to cake.

While I was sitting on a garden bench outside Norwich Arts Centre a woman with a sketchpad approached me and said she was going to be extremely rude. Like most people who approach you kindly and warn you of imminent rudeness, she was not rude at all, but wondered if I would sign her sketchpad. I said I would, but only if she would let me look at her sketches first. They were a riot of beautifully inked trees.

After signing books, Henry told me that someone had left something for me and handed me a sketch of a tree that is now my most splendid bookmark.

To rid my thoughts of dead llamas, I pulled a book out of my rucksack and started to read of the Promethea moth in Henry B. Kane's book: 'For a while, his battered wings stirred feebly, but at last, as the shadows grew deeper, they were stilled. The big Promethea had made his last flight, and the pale pink flowers of the partridge vine, hanging overhead, nodded a last farewell.'

CHAPTER 5

Mermaids and Mermonks?

Okehampton to Shoreham

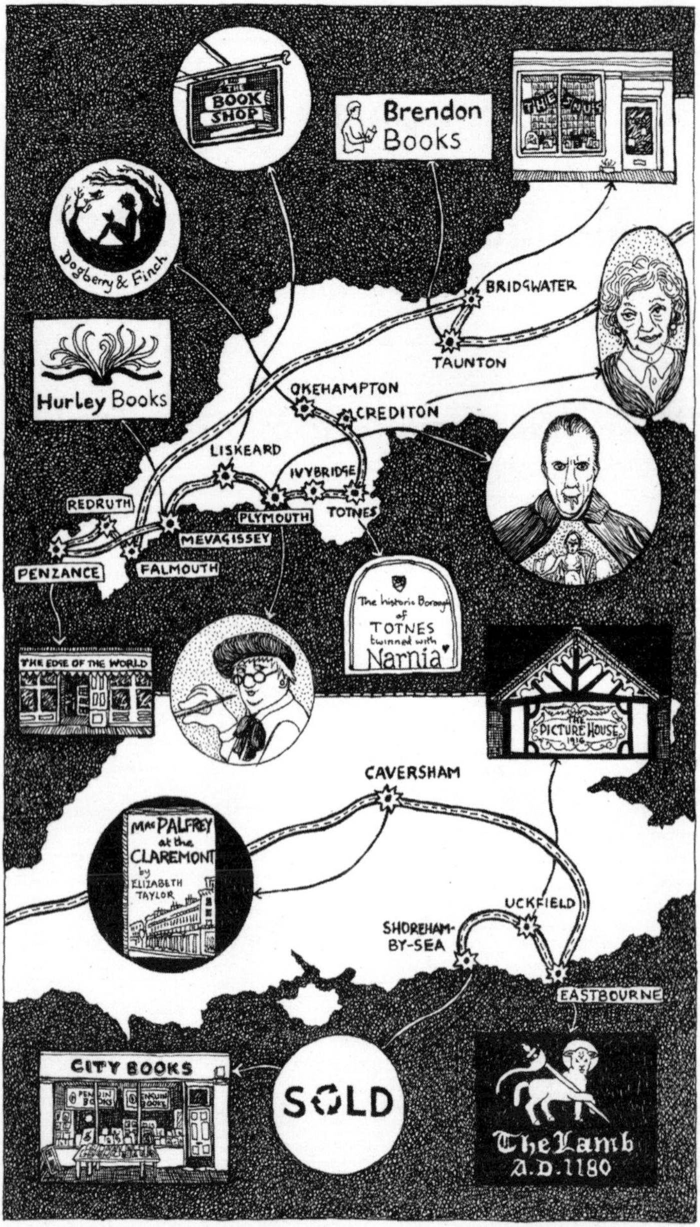
THE BOOK SHOP
Brendon Books
Dogberry & Finch
Hurley Books
BRIDGWATER
TAUNTON
OKEHAMPTON
CREDITON
LISKEARD
IVYBRIDGE
REDRUTH
PLYMOUTH
TOTNES
MEVAGISSEY
PENZANCE
FALMOUTH
The historic Borough of TOTNES twinned with Narnia
THE EDGE OF THE WORLD
THE PICTURE HOUSE 1916
CAVERSHAM
Mrs PALFREY at the CLAREMONT by ELIZABETH TAYLOR
UCKFIELD
SHOREHAM-BY-SEA
EASTBOURNE
CITY BOOKS
PENGUIN BOOKS
SOLD
The Lamb A.D. 1180

This week I have fifteen venues and six counties scheduled. I am exploring the West Country of England, which has a prolific number of independent bookshops. Dogberry & Finch Books in Okehampton is the first.

After a train journey troubled by a father and son who felt that their adored luggage deserved the comfort of a seat more than the people who were standing, I despise them and create a daydream in my head where I am played by Spencer Tracy, taking revenge for all the unseated. I am collected from Exeter by Linus, whose wife runs the bookshop. The big question when I arrive in Okehampton is: 'Where is Barometer World?' I was quite sure it was here.

When I ask Linus about the tourist attraction that celebrates the predictive nature of air-pressure measurement, he knows nothing of it. I first came across Barometer World before a gig I did in Hartland Point, where I had to hastily put together an act and used the tourist-attraction leaflets in the local pub as a resource. There was The Big Sheep farm and theme park, the Gnome Reserve and there was Barometer World. I then read about it in *Bollocks to Alton Towers: Uncommonly British Days Out*, in which the authors describe the Banfield Collection – the priceless barometers that form the centrepiece of the Barometer World exhibition – as 'a pretty baffling collection to the atmospheric novice'; but then go on to say that overall it is, fortunately, 'Just the slightest bit bonkers'.

I desperately want to go, but on further investigation it seems that Barometer World was on the outskirts of Okehampton, but is now closed for good. I waited too long. Mind you, had I been able to visit, I might have ended up buying an antique barometer and carting that around on public transport for a week, on top of all the books I will undoubtedly buy.

Dogberry & Finch's bookish name hails from the policeman in *Much Ado About Nothing* and the lawyer hero from *To Kill a Mockingbird*. It is a former florist's shop, and is now decorated with beautiful paintings of birds' nests. It is a bright and pretty shop. I imagine the bees still come back and bump their heads on the *Collins Guide to Wild Flowers*.

Kate opened Dogberry & Finch in September 2019. In the centre of the main window is an enchanting painting, a silhouette of a tousled-haired reader under a tree, being observed by a bird. It perfectly captures that spell when you are lost in a book, retreating into the shade and advancing into new worlds. The shop is the winner of the Muddy Stilettos Award for best local bookshop. Kate has made small cream-tea scones, which I use as energy pills.

Gilby and Jane are the first of the audience to arrive. Gilby has multiple sclerosis and is now a wheelchair user, yet still managed to get to the top of Belstone Tor with the help of a team from North Dartmoor Search & Rescue. It fills out to be an audience of teachers, retired teachers, scientists and one admirer of the current prime minister – a rarity. For the whole tour she will remain the only person to openly express admiration for the prime minister.

Crediton

> Dr Mortimer looked strangely at us for an instant, and his voice sank almost to a whisper as he answered: 'Mr Holmes, they were the footprints of a gigantic hound!'
>
> Arthur Conan Doyle, *The Hound of the Baskervilles*

It's dark when I get to Crediton.

Jean Rhys lived nearby in the village of Cheriton Fitzpaine. She described it as 'a dull spot which even drink can't enliven much', although locals beg to differ. She is buried in St Matthew's Church. I wish I had time to make a small pilgrimage, although I imagine she would have sneered at such frippery. The title of her fourth novel, *Good Morning, Midnight*, is carved into the gravestone, the phrase coming from an Emily Dickinson poem:

Good Morning – Midnight!
I'm coming Home –
Day – got tired of Me –
How could I – of Him?

The Bookery is a community bookshop in Crediton whose mission statement is 'to create an environment for enterprising, resilient and creative communities inspired by books and stories'. I keep thinking I should get a mission statement – it might give me a little more focus. Then again, if I had focus, I probably wouldn't be throwing myself around the country like this. If my diagnosis of ADHD is true, then I must start to acknowledge that the very things that I rail against, the manic intensity with which I decide on new quests, the inability not to be distracted by a new connection when I haven't finished explaining the previous five tangents, the snappy, judgemental inner voice, all play a part in getting things done.

The Bookery believes that brilliant books change lives, and I will not argue with that. I am being interviewed by a local folklorist whose most recent book is on Black Dog folklore. These Black Dogs are an omen of death, the kind of dog that Jack Stapleton wanted people to believe the hound of the Baskervilles was.

I risk having a glass of wine during our conversation, something I would never do when talking alone. I can't overrun too much, as my father-in-law is coming to collect me. At fifty-two years old, I still rely on parents and relatives to pick me up at the end of the day. I just don't have the kind of mind that should be in control of a car, with too many other thoughts to enable me to keep focused on the white lines.

As usual, my responses to the questions are more of a chain reaction than an answer. Only one purchase as I leave: a signed copy of Jeanette Winterson's *12 Bytes*. She always educates me.

Totnes

Totnes used to be 'Twinned with Narnia' – at least according to the elegant graffiti on one of the town signs. Sadly, this fabulous possibility was scrubbed off before the effect of the vastly increased sales of Turkish delight could truly be felt.

As I arrive in Totnes, as usual a past purchase flashes before my eyes: Les Dawson's *A Time Before Genesis*. Anyone who admired the comedian's eloquent turns of phrase would not be surprised that he was a novelist too. I first read his *A Card for the Clubs*, which was a grimily evocative look at the unscrupulous nature of show business. Every page puts dirt under your fingernails and soot in your eye, whether it's the pianist leaving the stage – 'Eventually she descended the platform with all the unconscious grace of a gouty hippo' – or the description of that night's digs – 'A mean crooked thoroughfare of terraced holes, that glared through dirty windows on to the cobbled street.'

A Time Before Genesis is his most surprising novel. It is a dystopian thriller about the coming of the Antichrist, sitting somewhere between the work of James Herbert and David Icke. The inner flap tells readers that we'll be entering a world where there 'is an evil force at work, exploiting man's basest instincts and promising youth, sexual gratification and longevity to its adherents, in order to undermine what goodness there is in the world and fight against the expected second coming'. It never made it into paperback but you'll be lucky to pick it up now for less than £50 online. I got it for six quid – another gazelle speared. It used to be Geoff's copy, a gift from Reg. Now it's mine.

The East Gate Bookshop window exudes friendliness. I could imagine my mother walking out of it in a headscarf with her wicker basket full of Wilbur Smith and Dick Francis novels on her way to buy an ox tongue. (Oh, how I hated ox tongue as a child – such punishment.) Nigel opened the bookshop twelve days before the second major lockdown closed him for more than four months, but he has survived.

It's 11 a.m. in half-term week, so there is a broad audience, from eight to eighty-eight years old. The talk is being held in Totnes Cinema, which was formerly a library and then formerly a cinema again. I can almost hear the ghosts of the librarians, but of course they are as quiet being dead as they were alive. Some of us hold shells up to our ears to hear the sea, but I hear the soft shushing of a librarian in my conch.

The room is a mixture of Art Deco and exposed brick. The balcony is decorated with an ominous lion roaring. I am not sure whether either Gregory Peck or Audrey Hepburn would have dared put their names forward, had *Roman Holiday* had its sequel in Totnes.

My family comes along today, including my wife, son, sister-in-law and parents-in-law. This puts on extra pressure. It is one thing to disappoint hundreds of strangers, but quite another to disappoint five members of your family, who might continue to bear a grudge until Christmas or beyond. Nina Simone is playing on the stereo, so I start my talk with *Nina Simone's Gum*, one of my favourite books of 2021. It is inspired by the chewing gum that Nina Simone stuck on the Steinway at the Southbank Centre; then she fought the piano into submission, until they became a singular thing of transcendent beauty. The gum, preserved by author and composer Warren Ellis, now has the wonder of a religious icon and is cast in gold.

People are touchingly open at the signing. I meet a beautiful dog called Stargaze, and hear from a mother and daughter about how important the communication of science has been for them during difficult times. When we lose our purpose, when we feel that we are pointless, it can be an agonizing struggle, and to hear that I have been useful to strangers means a lot to me.

Someone else buys the book for their ninety-two-year-old grandfather who couldn't attend. Later in the year he sends me a message to say that his grandfather told him 'this is the book I have been waiting for', which delights me. It is still early in the tour, but all these small bookshop events are creating vivid connections. As someone plagued by energetic negative voices, the memory of this warm camaraderie is something that I can call on, when in battle with them.

Totnes station is a plain station, but it has something that I delight in: a café in the old signal box. I have a fresh fried-egg sandwich on soft white bread – today's madeleine. I am not sure Proust would approve, as the ketchup gets caught in my beard. As John Hegley has written in *Can I Come Down Now Dad?*:

We're looking forward to our crusty rolls
We've got platform tickets and platform souls.

I have two hours to murder in Ivybridge, but it starts to close down at 3 p.m. I view cakes from a distance as the *Closed* sign rattles on freshly locked doors. Fortunately the river has no choice but to stay open, so I look at that for a while. The charity shops have nothing for me: bestsellers from a decade ago, Jeremy Clarkson's columns and Richard & Judy favourites.

The talk at the Ivybridge Bookshop* is at 4.30 p.m., and at 4.20 p.m. the shop is still empty. These ten minutes of dread expand to fill half my life. A watched chair is never occupied. Fortunately I look away and, when I look back, the chairs are filled with teachers who have hurried in with knotted bags full of marking, and people who are intrigued to know if I exist beyond being a voice on the radio. Is it possible that I could be solid?

The usual shock when people see the corporeal me is that I look very, very old for fifty-two, but I'll happily be as lined

* A couple of months after my visit the Ivybridge Bookshop was named National Book Tokens Newcomer of the Year 2022.

as Beckett. Good looks never played a part in my zigzagging career path.

Plymouth

> For 20 years, I have had the good fortune to live, work and play in Plymouth. Going shopping, walking the dogs, sitting in pubs, I am constantly entertained by the things going on around me. To see people enjoying themselves gives me the greatest pleasure, and the inspiration to paint.
>
> Beryl Cook, Plymouth Arts exhibition of her work, 2017

It would be hard for the people of Plymouth to be as joyous as Beryl Cook's representation of them, whether it's her punks on Plymouth Hoe or miniskirted clubbers under a green umbrella in the rain.

Matt and Wynnie, who run the Ivybridge Bookshop, also come to Plymouth to sell books at my event for the Plymouth Humanists, which takes place in a Chinese restaurant and bar. On the way they tell me about their previous life in Hong Kong and how they travelled to England by land – and some sea, obviously. They are unassuming people who nevertheless have an incredible story.

This is the first Chinese restaurant I've played on this tour, and I burn my tongue on a spring roll that I am too impatient with. I develop a vague lisp for the duration of the talk, so decide not to talk about seismic shifts, satellite systems or symbiosis. The third talk of the day is always the trickiest. My mind keeps saying, 'Didn't you just say that? Are they laughing because what you are saying is funny or because it is the third time you have said it tonight? Are you trapped in the loop of a single anecdote about Richard Feynman that you are simply saying over and over again?'

For the second time today I have a conversation with a member of the audience who is brimful of emotion. Onstage, and in the conversations I have with the audience afterwards, I can be at my most emotionally honest, before the shutters go down in order to survive the rest of day-to-day life. The genuine is often followed by a punchline, for fear that I've revealed too much. It seems safer to live my life 'only joking', although I am battling the habit.

I am staying with my friend Johnny tonight: archivist, author and my accomplice in the *Dead Funny* horror anthology series. He has a magnificent collection of book memorabilia, including original cover artwork for anthologies such as *Christopher Lee's Chamber of Horrors*. He is a relentless book enthusiast, but with more focus than my rabidly catholic tastes.

This time Johnny insists that I must take his copy of *Mr Bowling Buys a Newspaper* by Donald Henderson. Mr Bowling is a murderer who buys a newspaper the day after each killing to see if he is a suspect. Unfortunately, the chaos of London in the Second World War seems to be getting in the way of his being caught, and he really wants to be caught. Raymond Chandler loved this book and believed its failure to be a smash hit demonstrated that 'there is something wrong with the book business'.

On my last visit to Johnny's he gave me a reissue of Frank Walford's *Twisted Clay* with an introduction by Johnny himself. It was first published in 1933 in Australia and banned there for thirty years. Johnny summarizes the plot as being about 'a precocious fifteen-year-old lesbian who murders her father when she learns he wants to take her to Europe to undergo experimental hormone therapy'.

When Johnny thinks a book that has been long lost should see the light of day again, he often gets it republished himself, despite the sparse – frequently non-existent – financial rewards. Just in case the novels he generously gives me do not get me to sleep, knowing that I am struggling at the moment, he also gives me a yellow pill for emergencies.

Liskeard

On the way back to Plymouth, the taxi driver tells me about her inquisitive ten-year-old son. He's always finding out new facts from books, she tells me. 'He's always reading, telling me about space and monkeys and black holes. Mind you...' She describes the time he started asking her what she knew about Uranus. When she began to talk about the planet, he said, 'No, I mean your anus'; and then he told her, from his research online, exactly how much an anus could potentially dilate and what could be stuck up a bum. She told him to avoid telling the teachers at school. What a startling show-and-tell that could be.

Today I am getting off the train at Liskeard, St Austell, Penzance and, finally, Redruth.

Journeying into Cornwall, it seems rude not to be reading Daphne du Maurier. I choose Venice rather than Jamaica Inn and reread my first Du Maurier – still the same edition that I bought at the school bookshop thirty-eight years ago. She wrote in *Don't Look Now*: 'The creature was gibbering in its corner. The hammering and the voices and the barking dog grew fainter, and, "Oh God," he thought, "what a bloody silly way to die..."'

I am seven minutes early for Liskeard's The Book Shop, so plenty of time to browse the British Heart Foundation store. My instincts were right. I find a book from 1901, *The Story of the Heavens* by Sir Robert Ball. It has wonderful colour plates of maps of Mars and of the craters on the Moon; it is weighty, but irresistible.

The British Heart Foundation shops have taken to having one shelf of older, sometimes strange and sometimes mundane hardbacks, which it is always worth looking through. The spines have often lost most of the clues of the title, so you have to open them up and be surprised by the contents. Many are so weirdly specific that their appeal is almost immeasurable, but when that particular person comes in looking for *Practical Thoughts on The First Forty Chapters of The Book of The Prophet Isaiah* by Lady Frances P. Verney (1857), or a guide to cleaning the spark plugs of a Triumph Toledo, they will no doubt be ecstatic.

As usual, the bookshop owners are delightful and passionate people, who run a bookshop because they must, *and* I get a cup of tea and a chocolate biscuit. On entering the shop, you are dazzled by all the colours of the picture books. The invention and design of children's books get better and better and work as the perfect honeytrap to draw the adults in too. You can be dragged in by a child with book tokens, hungry for an adventure with a Gruffalo, or by a granny who has been keeping all the planets' wonders in a pickle jar and, while they are trapped in the devastating delight of having to choose which book needs to be theirs for ever, you distractedly start reading the back blurb of a Booker winner, or something about the minds of octopuses. Now you are both ensnared.

The small town of Mevagissey is near the Lost Gardens of Heligan, but, as the locals will tell you, the gardens were never lost; they always knew they were there, it's just that the tourists didn't.

Mevagissey is also the location of two of Susan Cooper's hugely popular *The Dark Is Rising* fantasy series – *Greenwitch* and *Over Sea, Under Stone*. She wrote, 'When we are children, we have a tranquil acceptance of mystery which is driven out of us later on, by curiosity and education and experience. But it is possible to find one's way back.'[1]

The original Puffin cover of *The Dark Is Rising* haunted many of my generation, even if we never read the book. It is a preternatural image of Herne the Hunter, described as having 'the head of a stag, the eyes of an owl, the ears of a wolf'. The artist was Michael Heslop, who made similarly striking covers for many Puffin books, including Joan Aiken's *The Shadow Guests* and Ian Serraillier's *The Silver Sword*. He now focuses on paintings of racehorses and golf, but hopefully an occasional Herne might be seen chasing a jockey.

Hurley Books is down a narrow street and mixes second-hand titles and records with new stock. I am told that I might be greeted by someone in their pyjamas and dressing gown when I arrive, as some days are 'Arthur Dent days' at Hurley Books.

All the local Mevagissians I meet are cheery and welcoming, but the faces of the tourists have that seaside grimness. The people walking along the quay have scowls that seem to say, 'It is half-term. We had to have a day out, and here we are… having a day out, like you have to. At least we have found a different view to look at while shouting at our children.'

The talk is happening in a pub's function room. There's an old man at the front who seems to veer between suspicion and sleep, as far as I can see, but then asks plenty of good questions.

I also meet Alex, who gives me a copy of his book, *Homemade Music: The Complete Home Recordings.* It is more a labour of disdain than a labour of love, as he reviews the back-catalogue of cassettes on which he recorded songs that he wrote – and he wrote many.

When Alex gave me the book, he had a look that seemed to say, 'I bet you never read it.' I did and, to make it worse, I thoroughly enjoyed it. I later asked him where people could get the book, as I was going to plug it, but his simple reply was, 'Who would want to buy it?'

That's true art. 'Who have you made this for?' 'Almost no one.'

I swore myself to parsimony after the big book of astronomy from Liskeard, but I see a stash of old science-fiction magazines as I'm leaving. I debate between buying *New Worlds Science Fiction*, which comes with Colin Kapp's *The Bell of Ethicona*, or an *Amazing Stories*, which comes with Miles J. Breuer's *The Hungry Guinea Pig*. Unable to decide, I buy both, and two more besides.

Penzance

Penzance is another town that I only ever seem to arrive in after dark, when everything is closed. Tonight's bookshop is The Edge of the World Bookshop, although the event will be at The Acorn Theatre.

Cornish audiences often feel excluded from tours, due to the long-held belief by most tour promoters and artists that the West Country ends at Bristol and all that exists beyond is wolves and moors. If you make the effort to go further, they will make the effort to support you. I have found an admirable loyalty in Cornwall, running along the lines of

'You've bothered to turn up, so we will too.' It's my experience that there are other areas of the British Isles where people often complain that nothing happens, but if you try and make something happen, they'll pretend it's not there, because they get far more out of complaining that nothing ever happens than from going and seeing something happen.

I've performed at The Acorn many times before and it always brings out an extra exuberance in me. Before I go on, though, I feel exhausted. I am beginning to find that being irrepressible during the talks leads to me being a shell of a human in between them. I turn on and I turn off very quickly. The moment I am out of sight of the bookshop, I become grey, inhabiting a liminal space.

Tonight I contemplate a measured delivery of the ideas in my book. I imagine tiredness creating gravitas, but, as usual, I go from exhaustion to ecstasy in the three steps from dressing room to stage. I tell the audience that, whatever happens, I can't keep them too long as I need to get the last train to Redruth. During the interval signing, numerous people offer me a lift to Redruth so that I can overrun as usual. Another Stockholm Syndrome night.

Two retired doctors drive me back to Redruth and tell me about the musicals that I should avoid, and recommend books I should buy. Redruth is dark and rainswept when we get there, but I know that I am staying near a bakery that works through the night. I get out of the car and find the rest of the way there by following the smell of bread.

Redruth

I have somehow ended up with just one bookshop to talk at today, but it is one of my favourites, Beerwolf Books in

Falmouth. With time in the morning to spare, I resign myself to a lie-in and read about murderous luggage in *New Worlds Science Fiction* 107: '"Good," grunted Greville, running his hands through his hair. He reached for his shoes and put them on. Then he picked up his deadly briefcase...'

There are many charity shops on Redruth's sloping high street and they have the promise of being unruly and disordered, with treasures hidden between cracked crockery, knitting patterns and a child's disembowelled toys. Disappointingly, there are a lot of murder magazines about Fred and Rose West near the Toby jugs, but nothing else.

In the shopping arcade there's The Redruth Idler, a bookshop mixing the antiquarian with a very impressive wall of comics. There is a pile of Commando Pocket Library magazines with titles like *Steeds of Steel* and *Journey into Danger*. It was in such magazines that I got my first German-language lesson, limited to 'Achtung!', 'Schnell!' and 'Aaaaaaaaaaaargh! Himmel!!!!!'

Uh-oh, there is more Colin Wilson – *The Geller Phenomenon* – and it's signed too. For once, I resist. The beautiful colour anthology of some of EC Comics' gorier spreads is also returned to the shelf, despite my delight at the promise to 'slide into the sloppy slimy crypt of terror, fiend fans' and to experience the grisly comeuppance of the vain, the murderous and the greedy.

Castigated, censored and forbidden in the 1950s, due to the belief that the fantastical and vengeful dead were warping the minds of the young, these comics had a very beneficial effect on my son. When he started reading my old *The Vault of Horror* series, his vocabulary became far more florid and grotesque and it got him lots of As from his English teacher.

Falmouth

I am in Falmouth early enough to discover the Maritime Museum and its *Monsters of the Deep* exhibition, a combination of real-life natural history and stories of the monsters that came from sailors' rickets-racked minds. I find out that as well as mermaids there were stories of mermonks – fish with the heads of monks and bishops.

My wife's family once owned a mermaid, or what was actually a dried and flaky monkey glued onto a wretched fishtail. They sold it to a hairdresser in North Shields. How this would lure in those debating which salon to get a perm, a beehive or a blow-wave, I do not know, but I've always respected their ambition.

On my way to Beerwolf Books I stumble on a third Falmouth bookstore in St George's Arcade: Rubicund Radical Bookshop and its coffee shop, a perfect mix of sublime orange sponge and revolutionary fervour.

It is the second transcendent moment of the tour, sipping coffee and seated by a shop window displaying a Robert Mapplethorpe photography book, as a sense of hope grows in me that there really could be a radical future with acceptance of everyone for whoever they may be, and quality cake for all. Rather than being a champagne socialist, I may become a Battenberg Bolshevik.

Though I was tempted by Arturo Escobar's *Designs for the Pluriverse* and David Boarder Giles's *A Mass Conspiracy to Feed People: Food Not Bombs and the World-Class Waste of Global Cities*, I leave them for now, knowing there will be much that I desire in Beerwolf.

Alice stocks Beerwolf Books with magnificent reduced-price finds. I first got to know her and Dom when they had a stall at the End of the Road Festival in Dorset. I would end up spending more time repeatedly browsing their books and drinking beer with them than I would watching the bands. Sometimes they would have their stall in the perfect position also to have a good view of the main stage, which allowed me to combine three of my favourite preoccupations: beer, books and bands. The comedian Arthur Smith once summed up the perfect amount to earn as being enough to buy the books you wanted, have a drink in the pub and still be able to afford a taxi home – a far superior aspiration to having a helicopter pad or a fast red car.

When Alice and Dom used to tell me of their ambition to have a bricks-and-mortar bookshop in Falmouth I imagined they were mere Cornish dreamers, but then they went ahead and did it. Now they have that most dangerous of things, a bookshop that serves beer. You finish your browse, buy a pint of Puxton Cross or Fun Sponge and start enjoying your new books. One more pint of Fun Sponge and discipline disintegrates. I find I really need that vast book on Pop Art and an encyclopaedia of Neolithic tombs.

The first time I played Beerwolf, it turned out that the microphone triggered some disco lights, so depending on my volume and delivery, I was bathed in blue, green or pink, and if I spoke too fast I needed to come with a seizure warning.

Tonight I am even more tangential than I was in Penzance, high on cake and political rebellion. The kindness of Cornwall is in evidence again, as Karl and Verity tell me to overrun as they will give me a lift home.

Two pints in, I return to browse. I manage to deny myself the vast Ralph Steadman collection, as my mind kindly flashes to a future mentalization of me lost in another town, weighed down like Buckaroo and swearing at cumulonimbus.

I leave with two Ursula K. Le Guins, a Rebecca Solnit and Sue Prideaux's book on Nietzsche.

Bridgwater

Is it Day 25 now? If I close my eyes and look back, I can walk around each shop and still take books from the shelves, but the details are beginning to fragment.

The train to Taunton is quiet enough for me to desert the vestibule. I start reading Ursula K. Le Guin's *The Lathe of Heaven*, a short but potent novel that is an aid to loosening your grip on reality. It concerns a man whose dreams change the reality of the world. I hear clanking down the corridor and look round, but it is only the buffet trolley, not a grumblin' Paul Newman puppet tied up with string.

Unfortunately there is an Oxfam shop directly on my way from the station to Brendon Books. I need a book of photographs of London in the 1980s with a picture of Francis Bacon on the Tube, and I need one on psychoanalysis and art – and, as luck would have it, the shop has both.

The assistant behind the counter is holding a copy of Patrick Hamilton's *Hangover Square* and I decide to make conversation with her about this bleak classic. This story of a damaged man surrounded by unpleasant people in 1930s bedsit-land is in Iain Sinclair's Top Five novels about London.[2] Sinclair is particularly drawn to Hamilton's portrayal of the derangement of London. Hamilton's life was plagued by misfortune, tragedy and alcoholism. Sinclair summed up the pleasures of Hamilton's final years as 'picking up his daily bottle of whisky from the chemist, re-reading Sherlock Holmes and Hopalong Cassidy, and watching pony club girls bounce around a rough field'.[3] Fortunately I was still some way off the story about the pony-club girls when I realized that the assistant had no idea what I was talking about. She didn't even seem to know that the book I was talking about was in her hand. Perhaps she had picked it up to defend herself, after becoming apprehensive when a man with a screaming suitcase and too many books entered the shop looking like a Bedlamite.

I have a driver in Somerset as I've squeezed in a late afternoon event in Bridgwater and need be back here by 6.30 pm. I drop my bags off at Brendon Books and then we drive the few miles to Bridgwater. Laura is a physics student and hairdresser and she insists that I once helped her with some of her degree work, which I find highly unlikely. She has offered to give me lifts for the day. Having detached myself from my over-Englishness when offered favours, I say yes right away. None of that tiresome rigmarole of 'Are you really sure? I don't want to be any bother'; I just go straight to the 'Yes, please'.

Fortunately the traffic on the way to Bridgwater's Snug Bookshop is terrible. This gives me time to hear more of Laura's story. If you mention to someone that you have met a hairdresser with a keen interest in astrophysics, people's faces veer between dismissive and utterly perplexed. 'But how could someone who cuts, fashions and dresses hair have an interest in Einstein Field Equations of gravitation or the coronal heating problem?' Humans seem to find it very difficult to imagine that people can be more than one thing at any one time.

The dire traffic around Bridgwater has had a knock-on effect on the size of the audience. It will be the most intimate conversation I have had on the tour so far. To anyone looking in, it would seem that a small family was being treated to tea and cake by a domineering uncle who wouldn't let anyone else get a word in edgeways.

The Snug Bookshop is run by Sam, a librarian with a lifelong ambition to have her own bookshop. The ambition was fulfilled in 2018. I am still to find a bookshop on this tour that is not gorgeously inviting. Sam is driven by wanting everyone to get the opportunity to experience books, to be encouraged to read, to get a taste of all the potential adventures and ideas there are within the covers of books. To have a bookshop really was her dream. Spending time with booksellers combats all those ugly thoughts that spill out of the news and social media. If I build an echo chamber, let it be full of book-lovers. In the weird world where the ability to infuriate and upset has been monetized and industrialized, the company I am keeping keeps that world at bay.

A month after my visit a storm led to some of Sam's roof caving in, damaging some books and making the shop unsafe to keep open. To see her on the news, talking about having to give up her bookshop dream, was heartbreaking. By the time you read this, I hope she has found somewhere else, and I could even hope that you are reading this book after watching me talk about it in Sam's new premises.

I have a hurried departure but, as I am almost out of the shop, my eye is drawn to a small box of second-hand books by the door. No time to browse, but a title grabs me: *The Autobiography of Ethel Firebrace*. I know nothing about it. I do not even open it. I just buy it.

What is it? I will find out later.

Walking to the Taunton venue, the only thing I know for sure is that the event with Brendon Books is in a church again.*

* I didn't leave Brendon Books empty-handed – I took with me a good pulpy horror called *Burn, Witch, Burn!* And some pleasing 1960s nonsense called *The Morning of the Magicians*.

Laura and I see a church and make our way towards it, but then we see another church and then another. We are on a street of many temples. I discover that the reason for such a varied denominational gathering along this road is because it is just over the town boundary and, in times past, this was the place where the Nonconformists could build and meet, although they were barred from voting.

I'm in the correct Methodist church. I extemporize in pleasantly godly surroundings, though I wish Laura was onstage rather than me when it comes to the quite specific questions I get afterwards on the nature of time. In the car to the station she tells me how I could have answered the questions more effectively, if I was up to date on the most recent research into black holes. She knows more than I do about the deformation of spacetime and how to create the perfect bob, and I confront my limitations again.

On the train home, I find out more about *The Autobiography of Ethel Firebrace*. It turns out to be a very rare book. There is one copy for sale online without a dust-wrapper and it costs £500. Another gazelle snared.

Ethel was the author of *Clothed in White Samite*, *Ecstasy's Debit*, *His for an Hour* and *An Airman for Averil*. But Ethel was not real. Published in 1937, *The Autobiography of Ethel Firebrace* is, like *Through Darkest Pondelayo*, a spoof. Firebrace is the creation of Malachi Whitaker and Gay Taylor. Taylor was a writer and publisher, while Whitaker was a prolific short-story writer from Bradford, whom Vita Sackville-West compared to Katherine Mansfield; she was once described as 'Bradford's Chekhov'. Gay Taylor was described as spending much time in poverty. She preferred buying books to buying food, and drank too much perry. By the end of my train journey, I was utterly fascinated by her and started searching for a copy of her book, *A Prison, A Paradise*, that was available for less than £200; another gazelle on the list.

Reading

Another Taylor, Elizabeth, is on my mind the next morning, as she is my favourite author from Reading. I came to her late with *Mrs Palfrey at the Claremont*. It is an elegant and honest novel about the frustrations of being old. I read it when I decided that, for one year at least, I must only read novels by women, as I simply hadn't read enough. I remember a friend of mine telling me that the issue for women writers is that stories by men are generally considered to be stories for everyone, but stories by women are presumed to be stories for women. It was a grand year of reading novels by Jean Rhys, Flannery O'Connor, Marian Keyes, Alice Walker, Doris Lessing and Octavia Butler, amongst others. Some of you reading this must be thinking, 'What nonsense! Doesn't it all balance out anyway?' Well, somehow I don't think it had for me. I picked Elizabeth Taylor's *Blaming* to dip into for my trip. Being unable to find an independent bookshop in Reading proper, I had booked Fourbears Books, a short walk over the river in Caversham.

I walk across an autumnal park that feels like it could have sprung from the pages of a 1970s children's picture book, all swings and slides, ducks and Shirley Hughes.

At the shop, I find that my signing armchair is occupied by a teddy bear. I am also being watched over by a two-dimensional Jimmy Carr. His promotional cardboard cutout has been a regular guest on my tour, often nestling next to a quizzical-looking and equally flat Michael McIntyre. One day maybe I'll be a full-sized cardboard cutout too.

If I behave correctly during the signing I am promised a cupcake.

The people of Finland are the first to come up for the signing, or at least their representatives are. I am asked to dedicate a book to 'The inquisitive people of Finland'. I hope they pass it around.

A few weeks before the tour I picked up *Picturesque Finland* at a jumble sale. It is a 1950s book with many photographs of Finland and the Finnish people. There are lots of pictures of factory workers, with captions about the Finnish traits of 'humor, obstinacy and vigilance' and much tending of fields too: 'The monotonous drone of the farm tractor fills the air, while the delicate fingers of the rowan leaves open toward the sun...' The summer in Finland is apparently like 'a blushing schoolgirl... eyes shining like our blue skies and breasts tremulous with anticipation'.

After signing some books for the school library I feel have earnt my cupcake.

Eastbourne

It becomes a day of standing on trains, and the rickety bustle makes it difficult to find space to read. I don't like such times; it feels like time wasted when I could be reading Rupert Thomson's *This Party's Got To Stop*, a memoir of family and loss based in Eastbourne. The thoughts that I conjure up, looking out of the window at the Haywards Heath Waitrose car park, have nothing on Thomson's striking and stylish prose.

Any frustration vanishes when I arrive at the coast and see two men in *Star Trek* costumes (from the original series – one Kirk, one Scotty). They have a dignity, seriousness and composure that suggest they are not merely part of a stag-night.

This will be the last time that I arrive at an evening gig in daylight as the clocks go back tonight and, while I will get a useful extra hour in bed, from here on in, evening bookshop visits will be in the darkening gloom. The bookshop hosting the event is the Hastings Bookshop, but the venue is the Lamb Inn. This is high on my list of favourite pubs in England, due to its remarkable friendliness, long history, big old chairs, open fire and excellent beer, and its brilliant and kind owner, Natalie. For me, it is the closest version to Orwell's perfect imagined pub, from his essay 'The Moon Under Water'. You can tick off much of his checklist of what makes the perfect pub, although I don't think the Lamb sells aspirin and stamps.

It is also not too far from my favourite second-hand bookshop, Camilla's, a wonderfully overstocked bookshop that has an occasional guest grey parrot to greet you and, on each visit, seems to teeter further and further into the street under the weight of its stock.

I perform for seventy minutes for the first half of the event – a sort of book talk, though slightly more stand-up than of late – and the second half is the comedy-club jamboree, led by my friend Joanna Neary, who once gave me a beautiful Victorian pocket book on the life of coal.

The people from Hastings Bookshop are with me again today. Does this count as another bookshop? Technically it only counts as one, but as I am at a totally different venue and they have sent a different bookseller, I will count it as two. Even without this cheat, I am still certain that I will make the 100.

I am playing Screen 2 at Uckfield Picture House, a full 3D

presentation. Kevin, whose family have owned the cinema for more than fifty years, collects me from the Lamb Inn. He has wonderful diaries that his father kept, which have every screening noted – the main feature, support feature and shorts – and the pounds, shilling and pence they made. On the day I was born, *Thoroughly Modern Millie* was showing. Sadly, I was just a little too early for Rod Steiger in *The Illustrated Man* or the double bill of *Frankenstein Must be Destroyed* and *Sons of Satan*.

Kevin celebrated the cinema's 100th anniversary with a season revisiting the cinema's double bills. I introduced Vincent Price in *The Masque of the Red Death* – 'How many evils can you count in this vile face of evil lust?' – and Ray Milland in *X-Ray: The Man with the X-Ray Eyes* – 'He stripped souls as bare as bones!'

Conversations during the signing include a discussion about the influence of Vonnegut's *The Sirens of Titan* on Douglas Adams. A fourteen-year-old shows me an app that propels you through the comparative size of things in the universe. Apparently humans are pretty much in the middle, when it comes to the size of things in the universe, between the smallest particles and the most massive of supermassive black holes. It seems counter-instinctual, but it is facts like these that I glean at the signing table that stop my mind from atrophying beyond repair.

Shoreham-by-Sea

I have mistimed my trip to Shoreham-by-Sea. It is home to one of my favourite charity shops – SOLD – but it is closed on both Sundays and Mondays. SOLD always has the most splendid window displays. It inherited a garage filled with spectacular fake flowers and bouquets and, before these all got sold off, the shop looked like a garden centre for Autons for at least a year.* But it's just the traditional charity-shop Hallowe'en window tonight, with zombies, cobwebs, bloody smears and handprints on the glass – never less than vivid.

City Books of Hove have organized the event at Shoreham's Ropetackle Arts Centre. It is one of my favourite destinations because all the volunteers who run it are delightful and often have a story to tell. We discuss how a good way to judge people coming for events is by observing the disparity between how they treat the most powerful people in a room compared to the least powerful. Most performers are remembered fondly; a few less so.

Tonight I am back behind a lectern. I start to worry that I have talked about these ideas too often. I try to make sure that every talk is different, but now that I am at the fiftieth talk (or fifty-first or fifty-second?) there is a rhythm that is harder to elude. Perhaps I am getting complacent?

The tangents have begun to harden. In the first couple of weeks the talk was more fluid, but now that I am at show fifty-one I can feel the repetition. There is much at the events that I have not touched upon in *The Importance of Being Interested*, and I think it is time to remind myself of what I have forgotten I wrote in the first place.

I reread my own book and look at sentences that I have no memory of writing. Some of them I would cut out now,

* If you are Auton-unaware, Autons were robots from *Dr Who* that looked like window-display mannequins – terrifying in itself – and used a weapon that looked like a daffodil. The daffodil would spray out a film of plastic that would cover the nose and mouth and suffocate the victim. The dying breath would then disintegrate the plastic, leaving no trace. As you know, the Autons were animated by the Nestene Consciousness.

while others make me feel quite impressed by whoever was in charge when I wrote them. I'm sure it can't have been me.

At the signing table, someone else tells me their theory of the nature of time travel. One day – perhaps in 2039 – I hope to suddenly recall that the young man telling me his theory of time travel looks unmistakably like the old man I met many years before.

After the signing I have a drink with the neuroscientist and author Anil Seth. In his most recent book, *Being You*, he worries that 'We're all hallucinating all the time; when we agree about our hallucinations, we call it "reality".' Depending on the day, that can be either comforting or horrifying.

On the way back I am sure that I notice a new bloodied handprint on SOLD's window.

CHAPTER 6

What is Avuncular Knitwear?

Margate to Southwold

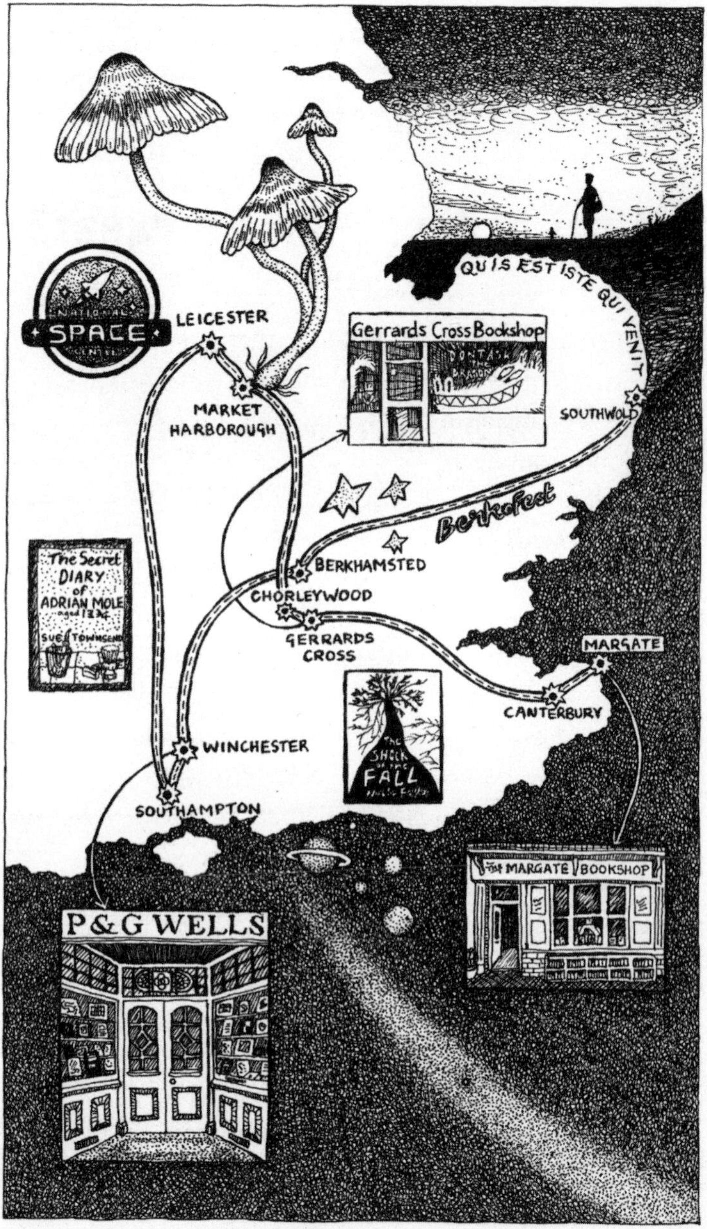
QUIS EST ISTE QUI VENIT
NATIONAL SPACE CENTRE
LEICESTER
Gerrards Cross Bookshop
MARKET HARBOROUGH
SOUTHWOLD
Berkofest
BERKHAMSTED
CHORLEYWOOD
The Secret DIARY of ADRIAN MOLE aged 13¾
SUE TOWNSEND
GERRARDS CROSS
MARGATE
CANTERBURY
WINCHESTER
SOUTHAMPTON
FALL
THE MARGATE BOOKSHOP
P&G WELLS

There are a number of books that, when I read them, struck me with such force and such surprise that I relentlessly bang on about them, finding any excuse to squeeze them into conversation – books such as *Picnic at Hanging Rock*, *The KLF: Chaos, Magic and the Band who Burned a Million Pounds* and *Bee Season*.

Near the top of that list is David Seabrook's *All The Devils Are Here*. It tells stories of Thanet, the region of Kent that takes in Margate, Broadstairs and Ramsgate – towns that I have been regularly drawn to for holidays. When last in Broadstairs, I visited the location of the Bleak House in Dickens's novel, to find that it was currently a Bikram yoga retreat. I could not imagine anything bleaker. In Ramsgate I found a second-hand copy of Heathcote Williams's *Whale Nation*, signed and dedicated by the author:

For Joseph (7) and William (5)
Heathcote Williams (47)
DECEMBER 1988

It is written in a beautiful hand, the antithesis to the scribble that I scrawl in my books. There is calmness and intelligence in his ink.

When David Seabrook went in search of the seaside shelter that T. S. Eliot used to write in, he wrote, 'There's no money in Margate. Eye contact has replaced it as the root of all evil and, yes, this town's as ripe as ever for a low-budget remake of *Brighton Rock*: the joyless amusement arcades, the facial scars...'[1] To the outsider at least, Margate has changed. In the summer the sandy beach that Turner painted, under that vast sky, was hectic with joy, ice-cream and inflatable dolphins, and Dreamland's rides were being oiled and readied for a visit by The Specials.

Margate also has one of the trickiest holes of any crazy-golf course. On a busy day the shame of the lengthening queue at the first hole, as you're on your twelfth shot, can burn hotter than the sun.

The clocks have gone back now and the town is definitely out of season for my return. It is dark and Monday-quiet by the time I arrive for my talk at the Margate Bookshop. The crazy golf is closed, the dolphins are deflated and there are no rollercoaster screams from Dreamland.

I had hoped that the journey from Shoreham-by-Sea to Margate would take me on a coastal route and that I might wave as I passed near the Dungeness cottage of Derek Jarman (a diarist I have read nearly as many times as Kenneth Williams). But it turns out that I have to leave the sea, go back into London and then return to the sea.

It's 1 November. On Jarman's final 1 November, he wrote in *Smiling in Slow Motion*: 'All Hallows. The dead circle the cottage in a high grey wind. I walk along the shore, the maroons go off and the lifeboat topples into the surf; all those lost at sea in the iron-grey waves. A calm has swept in.'

I was fifteen years old when Jarman's work started to be screened on Channel 4 and his interviews appeared in the magazines that I read. There was both elegance and activism in the way that he said 'Fuck you' to the conservative, the petty, the judgemental and the oppressive. Like so many writers that I adore, he is something I am not and can never be, but Jarman is one of the authors who allows me an excursion from my timidity.

The Margate Bookshop is the smallest of the evening gigs. It can just manage to seat double figures, if I do the talk from halfway up the staircase. The bookshop is a former textile studio. Francesca used to run a pop-up bookshop in the Turner Gallery and is a fine-arts graduate. Her frustration at finding a job in the arts led to her becoming a bookseller. Bookselling is driven by a desire to inflame a passion for reading. When I visited, she had begun a crowdfunder to get more books into Thanet schools.

Lift the bohemian curtain that can skirt Thanet and you'll discover that it has the lowest children's literacy rate and the highest child-poverty rate in all of Kent. Francesca was first drawn to books at school by her teachers, who instilled in her a love of reading. She knows how this shaped her identity and her friendships, and she wants to increase the opportunities that she had in those cash-strapped schools.

The shop is intimate and full. I have taken a few books off the shelf to inspire some tangential digressions. I start with something inspired by Octavia Butler's *Kindred*: 'Sometimes I wrote things because I couldn't say them, couldn't sort out my feelings about them, couldn't keep them bottled inside me.'

The Margate audience has many questions. Terry wants to know what the phrase 'avuncular knitwear' means – something I had written on my blog a few days before. He had looked up the words, but could not make the connection to what I was trying to describe. I tried again and described it as woollen jumpers that create a non-threatening appearance, which I hope gave some satisfaction.

The author Daisy Buchanan is in the audience. Her novel *Insatiable* has been described as 'gratifyingly grubby', so I imagine it may be short on avuncular knitwear, though that is apparently made up for by 'a great deal of cunnilingus'.[2]

Walking up the stairs to my hotel room in Canterbury, I see a portrait of Margaret Rutherford, which is always reassuring. (I think this is the shortest journey from cunnilingus to Margaret Rutherford that has ever appeared in a book.)

Canterbury

And sodeynly anon this Damyan
Gan pullen up the smok, and in he throng.

Geoffrey Chaucer, 'The Merchant's Tale'

In Canterbury I recite Chaucer, but only a tiny bit. I studied 'The Merchant's Tale' for A-level English, and all that I can remember are the two lines about smocks and thronging.

Don't blame me – I was sixteen years old and frustrated, and there was a certain dryness to how it was taught, so what stuck with us puerile youths was the sex. The puerile youths grew up, and now you can read learned texts in academic journals about how *Carry On Up the Jungle* and *Confessions of a Window Cleaner** are the twentieth-century Chaucer equivalents.

* Robin Askwith starred in both the *Confessions* movies and in Pasolini's *The Canterbury Tales*.

Today is a divided day – a lunchtime book talk at Christ Church University Bookshop and then off to punch a melon at the Gulbenkian Theatre for a lecture about comedy. The question is: what kind of melon? Should I punch a Galia melon or a watermelon? This is the sort of question that gets you thrown out of greengrocers'.

I sit alone at breakfast while couples argue over the diets they had imagined the other was on, and whether kippers are allowable, and can he have a strawberry yoghurt? Alone as ever, I imagine that I am in a Terence Rattigan play, but with Coco Pops. I scribble notes for the Linda Smith lecture I am delivering tonight.

After breakfast, I walk the Canterbury streets in search of a crooked house. I can't remember which lane it is down, but I am determined to find it because it is an architectural oddity and an excellent bookshop.

I find it and remember that it is only when you are halfway through the shop door that you notice the building's Dr Seuss-like skew-whiffery and then you wonder if you are stepping into another dimension, discreetly hidden from the street outside. Perhaps it's a dimension with a slant that is somewhere between the fourth and the fifth.

I buy some Doris Lessing science fiction, Liv Ullmann's autobiography and, for the purposes of balance, a book on the films of Danny Dyer. The equilibrium of the universe will be maintained if I read a few pages of Liv Ullmann on Ingmar Bergman and then dip into analysis of *The Football Factory* and *Pimp*.

Here is Liv Ullmann writing about the Moon: 'When it was quite new and thin, I would stand by the window and curtsy to it three times.'

And here is something from *The Films of Danny Dyer*, on *Dead Cert*:

> Retired villain Freddy Frankham agrees to a bare knuckle fight between his protégé Dennis Christian and a monstrous member of an eastern european gang for the rights to his new club The Paradise. Dennis loses and is killed in the fight, but Freddy soon discovers that his opponent had a supernatural edge – he is a vampire.

Freddy swears vengeance. Liv swears continued allegiance to the Moon's beauty.

I like skipping back and forth between the incongruous. I recently read a biography of the Pulitzer Prize-winning poet, depressive and author of 'Menstruation at Forty', Anne Sexton, whilst also dipping in and out of the autobiography of the foul-mouthed, race-baiting comedian and composer of *You Fat Bastard*, Roy Chubby Brown. Sometimes, when reading too many books back-to-back, I can forget which one is which, but this never happened with these two.

I have met Craig and Colette from the University Bookshop before, when they were selling books at festivals in Folkestone and Canterbury. The shop is filled with the usual textbooks that you would expect to fulfil academic needs, but it is also stocked with many things of intrigue and wonder – another example of combining the practical with the beautiful.

They place me on a bench and I drink coffee and listen to students planning a play, with a mixture of despair and ingenuity. Maybe they would know what sort of melon I should punch at the theatre tonight? After my talk, Craig gives me some beautifully wrapped books as a thank-you present. They know my tastes well: Alan Garner's *Treacle Walker*, Baxter Dury's autobiography, a book on the psychology of horror and a hardback of Ursula K. Le Guin's *Orsinian Tales*. When asked what inspired her to be a writer,

Le Guin would reply, 'Learning to write, when I was five', as if the very act of writing was all the ammunition she needed to run riot in our minds.

The audience is a mix of interested academics, radio-listening locals and teenage students who have probably been told that filling out the room will count towards their course work. I sign books and talk to a middle-aged academic who has only recently been diagnosed with ADHD. She tells me that having the diagnosis has changed her life, and gives me the name of some pills that might help to change mine.

Up the hill, on Kent University campus, I am mistaken for a bookseller. There is a large outdoor bookstall catering for upcoming lectures. As I browse, a young man asks me about the price of a book titled *Wombs and Alien Spirits: Women, Men and the Zar Cult in Northern Sudan* and another titled *The Field of Cultural Production: Essays on Art and Literature*. I acknowledge that if anyone looks as if they've written the pencilled prices in the books, it was me, but I am not the man he is looking for. I point to the bookseller on his folding chair. The student agrees that I look more like a bookseller than the bookseller, which reminds me of something Sartre once said about a waiter, but not enough for it trip off the tongue fluently, so I keep it in my head.

Looking at the young browsers searching modern texts and old philosophy at the stall, I feel nostalgic and a little melancholy. There is that late-teen fear and excitement of being able to become who you wanted to be, now that you are away from home and from your past. That distance brings a dizzying freedom – your sexuality, politics, piercings: so many possibilities.

I think of some of my awful overcoats and experimental haircuts that led to me being the bald man in a duffel coat that

I am now. I am glad I was able to have those awful haircuts while I could.

The Linda Smith lecture is not officially one of my 100 bookshop talks. The subject matter is entirely different, save for a three-minute overlap. I have a huge stack of notes about why I love comedy, my inspirations and three different types of melon. I will sit behind a desk for the duration of the talk, and the desk is covered in books and rare comedy LPs that were like white gold to me in my childhood and adolescence.

I wanted the lecture to be ultimately about love, and how comedy can be something that gives freedom and makes people feel less alone. I talk of how what you create is never (for me at least) what I thought my head might hold; of when being a fool onstage connects with people in the audience who realize that they are not the only one in the world with freaky thoughts. My favourite comedy, like my favourite books, takes me into otherness, lets me explore other worlds and other ways of thinking, lets me walk in others' shoes.

Oh, and it lets you punch melons for a living. I shouldn't have gone with the watermelon – it went everywhere... but not on those rare comedy records, thank God. Always remember to aim an unpredictable watermelon carefully.

The campus Blackwell's staff come to sell my books and, finding the Wi-Fi hampered by the brutalist architecture, each purchase requires a walk outside. Everyone is patient, and young people tell me they are glad that an old man like me is not entirely lost in the 'kids nowadays!' wing of the culture wars. I still find poverty more troubling than potentially having to change a personal pronoun.

Gerrards Cross

I first came to Gerrards Cross bookshop when I was thirteen and excitedly bought a copy of a brand-new film annual called *The Film Year Book 1983*. I still have it and I still read it, although I have stopped giving the films that I've seen a rating in pencil. I was more impressed by *Halloween II* than by *Herbie Goes Bananas* and was ambivalent towards *On Golden Pond*.

Although both Chorleywood Bookshop and Gerrards Cross Bookshop are owned by the same person, the stock is far from identical. Gerrards Cross has a whole wall of past and present Booker Prize nominees. The people of Chorleywood seem less attracted to the potentially highbrow; they'll take a Booker or two, but not a whole darned wall.

It is a quiet weekday signing. Fortunately one couple need six signed copies. Browsing to pass the time, I am again mistaken for a bookseller.

'Could you help me with the Paddington Bear books? I have a granddaughter in Perth.'

Of course I can. We find the adventure that seems exactly right, and then the lady asks me how long I have worked here. I explain that I don't – that I've simply been signing my book.

'What's it about?'

Luckily I start by mentioning that it is about concepts like the nature of time, and it just so happens she is studying that as part of the philosophy course she is doing at the community hall. Another sale.

One day I'll come for a signing and, seventeen years later, the shop owner will realize I have never left and have been recommending books about bears and the spacetime continuum to anyone who might want one. They never employed me, but I was always there – a ghost before I died.

Chorleywood

There's a nice sold-out gathering in the Chorleywood Bookshop, including my eldest niece who is on a date. It shows a great deal of trust in an uncle to risk taking a possible partner to watch him give a talk about the potential of extra-terrestrial life and the possible existence of spitting night-hags when suffering from sleep paralysis. I decide to drop the bit about night-hags – it might be introducing too much family madness for a first date.

At the signing a mother shows me the most beautiful tattoo. It is the pale-blue dot colliding with the mind of Douglas Adams. It is in memory of a child she lost. Times like this crush cynicism. I stand up in front of people and spill out the stories in my head, and then afterwards they often give me their stories. I am glad people feel they can share their stories too.

Market Harborough

I haven't disembarked at Market Harborough before. Like Crewe, it is frequently passed through, but is rarely the destination. It is prettier than I expected, even in today's drizzle.

Some market towns with pleasingly rural names turn out to be unwelcoming, with any hint of oak trees, maypoles or indeed a market long since concreted over, replaced by the progress of zero-hour contracts, soulless novelty and a sense of perpetual stasis. The name from the past mocks the bleak surroundings of the present.

Linda Smith gave just such a celebrated summary of her home town, Erith: 'It's not twinned with anywhere, but it does have a suicide pact with Dagenham.'

Without Market Harborough, I wouldn't have known what a cryptogamist is. Miles Joseph Berkeley was a vicar near Market Harborough and a pioneer in the study of cryptogams, plants that reproduce using spores. His daughter, Ruth Ellen Berkeley, was celebrated for her illustrations of fungi. She would probably be busy again now, as mycology is experiencing a renewed period of public fascination. Merlin Sheldrake's *Entangled Life* is about fungi and was a bestseller, and one year since it was published it is still on the front tables in many of the bookshops I visit. In it he writes, 'We can't adjust to life on a damaged planet without forging new fungal relationships.'

The Mushroom at the End of the World by Anna Lowenhaupt Tsing, published in 2015, also grabbed the public imagination more than any publisher might have imagined, for a book that 'describes and analyzes the globalized commodity chains of matsutake mushrooms'. You could also be lured into acquiring the two-volume *John Cage: A Mycological Foray: Variations on Mushrooms* published in 2020. It was on my wishlist, and I had an opportunity once to pick it up cheaply, but foolishly I hesitated and now it sells for £200 and more.

With mushrooms in mind, it seems apt that my event with Quinns Bookshop is set among a broad range of organic vegetables. I have rarely performed with so many carrots beneath me. This is in Market Harborough's new Eco Village, which before the talk begins offers me the opportunity to browse chutney and honey, rather than books. I see a blackberry-and-rosemary muffin that I know will one day be mine, but not yet, not yet. Any digestion may rob me of the energy I need to generate a talk.

The room takes about sixty people and is, fortunately, sold out, which is good for a daytime school-day appearance.

Signing books afterwards, I get to discuss Darwin again. This time the discussion is about the story of the cruel sailor who bullied monkeys during his week's leave. On his final day, walking back to the ship, a monkey relentlessly pummelled him with balls of monkey shit. According to Darwin's penpal, who sent this story to illustrate the ingenuity of monkeys, this vengeful ape had been piling up balls of dung, like sailors piling up cannonballs, for a week, planning and waiting for his opportunity. Intentional shit-throwing is a sign of self-awareness.

There is an Age UK shop on my way back. I pick up a book by Houdini about psychic mediums; something about the quest for the Holy Grail; a Jungian guide to grotesques in literature; and Yukio Mishima's *The Sailor Who Fell from Grace with the Sea* (perhaps because I referenced it the day before, when talking about Sarah Miles's plan to chain Richard Dawkins to a bed in a haunted house to convince him of the existence of ghosts).

Leicester

Three writers from Leicester encouraged and supported me through my teenage years. The first was Sue Townsend, then Colin Wilson and finally Joe Orton. Two created brilliant diaries that had a fascination with male genitalia: Joe Orton with other people's, Adrian Mole with his own. If I see a disused public toilet in a park in Leicester I wonder if there should be a plaque in memory of Joe Orton's cottaging. I first read his diaries on the Metropolitan Line, going in and out of central London for my summer holiday job. I would anxiously wonder if any of the pinstriped, dour-faced City gentlemen knew the words I was reading: 'No more than two feet away the citizens of Holloway moved about their ordinary business… When I left, the labourer was just shoving his cock into the man's mouth to keep him quiet. I caught the bus home.'

My late-teenage reading was full of voyeurism – injecting heroin with William Burroughs's *Junky* or hallucinating bats in the desert with Hunter S. Thompson in *Fear and Loathing in Las Vegas* – but I always knew I was more of a Mole. I'll still be in the library when Bukowski's raging in the bar.

Arriving early at Leicester, I suppress my fear of a sudden swan attack and walk a circuitous but picturesque route along the River Soar to the National Space Centre. I imagine Orton walking this path and spying furtive men lurking in the shrubs. The more you read, the more ghosts you can walk with.

A couple of friendly Deliveroo riders speed by me and say hello, and I look down at my feet as I pass a couple who are smooching under a lamp post and look like a pencil sketch on the cover of a 1930s song sheet. It feels right to be walking through this old world before being confronted by a gleaming building celebrating our hopes of travelling to Mars. Having been above the carrots, I am now beneath the constellations, performing in the Sir Patrick Moore Planetarium. The gift shop is my bookshop tonight. This afternoon I was browsing chutney before my talk, but tonight I'm able to look at the Soyuz 7K-OK(A) spacecraft. I adore both, but, sadly, only one is coming home with me.

The collection of space-related objects includes something else I covet: a book that has been into space twice, once with Helen Sharman and once with Tim Peake. It is Yuri Gagarin's autobiography, *Road to the Stars*, signed by Gagarin. Sharman took it to the Mir Space Station with her and then loaned it to Peake when he went to the International Space Station. When

I've asked astronauts about reading habits in space, they've told me that they go with good intentions, but it's very hard not to spend all your time looking out of the window.

There are no new tattoos to see after the show tonight, but I have a happy conversation with a shy young person who has recently become inspired to study horticulture. This leads to yet another conversation about Charles Darwin, this time about his earthworm experiments – any excuse to bring up the bassoon.

Southampton

I get collected from Southampton Airport Parkway by John, a former soldier and engineer who now puts lifts in at stations. During my journeys he'll tell me whether or not to keep an eye out for an elevator that he has installed. I have written about John before, and how he and his family dealt with the death of his son, Jamie. During the book tour I have tried to talk about this whenever it has felt right. John is pleased to know that Jamie's name is still being spoken and his stories told.

This is one of the wonders of books: the delight of being a species that can chronicle and preserve. I pick up a book from a shelf, and someone who is no more than ash or bone can still change me.

Today's talk is at October Books, Southampton's leading political bookshop, which operates with military precision. I have never had such specific timetabling. The revolution may not be televised, but it will follow the schedule exactly as listed in the *Radio Times*, with no deviation for regional variations.

October Books has an impressive front of concrete pillars. It is a solid, determined façade, a bookshop to be painted for the 'Reading is good for you' propaganda posters of 1960s

Russia. Upcoming events include 'Transgender Marxism', a film screening of *Mothers of the Revolution*, a Vegan Community Café and there is a regular radical reading group. This is the bookshop that the *Daily Express* warned you about. Jordan Peterson will not be appearing soon. One of the weapons against locations like this is to stress the humourlessness of it all, but going inside and wandering about, I find a very jovial atmosphere. I seem to be surrounded by people delighting in new finds and by strangers striking up conversations. You can get your wholefoods here too. As a politically active bookshop, its shelves have many books from small presses containing both original and independent thinking.

Sometimes when I turn up booksellers look worried, especially if they have only done a few – or indeed no – previous events. They imagine many obstacles or demands or presume that I'll be trailing an entourage. I tell them, 'You just say where you would most like me to stand and everything else should work itself out.' That either subdues their anxiety or terrifies them. It's not *Starlight Express* – merely a man talking.

In the back room, I am told very specifically how my talk will run. It is the first talk the shop has had for a while, and the first one the organizer has ever put on. There will be no mistakes.

There are no mistakes. I make a book stack including Merlin Sheldrake, Octavia Butler and Pragya Agarwal. Today, should my tangents stretch the margins of the timetable, a hand will go up in the air, making it clear it is time to move on to questions.

Forty-six minutes in, the organizer puts up her hand to tell me that I should start thinking about taking questions, if we are to keep to time. Fifty-nine minutes in, the hand goes up to stress that this must be the last question, if I am to get to the signing table at the back of the room anywhere near the timesheet schedule.

I enjoy the customized face-masks at the signing, which include face-masks for the bands The Mission and New Model Army. I embarrass myself by attempting to name a New Model Army album that I particularly enjoyed, but can't remember its title or any of the songs on it. As I am talking so much every day, my mind has a habit of switching off my memory unless it's needed for an event.

Karen, who helped me understand about the psychology of pain when I was writing my book, is in the audience too. She brings me a lovely present of Christopher Isherwood's *Mr Norris Changes Trains*, renamed and adapted to reflect my own journeys.

This afternoon I need three books from October Books' second-hand shelf: a series of essays on Tabloid Culture; something on the 1960s, with a lengthy piece on *The Avengers*; and a book on galaxies and quasars, which is forty-two years old, so perhaps a little out of date, but has a beautiful dedication written on the first page, which makes up for its possible shortcomings in terms of quasar education:

> To Mammy,
> From a quarrelsome and recalcitrant, if not positively contrary offspring.
> In gratitude for all your efforts before and after and during the 27th August, 1981.
> If I do not lay the world at your feet, it is because I send you galaxies and quasars,
> with love [squiggle signature]

I cannot make out the squiggle signature, nor can anyone behind the counter. I am told the book's dedication has been pondered about ever since it came into the shop. Would Squiggle Signature ever have contemplated that strangers in a new century would be intrigued by them and their mammy?

I am also given *A New Index for Predicting Catastrophes* by Madhur Anand, from a man who tells me that he has been carrying it with him for three years. He has been waiting to pass it on to me since he saw Anand give a talk and thought I should know her work. It is a meeting of poetry and theoretical ecology, of science and art.

The giver has kindly included a printout of a review of the book from the *Journal of Humanistic Mathematics* and a card: 'It has taken me three years but if you are reading this then I finally managed to get the book to you. The author was very kind to me during a very bad day. I'm passing this book on to you as a way of paying back a very small part of that kindness.'

I adore the necessity of passing on books, of hearing an author and thinking, 'I know a stranger who needs to hear this voice.'

Winchester

P&G Wells is the oldest shop in Winchester and the oldest bookshop I will be visiting. While many of the independents I am visiting began operating in recent years – some just before or even during the Covid pandemic – P&G Wells has made it through cholera outbreaks, Spanish flu, numerous wars, rebellions and turmoil, though it was founded a little too late for the last major European outbreak of the Black Death in 1720. Book printing, binding and selling have been going on here since 1729. They don't know definitively whether Keats ever visited, but they believe he would certainly have walked by as 'To Autumn' was shaping in his mind.

I am disappointed that no one working here has half-moon glasses and a dapper little moustache. I hoped to see them tutting as they looked at their pocket watch. It is a very wooden bookshop, with wooden shelves, wooden floorboards and an Everyman Classics carousel in the centre of the ground floor. I am proudly shown the historical wallpaper that was revealed during redecoration. I have a fondness for bygone wallpaper revealed.

This is a bookshop that is an escape – where time can pass how you wish it to, rather than being tethered to the laws of physics. The yellowed photograph of Wells in 1900 could happily have been used in the opening credits of *Bagpuss*, and a marvellous mechanical mouse organ would not look out of place here.

The peace of P&G Wells makes the transition to a drunken Saturday night on the London Underground spiky. It is the worst of England – the antithesis of the kindly readers of Winchester. It is boozy, arrogant, selfish, an ugly spectacle of swigging cans and bullying laughter.

Did this happen to Mr Norris in *Mr Norris Changes Trains*? I turn a page and start to find out: 'Like a long train which stops at every dingy little station, the winter dragged slowly past.'

Berkhamsted

Today I have four events, but the commute is easy as I merely need to walk across a corridor in Berkhamsted Town Hall to get between them. Despite that, I do not have time to visit the grave of Peter the Wild Boy in St Mary's Church, but I do find Edward Popple in the Rectory Lane Cemetery.

It is the BerkoFest Book Festival and, as well as presenting a talk about my own book, I have to interview three other authors: psychologist Claudia Hammond, novelist A. L. Kennedy and the therapist and cricketer Michael Brearley.

At 10.15 a.m. I am the first talk of the day and am relieved to see a crowd, including the mayor in the front row. He is the first and last mayor in attendance during this tour – in chains, at least. There may have been others undercover, in other towns, quietly clanking. It feels very early to be vivacious and engaging, but, like a lycanthrope at full moon, the transformation occurs and the evidence-based howling begins.

The speed of change in my mental temperament is an intriguing thing to me. I can be tired or melancholy, anxious or furious, but making rapid connections to all the ideas that I have fizzed up in my head is when I am at my most content. I have rarely carried the fog of any offstage mood with me onto the stage. I love hearing the stories of ancient crooners and comics who doddered into theatres, with the stage crew looking startled that these tired and ancient figures might even consider taking to the stage. And then the lights go up, the introductory music blares and they bound on, dynamic, coherent and splendid.

There is an encouraging nonagenarian in the front row, whose nodding, smiling and sometimes questioning looks conduct me through my talk as if she were Daniel Barenboim. She comes up to me at the signing table and explains that she was not allowed to do science at school, but was instead pushed into languages – 'two of them dead' – and so she was made to become a diplomat rather than a cosmologist. 'But now I am ninety I can I do whatever I want.' She's another inspiration.

I have a three-minute turnaround and then take to the stage with Mike Brearley. We talk of racism in sport, bowler Bob Willis and ventriloquism from a Freudian perspective.

In a one-day festival with a packed bill across three spaces, the green room becomes increasingly energized by the presence of Marxist comedians, classicists and William Blake experts. John Higgs's most recent book is *William Blake vs the World*. It was thanks to him that I was able to stand at the altar of Blake's notebook, which is secured at the British Library. I was with poets Salena Godden and Kae Tempest as the archivist carefully turned the pages of a notebook whose survival defies the odds. Blake was not celebrated at the time of his death, and was buried in a pauper's grave at Bunhill Fields, so the fact that anything survived is a small miracle.

Salena and Kae both wept as they saw the crossings-out around 'O Rose, thou art sick' and other now-famed lines that were most likely leaving Blake's mind and appearing on paper for the first time. Both were permitted to hold this sacred relic. I declined the offer to touch it. I am inherently clumsy; I was banned from using ink pens at school, due to the blotty chaos I left across the page. I didn't know how I would ruin the notebook, but the fear was too great. I had a mental image of Thomas Harris's *Red Dragon* and, with incomprehensible hunger, saw myself starting to devour the notebook, like Francis Dolarhyde, the Tooth Fairy. I couldn't take the risk of the impish thought becoming reality.

No such notebooks at the festival today, not even Graham Greene's tally for his rounds of Russian roulette.

I talk to Claudia Hammond about *The Art of Rest*, one of the few arts that I am content to have failed at utterly. I then move back across the corridor to talk to A. L. Kennedy, and much of the front row does the same. Kennedy is on the shortlist of authors whose work has almost made me cry. I don't think I have ever actually cried when reading a book, as I am too repressed, whereas my copy of Nathan Filer's *The Shock of the Fall* is badly water-damaged from the cascade of tears that came from my wife when she read the final two chapters on the train from Camborne.

A. L. Kennedy's *The Little Snake* is inspired by the snake in *The Little Prince*, my mum's first favourite book and one that I read from at her funeral:

> All men have stars, but they are not the same things for different people. For some, who are travelers, the stars are guides. For others they are no more than little lights in the sky. For others, who are scholars, they are problems... But all these stars are silent. You – You alone will have stars as no one else has them... In one of the stars I shall be living.

The beauty and poignancy of Kennedy's writing, and the connection to my mother's birth and death, created the heady cocktail that overwhelmed me. A. L. talks about the art of writing and connecting with humanity. She ends by recalling how her mother still jumps when she hears a loud bang. It reminds her of when the orphanage next to her childhood home was bombed. She asks us to think then of all the other mothers in the world, in so many countries, who jump when they hear a loud bang, living in constant expectation of confrontation.

The audience are moved and silent. There is no need for anything more to be said.

Southwold

After enjoying a day in just one place, I have to move fast to get to Southwold, as I am talking there at 11 a.m. the next day. Suffolk is a county populated by towns and villages with names on the cusp of rural parody: Coddenham, Gipping, Framlingham and Boulge.

I am on the way to Darsham. M. R. James is even more present than he was at Wivenhoe. The station is a lonely platform and I am the only one to disembark on this cold, dark night. A little steam billowing around my ankles is all this scene is lacking. James was brought up in Great Livermere, a little way north of Bury St Edmunds, a village that is also home to 'The Insect Circus', a bizarrely wonderful comedy circus. Whenever I walk along Southwold beach I think of the acclaimed Jonathan Miller adaptation, *Whistle and I'll Come to You*, filmed only a short stroll away at Dunwich (not the Dunwich where H. P. Lovecraft set his horror, but despite this geographical error, it still brings Cthulu to mind).

I am the only passenger to disembark at Darsham. It creates a perfect pudding of romanticism and threat. A taxi is waiting in the car park, but the driver was expecting me to be a woman. He proudly asks if I noticed how fast he was going when we were on the main road. I did. Then he gets distracted by a nocturnal swan, and I grip my knees tightly. As usual, it turns out the real threat are the living, not the dead.

I have put off eating, as I had been told I would arrive in time for a meal at the festival hotel. It turns out that the kitchen is closed, but I'm given a very cheesy cheese sandwich – the sort you can feel in your bowel before you bite in. The rest of the authors and volunteers are seated in front of their empty pudding bowls and I am envious of their feast.

I am sober and hungry, and they are full of wine and conversations that are on their final echo. I drink enthusiastically, happy to catch up. Before long we get to the subject of ghosts.

Irving Finkel is at the table. Looking quite perfectly like an academic who studies the ancient – white-bearded and bespectacled – he is an expert on cuneiform. This is exactly who I am meant to meet in this M. R. James landscape. He promises to tell me more at breakfast. Isn't that what always happens in the movies before the academic is found dead, the secret that he promised to tell still on the wrong side of his lips? As James wrote in 'Number 13': 'I heard one cry in the night, and I heard one laugh afterwards. If I cannot forget that, I shall not be able to sleep again.'

CHAPTER 7

Where Orwell Ate His Chips

Southwold to Leeds

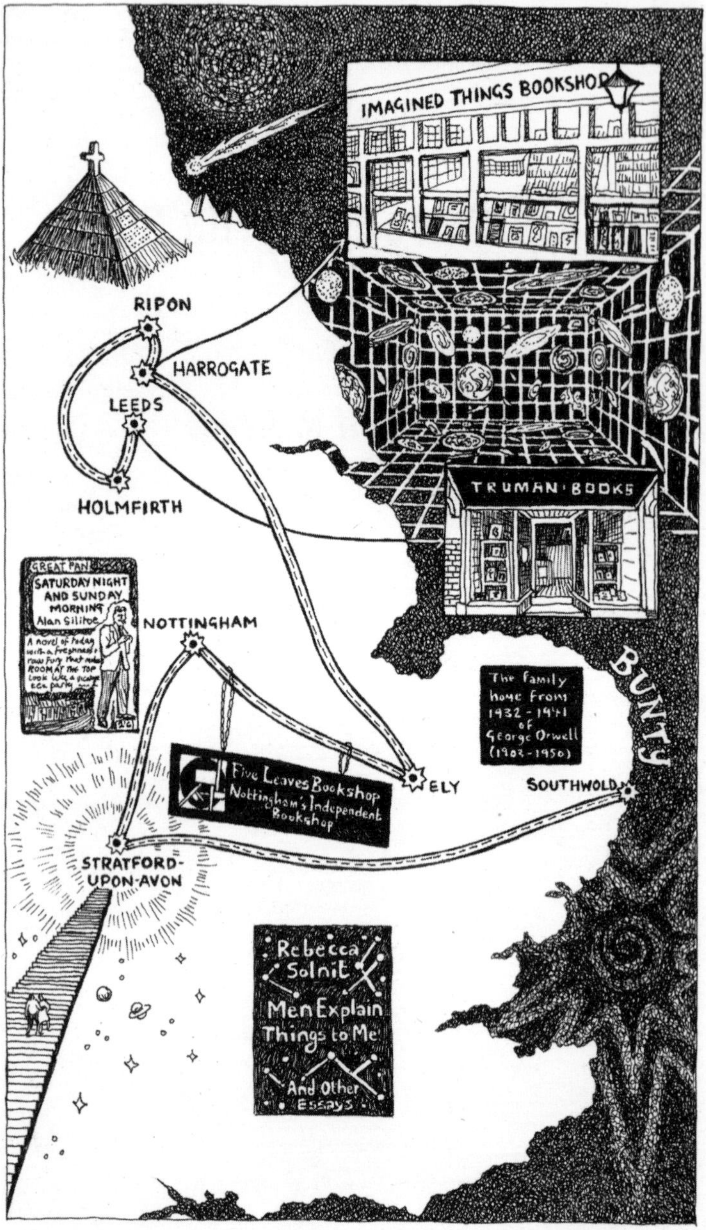
IMAGINED THINGS BOOKSHOP
RIPON
HARROGATE
LEEDS
HOLMFIRTH
TRUMAN · BOOKS
GREAT PAN
SATURDAY NIGHT AND SUNDAY MORNING
Alan Silitoe
NOTTINGHAM
BUNTY
The family home from 1932 - 1941 of George Orwell (1903 - 1950)
Five Leaves Bookshop
Nottingham's Independent Bookshop
ELY
SOUTHWOLD
STRATFORD-UPON-AVON
Rebecca Solnit
Men Explain Things to Me
And Other Essays

Irving has survived the night.

I eat my breakfast alone, thinking of the marvellous noises Michael Hordern made when eating grapefruit as the academic in, 'Oh, Whistle, and I'll Come to You, My Lad'. Then I approach Irving to hear about more of his ghost studies. I am disappointed at how quietly he eats his cornflakes, but I enjoy the pugilism he shows between spoonfuls as he suggests that Brian Cox doesn't know quite as much about ghosts as he thinks. Irving is ready to challenge physicists over their reluctance to explore apparitions just because their existence would break the second law of thermodynamics. I depart, eager to aid Irving with his throwing down of a gauntlet.

Oddly, I am the final event of the Southwold Literary Festival at 11.15 a.m. on a Monday morning. I have a lovely audience of people with nothing better to do. After selling a few books and talking to some retired science teachers with far better ideas for the science curriculum than the last decade of Education Secretaries, by the time I leave the hall the banners are already coming down. Should I mention to anyone after 1 p.m. that I just spoke at the book festival, they will tell me there has not been a book festival in Southwold since 1954 – the day Somerset Maugham exploded and the festival burnt to the ground.

It's good to be back in a ghost story.

Cancelled trains mean that I have time to wander and watch the dog walkers and the waves. I notice a plaque for George Orwell next to the chip shop. My head has obviously been buried so deeply in my mushy peas on previous visits that I've never noticed it before.

Like Sidmouth, Southwold has been fictionalized. It is Knype Hill in George Orwell's *A Clergyman's Daughter*. Before breakfast this morning I had read up to the moment that Dorothy, the Clergyman's Daughter herself, is feeling underwhelmed by the children she's teaching: 'the frightful abysses of their ignorance. For they knew nothing, absolutely nothing – nothing, nothing, nothing, like the Dadaists.'

No Orwell in the local hospice shop, instead I buy two *Bunty* annuals (1979 and 1988) and a 1979 *Return of the Saint* annual with really useless illustrations, as many TV spin-off rip-off annuals at the time had.

However, I am not disappointed by the *Bunty* comic strips: *Georgie and Griff* – the story of a girl coming to Camelot Ladies' College, but she brings with her Griff, 'her pet Griffin – a mystical creature, half eagle, half lion. Griff had one other strange quality – he was invisible!'; *Sarah the Sound Seeker* – Sarah gets the dream job of working for her local radio station, where she has to collect unusual sound effects from the local area; *Nearly New from Netta* – the exciting adventures of Netta, who works in the nearly-new shop where things sort of happen for a bit.

To hell with the Marvel Universe. If Hollywood had real vision, it would be making millions from the Bunty Universe.

By 1988 Bunty has morphed somewhat, and we have *Wings of Fear* – since the death of her dad in a climbing accident, Kelly Mason's strange cousin Leonie has the power to control birds. *Return of the Saint* is very pale in comparison.

I am dropped off at Darsham station by one of the many ebullient festival volunteers, who drives with care and without being distracted by swans. I try to tease out of her who has been the most problematic guest. There is often someone in a programme, and I think, 'I bet they're a nasty piece of work when they're not in public.' But according to my driver, it seems everyone this time was kind. And then I think, 'Oh no, maybe I was the one?'

I end up reading more of the *Bunty* annuals than of the Orwell; if only he had included more invisible griffins after the Dadaism.

Stratford-upon-Avon

Comedy writers are tortured by puns. If they spend enough time working for BBC radio comedy, they will eventually see puns everywhere. Reality becomes obscured by screeds and screeds of wordplay. Every year at least two comedy writers die, walking off a cliff after being blinded by potential puns confusing girls and gulls. Walking through Stratford-upon-Avon with a comedy writer once, I saw a shop called 'Much Ado About Toys' and we then spent the rest of the afternoon unable to write our screenplay, as the bits of our brain that we wanted to use to actually create something were jammed. Puns on the brain are like pouring sugar into a petrol tank.

We came up with the DIY store Taming of the Screw, estate agent Ham Lets, Toys R Us and Cressida, chiropodists Two Gentlemen of Verruca, sports shop Merchant of Tennis, kitchenware store The Merry Knives of Windsor, fast-food outlet Big Mac Beth, and skiwear shop Two Snowball Kinsmen. It was a terrible wasted day, and this short paragraph openly exists so that your day can be destroyed too as you accept the pun challenge – whether you wish to or not – and I find my social-media account on intermittent days buried under your superior bard-based retail outlets.

This is a slow day. I was the last of Southwold, and now I am the first of the Stratford Literary Festival. It is a one-event day, which feels like a day off.

There is a hospice charity bookshop opposite the venue and I go straight to the glass cabinet of treasures. No books, but I am struck by the plastic bag of vintage film star post-cards. There is a photo of Sylvia Sidney next to a whippet, and of Dennis Price seated louchely in the guise of Bad Lord Byron. I rifle through these and decide that some will make delightful new bookmarks, including what appears to be a signed photograph of an achingly young Dirk Bogarde on the way to being Dr Sparrow, before continental cinema darkened him towards deathly crack-ups in Venice and Nazi night-porter shame.

I also need a book on the complete works of Leonard Rossiter, from *The Clandestine Marriage* at the Bristol Old Vic to *Loot* at the Ambassador's Theatre, as well as all his film, TV work and Cinzano commercials with Joan Collins in between.

In Swansea I picked up a similar but far heftier book dealing with everything Kenneth Williams ever did. *The Kenneth Williams Companion* is remarkably complete, including as it does every advert he ever did – from Terry's Pyramint to Fiesta Kitchen Towels, to his ad encouraging us to go to Hull to take the ferry to continental Europe. You can also discover that his only mime in the TV charade game *Give Us a Clue* was for Whiplash Willie, correctly guessed by Bernard Bresslaw.

I am in the annexe of a church that is now a small arts centre. The show is in the round and I have a magnificent oak chair all to myself, practically a throne, to sit on and cast out my words like pearls to the audience. I believe this could be my Lear day, or at least my Monty Python version of it.

The audience has in it many young people from a local grammar school, so I become aware that some tangents I usually veer off into will have references that teenagers will find utterly perplexing. Despite this, I decide to deal with the size of the universe by using a lengthy reference to the David Niven film *A Matter of Life and Death.* If this talk leads to just one teenager experiencing that masterpiece, then my status as an educator will have been confirmed.

I am aware that my references might be perplexing to all age groups. When I am working in other countries I will often fall into conversation with people who tell me, 'If I am honest, there were some references I didn't quite get, but I suppose that is because I am not English.' I will then explain it's not because they are not English, but because they are not me. Sometimes I am even too specific for myself – references emerge from recesses in my mind and I have no knowledge of their origin.

Nottingham

Alan Sillitoe is part of the psychogeography of Nottingham. On any street my imagination can overlay a scene of 1,000 Raleigh bikes racing along, all fresh from the factory. Then I can hear Arthur Seaton call, 'What I'm out for is a good time – all the rest is propaganda!' Did I read that in the book *Saturday Night and Sunday Morning* first or hear Albert Finney deliver it in the film?

On some absurd version of *Desert Island Discs*, where you had to choose eight pieces of book-cover art to take with you, my number-one choice would be the Pan artwork for the novel. In racy bright-orange font there's a quote splashed across the front from the *Daily Telegraph*, reading, 'A novel of today with a freshness and raw fury that makes ROOM AT THE TOP look like a vicarage tea-party' next to a painted Finney, with him wearing brown slacks, brogues and a grey flannel jacket, cupping the flame for a cigarette, challenging the world to take him on – our very own Rebel Without a Cause.

On my way to the Five Leaves Bookshop I pop into the nearby Oxfam. This Oxfam has never been lucky for me, but today I look in the window and see a rare Philip K. Dick book: *The Dream Connection*, an interview with him filled out with memories from others. It's £30 and so, digging deep, I justify the purchase in the knowledge of another well being dug – and I did take the cheap train.

I find *another* Colin Wilson book of mysteries, the greatest mystery being exactly how many books about mysteries Wilson put his name to. My inability to decline this purchase reveals how tired I am, and it's made worse by buying a book that is considerably larger than it needs to be, combining two interviews with André Malraux, a man I know almost nothing about, bulked out with lots of reasonably dull photographs of his face.

I do not need this. At moments like these, I am taken over by a voice that says, 'This may be rare and strange – grab it now, you may never see it again. What if you later find out it is worth hundreds of pounds and you left it behind?'

Desmond Morris will say that I failed to spear the gazelle and I will be expelled from the tribe. Fear of regret drives many such purchases. And being too tired for my reasonable self to win the argument. A beautifully illustrated and wildly colourful 1950s look at evolution, *The Story of Living Things and Their Evolution* by Eileen Mayo, with a chimpanzee mother and baby and butterflies on the cover, is too lovely to leave behind too. It looks delightful, and I assure myself that even if I find this for one pence at some future date, this is a book to be treasured. That is how my purchases are made: through a combination of fear and delight, and any notable paintings of orchids and their duplicitous ways.

In the end no gazelles bagged here, but maybe a plump rabbit or two.

Back in Five Leaves, I drink tea and eat Welsh cakes. The shop's focus has been on politics and activism, but with lockdown and having to operate online, its stock has broadened. A few bestselling thrillers nestle amongst the Noam Chomskys and Naomi Kleins, not to say that Naomi and Noam aren't thrilling too. The shop won Independent Bookshop of the Year in 2018 and also publishes its own books.

Ross gives me a copy of *The Hosanna Man* by Philip Callow, his debut novel. It has a troubled history. Published in 1956, it received good reviews, but then a local Nottingham newsagent complained that he formed the basis of the character who surreptitiously sold under-the-counter pornography, which in those days included the work of D. H. Lawrence. It took a lot less to be pornographic then. Surely the newsagent, by pursuing the complaint, was only drawing attention to his nefarious activities?

The book was pulped, though, and Callow's contract for a second book was cancelled. Fortunately, Callow got another book contract and, as well as novels, went on to write biographies, including one of Walt Whitman, *From Noon to Starry Night*. He never allowed *The Hosanna Man* to be reprinted in his lifetime.

Ross and I get talking about Ray Gosling, a notable Nottingham inhabitant, activist and documentary film-maker, and someone whose humane and compassionate voice I admired a great deal: 'I was for the working classes, for the underdog, for the seedy and the left behind.' Ross tells me that you knew you were going places in Nottingham when you joined the list of people Gosling owed money to.

His youthful autobiographical novel, *Sum Total*, is an illuminating insight into post-war youth culture and comes as close to a British beatnik novel as there is:

> Standing at bus queues, on railway platforms, airport lounges, on quaysides, at coach stops never feeling quite at home. Coming from and going to but never arriving, never departing, always passing through. Seedy, unpresentable, holding the tipped cigarette as if it were love like the singer holds the hand mike, and then drawing on it like it contained some secret quality, everlasting life or death, or complete immunity.

This is not dissimilar to my own bookshop-tour experience.

Five Leaves republished the follow-up to *Sum Total* – *Personal Copy*, which takes us through Gosling's 1960s, including his fight to get rid of slum dwellings and his stand on gay rights.

Gosling seems overlooked at the moment and I hope that will change. Sadly, his career ended ignominiously. His 2007 documentary, *Ray Gosling: OAP*, won the Jonathan Gill award for most entertaining documentary at the Grierson

Awards, but his later years were marred by heavy drinking. In 2010, while making a television film about assisted dying, Gosling spoke movingly of suffocating a former lover who was in agony, dying from AIDS. This was investigated by the police and found to be untrue, though I think Gosling believed it as he said it. When asked why he said it, he explained that his problem was that 'My heart was bigger than my head.'

I am the first live show that Five Leaves have put on since lockdown: started and stopped, stopped and started eighteen months before. We are at Peggy's Skylight, a beautiful jazz club, which allows me to imagine that I am Lenny Bruce, though obviously if you want to smoke you have to go out into the rain now.

Geri, a frequent visitor to my Nottingham shows, gives me a copy of Polly Barton's *Fifty Sounds* afterwards because she thinks I'll like it, and she is quite correct.

I have to get the last train, so the show is hasty but fun. I am accompanied to the station by Callum Cooper, an academic with a keen interest in death, amongst other things. We have a hurried conversation about ESP as we follow the tramline. He gives me my final book of the day as I walk through the station gates: Craig Weiler's *Psi Wars*, an investigation into notions of scientism and Rupert Sheldrake.

Tonight I dream I am hanging out at Kenneth Williams's flat and he is cross because a smashed mirror has been delivered. My celebrity dreams have grown up. I remember when I was nine, dreaming that I was flying the *Millennium Falcon* through space with Han Solo, and being so sad when the dream ended. Now I dream of a dead melancholic celebrity's delivery annoyances. Reality gets closer in sleep.

Ely

> I am much troubled in sleep. No definite image presented itself, but I was pursued by the very vivid impression that wet lips were whispering into my ear with great rapidity and emphasis for some time together.
>
> M. R. James, 'The Stalls of Barchester Cathedral'

I like the flatlands of Ely, and the cathedral makes me think of 'The Stalls of Barchester Cathedral'. This tour has thoroughly brought home to me that almost none of my destinations are fresh to my eyes, whether I have visited them before or not. Almost every landscape is already populated by someone else's imagination. Every town is layered.

It is eight years since I last trawled the charity shops here. At that time I bought an illustrated biography of Derek Jarman, a book about the cultural myth of the mad scientist, and a boxed set of lyrical literature, including Thomas Gray's 'Elegy Written in a Country Churchyard'. I gave that to my dad and it sits on a shelf outside his bathroom in case anyone wants to read rural prose and poetry while waiting to use the loo.

I have thirty minutes to get through all the charity shops before closing time, so I need to be impulsive. I later regret not buying the 1966 *Buster* annual with the Charlie Drake comic strip in it. My son and I used to count *Buster* annuals as the Holy Grail of comic annuals because they seemed so rare. He remained in deep umbrage when we found one in Hastings that was way overpriced and would have dug too deeply into our money for the crazy golf. That bookshop was blacklisted after that.

I find Michael Freedland's biography of Kenneth Williams and, having only dreamt about him last night, and knowing that it is the only Williams book I don't have, I take it to the counter. I also buy *Reality Through the Looking Glass* by C. J. S. Clarke. This will be the third time I have bought it, and next year will probably be the third time I donate it to a charity shop, as it always seems the first on the sacrificial book pile when the stacks of books at home go above the floodline of my family's sanity. The new find is *Unaccompanied Minor* by Alexander Newley, the son of Anthony Newley and Joan Collins, as well as being a rather splendid painter with a hint of Lucian Freud.

I need another Rebecca Solnit too. This time it is her biography of Eadweard Muybridge, the early photographer of things in motion. The book plays a part in the first essay of her collection *Men Explain Things to Me*. After telling a man at a party that she has written about Muybridge, he proceeds to lecture her on a new book all about him. Her friend attempts to explain that the book he is lecturing her about *is* Rebecca's book, but he continues to extemporize and, when the information finally penetrates his thick exterior, he simply moves on to something else. It is a story that almost every woman I know has some version of, and Solnit's essay is a reminder for me to shut up and listen, even if my fizzy mind is demanding airtime. It's a lesson that I am still learning.

Topping's bookshop in Ely, like Blackwell's in Oxford, has a small, unassuming door leading to a lavish world inside. It doesn't unfold its spacetime quite as much as Oxford, but it has hints everywhere of being designed by M. C. Escher. I am placed up in the art section to sign pre-ordered books and stock, and I am immediately surrounded by temptation. The room becomes my office, and I write a little while nibbling on complimentary Brie and charcoal biscuits. There are plenty of little pots of tea too. This is closest to my dream of what it is to be a travelling author.

The evening event is in a church a small distance away, where I have spoken before. The audience get elderflower pressé as they enter, and I am behind another lectern. It is splendidly civilized.

The audience's questions are many and varied, from asking my thoughts on mental health (my own and in general), to why human beings feel the need for gods. These are some of the favourite moments in my life because, as much as I write to release the pressure of thoughts inside my head, when I start talking, things just pop out and eventually I can discover afresh what I think about things. Some days on this tour I find out that I think something totally different from what I had previously thought in Market Harborough or Pontypridd, and I want to send those previous audiences footnotes, updates or apologies.

I am quite surprised that my frantic mind, working at full throttle while I am being stared at, often does much better thinking than the mind that calmly looks out of the window alone and carefully contemplates.

I am staying in a hotel in Peterborough and find myself walking the uninviting back streets, grumpy and confused, having misjudged the direction it was in. I am alone and free to swear loudly at the dark. When I finally arrive, the receptionist has a furious face, which lightens when she tells me that the bar is closed. Like so many English people, bad news may be her only happiness.

I remember that over the bridge is a riverboat bar that is so debauched it serves beer after 9.45 p.m. A busy pub quiz is in full confusion when I arrive, so I buy my pint and then go out and sit on the bank. I read about Dame Edith Evans's appreciation of Kenneth Williams's late-night cocoa-making, and I listen to the quiet river. It is a perfect moment to romanticize being a British traveller alone on the road, and on the rails. At times like these, I know where I most belong.

Harrogate again

> I am dreaming of the edge-land again. It has begun to colonise my sleeping mind. Dreams take place in the midst of Scots pines and down among the cold, scrub-scattered banks. I am following a fox...
>
> Rob Cowen, *Common Ground*

I took advice on Yorkshire books to read on my way to Harrogate and I was told to read Rob Cowen's *Common Ground*, set in the edge-land not far from Harrogate. I got my hands on an ex-library copy from Bromyard in Herefordshire. It has plenty of date-stamps – the final one before being withdrawn from circulation happens to have been on my fiftieth birthday.

I read of the spring equinox, a day that the author feels to be strangely hallucinogenic, and I consider that most days feel like that to me, particularly whilst on this trip. There is always a sense of being detached when I travel, of never quite being solidly in the streets. Some days, each moment of physically connecting with reality seems to be a surprise, as if I was expecting it to fall away, as if it was vaporous. The first time I heard about the holographic principle – the concept that we are two-dimensional projections from somewhere else – it didn't seem so strange to me, and that's how I feel, back in Harrogate again.

I am slightly late for Imagined Things bookshop, but there is no heaving queue outside. It is a quiet signing, mainly pre-orders, although a handful of people pop by to get dedications to sons, daughters and even themselves.

Imagined Things is a pretty shop in Harrogate's last Victorian arcade, and it is as colourful as candy floss and invitingly bright. It has an atmosphere that makes you smile as you walk in. Like many independent shops, it has had its battles and nearly didn't survive its first few years.

Although social media can often seem like a festering sore, it is not just there for the vicious and the sure. Back in 2018, a tweet from Imagined Things was instrumental in its survival. After eleven months of being open, the shop was beginning to struggle and the owner, Georgia, tweeted: 'We only took £12.34 today... if anyone was thinking about buying a book now would be a great time! Things have been tough recently – today the worst day ever. A card, a book, anything makes a huge difference to a small business like ours. We'd be very grateful for your support.'

This went on to be re-tweeted nearly 7,000 times. The next day the shop was hectic with locals, and the telephone was ringing with people from further afield buying books. Books were sent as far as Kazakhstan. For Georgia, the most important thing was the local interest. She wrote, 'I opened an independent bookshop – for people to come in and find books they didn't know existed, to experience the wonder of being somewhere that celebrates books, and to be a part of the community and unite book-lovers. To keep the high street vibrant and interesting for now and the next generation.'

Meg is behind the counter today, and we talk about the size of the universe and the fabric of spacetime. Other people's understanding of ideas never bores me. I am still at such an early stage of comprehending the universe – a position that I am unlikely to move from, however much time I have left. After all, it just won't stop expanding. Hearing how other people react to these incredible ideas – as with Meg – gives me a better understanding of how to understand.

Mik and Angela are there too. Mik is a regular at my gigs in the north-west, so much so that I have often told him to stop paying for tickets, but he is stubborn (my agent will be glad to hear). The rooms that I play may not be grand, but they are frequently filled with really lovely people, and some, like Mik, attend many shows in a year.

Mik is going to come along to Holmfirth tomorrow too, which is useful, as whenever I see him and his wide-brimmed hat in the audience, I know not to trot out the same old gubbins again. He assures me that the gubbins is in a state of constant flow and that it's okay – two shows have never been the same. I hope so.

There is a clash of authors while I continue to leisurely sign. Aaron Reynolds pops in to sign copies of his book *Effin' Birds*, which is beautifully illustrated and flamboyantly sweary. The book combines illustrations of birds, in the style of Audubon or Gould, with bursts of invective. Fine-plumed red birds appear to declare, 'Settle down, you fucking idiots' while chickens exclaim, 'Eat my fuckin' turds.'

Despite the title appearing to be a dead giveaway that this might not be the usual bird-spotter's guide, Reynolds tells me he still gets complaints from sensitive ornithologists who were not really expecting finely painted feathers and overt scatology to be in such close proximity.

I walk by the Oxfam bookshop and, despite having visited only a fortnight before, decide that I should have a hasty browse, in case something vital has been donated in the interim. It appears that the hardback copy of Keith Thomas's *Religion and the Decline of Magic* is still on the shelf. This means it was always meant to be mine, as is Parker Posey's *You're on an Airplane*, an autobiography in which the actor tells her story as if seated next to the reader on a plane. This approach seems inspired by Posey's dad, a car salesman. She describes him as someone who could sell ice to water, and perpetually gregarious. Despite having no idea what he was doing, he confidently gave a stranger an impromptu chiropractic adjustment at a party. As she walked away in obvious pain, he scarpered. When selling cars, he would place faux used nappies in the boot of the car just to get the conversation started. File him under 'chutzpah'.

Ripon

The rail line to Ripon fell under the Beeching axe in the 1960s and, with no public transport, my friend Julia has kindly offered to give me a lift to her home town. She is another person I have got to know from meeting her regularly when I've been performing in the north of England. During our journey the conversation gets to the great ethical problem of 'At what age should you buy your child a bottle of vodka?' My son is still more for Minecraft than Morosha.

Ripon was Wilfred Owen's home after his convalescence in Scotland, having been sent home injured from the front. He was billeted in a cottage at 24 Borrage Lane. According to David Winpenny's *Secret Ripon*, although he found it difficult sharing with thirteen other officers, Owen eventually found a corner where he could have tea 'and contemplate the inwardness of war'. He drafted the preface to his war poems in Borrage Lane. 'My subject is war, and the pity of war. The poetry is in the pity.'

There are many charity shops to visit, but I'm relieved that few have what I need. I cannot resist, though, a *Woman & Home* Cordon Bleu cookery book from the late 1950s or early 1960s. I'm a sucker for those gaudy images of overly decorated pieces of ham that look like a roadside-diner Knickerbocker Glory. This purchase makes up for my leaving behind in Reading the book about multiple ways with cream. The most repulsive colour photograph within is for Escalope de Veau Valentino, 'a good party dish; the escalopes are heaped on pommes mousseline, and served with cream sauce, asparagus tips, and mushrooms'. The suggested wine is Schluck.

In Oxfam I find a book of Will Kemp's poetry, a book on forms of fundamentalism and something about free will with an introduction by Mary Midgley, and I realize that I will only know at the end if I had any choice in buying it.

I eat a piece of cake that's as gaudy as anything in *Woman & Home* in a nearby café while schoolboys slurp milkshakes and I am given that look of 'He's not from around here'. Further suspicion is aroused as I open my copy of *Religion and the Decline of Magic*. The mobile phone seems to have caused a sharp decline in public book-reading, which has made the public reader an even greater figure of suspicion.

I feel as if I am in the old Bill Hicks routine where he's reading in a diner and a waffle-waitress comes over and asks, 'What you reading for?' I wait for Hicks's surly mob to appear and jab their fingers at my pages and spit with menace, 'Looks like we got a reader here!' It's never happened yet, but I always keep one big book with sharp pages in my bag, in case I need something to defend myself with.

The Little Ripon Bookshop is not so little any more, but it's not quite big enough for tonight's event, so I am at the Ripon Arts Hut in between this month's amateur light opera, *HMS Pinafore*, and the next youth-theatre production of *Death of a Salesman*. It is an excitable crowd, in the best way, and more like a Friday-night gig than a book talk.

Back at my hotel, I find out about the death of Abi. Like Mik, Angela and Julia, Abi has been a regular in the audience at my events for years, though mainly in the west rather than the north. She was a popular science teacher and was one of those people who added extra energy to any audience. I had last spoken to her a few months before at the Cheltenham Science Festival and she was as animated as ever. The relationship between act and audience is not as one-way as it may sometimes seem, and whilst it can be flighty and occasional, it has a concrete tangibility to it as well. Sometimes people drift away and you don't see them at an event for years, and then you notice them return and, at drinks in the bar afterwards, they'll tell you of those missing years almost apologetically. 'Sorry I wasn't buying tickets for your shows between 2007 and 2018, but I met a man and went to live in Budapest.'

Sometimes there is sadness: 'Do you remember a gang of us always used to come to your gigs in Penzance? I thought you'd like to know...' And then you'll hear sad stories of an early death. Sometimes you only notice the face in the crowd when it is gone. I know that every time I am in the West Country I will expect to see Abi and then I'll remember that she can't attend any more.

Saturday morning and, sadly, I have found out about the grave of Charles Piazzi Smyth too late to make a visit. He was

Astronomer Royal for Scotland, but he was also christened a 'pyramidiot' for his belief that the measurements of the Great Pyramid of Giza held all the secrets of the universe. His fascination with pyramidology led to him being buried under a pyramid tomb in nearby Sharow cemetery.

Holmfirth

I need to take three trains to my first gig – Harrogate to Leeds, Leeds to Huddersfield, Huddersfield to Brockholes. I pull *The London Nobody Knows* out of my rucksack. Although the subject is not Huddersfield, Geoffrey Fletcher's book is linked to it by Huddersfield's famous son, James Mason, who presented a documentary based on the book. He visited decayed and pigeon-spattered music halls, sewer-ventilating street lamps* and the public toilet of Star Yard.

The boozy men of Saturday board the train at Leeds. They are happy with their bottles of beer and are good-natured, but my anxiety gets in the way of my ability to read. I create the illusion of scanning pages and turning them, but I see no words, as I'm anxiously playing out imagined interactions with the men in my head. Outwardly they are as men should be. Are they thinking, 'What are you reading for?' Or could they be thinking, 'I wish I was reading instead. I bet I get drunk and drop my phone down the toilet in Headingley again and wake up without my trousers.'

The third train looks increasingly elusive, with the

* These were lamps that would burn gas coming from the sewer, increasing illumination and decreasing intoxication.

platform indicator moving from a fifteen-minute delay to a thirty-minute delay, until eventually it just shrugs and says, 'I dunno.'

An alternative plan is devised and Clare from the bookshop comes to pick me up. Bookshop people apologize for their cars almost as much as they apologize for their toilets, but they don't need to. I've been in many touring comedians' cars and it takes a lot of half-eaten pasties, shattered CD cases and syrupy Lucozade seat-stains to outdo their chaos.

Mik's hat is in Holmfirth, and Mik is beneath it.

Read, run by James and Louise, wants to be a welcoming family bookshop and it is. They have a website where you can find out about the reading habits of everyone who works there. James is someone who always has a book in his pocket, preferably Le Carré or Atwood, while Louise reads Sarah Crossan and Mary Lawson, when not painting pebbles and hiding them around the town. Clare loves Tolkien enough to call her dog Bilbo, and Penny loves jazz and F. Scott Fitzgerald. Sadly, I don't meet Penny to talk about *The Great Gatsby*, because talking about *The Great Gatsby* is never time wasted, as far as I'm concerned.

Mik offers me a lift into Leeds, which gives me time to look in another Oxfam. Today I need one more Johnny Cash biography, a collection of off-off-off-Broadway performance texts, a book of conversations with Truman Capote and a copy of Colin MacInnes's novel *Absolute Beginners*. By coincidence, I remember that the episode of the TV quiz show *Pointless* that I appeared on is airing tonight. *Absolute Beginners* played its part in the proud victory of Josie Long and me. I happily recall that our best answers included Arundhati Roy, Alderney and Eve Ferret.

Leeds

Mik drops me at Truman Books in Farsley. Will I find a copy of *The Killer Wore Nylon* or *Miss Fandown Takes the Drop* here? Or maybe they'll have *Death Cab for Cutie*? These books are the creations of one of Leeds's most celebrated writers, Richard Hoggart, though you'll be hard pressed to find copies.

All of them exist as titles only in Hoggart's influential examination of the post-war spread of mass media, *The Uses of Literacy*. Sixty years after it was first published, D. J. Taylor described it as 'still one of the great interpretative tools brought to considerations of post-1945 British life'.[1]

During the set-up for my event at Truman Books there is the first shelf accident of the tour. Someone is briefly buried under a free-standing bookshelf that gives up its wish to stand freely. This is probably the moment of highest drama and peril that you will find in this book, so enjoy re-creating the scene in your mind.

A sudden crash.

A human floored.

Books spread across the floorboards.

Anyway, everyone is all right, so that's the dramatic moment of the narrative over and done with. I'll turn it into an explosion in a dictionary factory for the movie version. Back to browsing.

Poet Matt Abbott, author of *A Hurricane in My Head: Poems for When Your Phone Dies*, wrote that Truman Books was one of the five best things about Farsley. When Amanda opened the shop in June 2021 there were people queuing down the street. She had worked in the travel industry, but when it collapsed during the pandemic, she decided it was time 'to be brave, try something new and follow a dream'.[2] Looking along the shelves, I can see that she has achieved her aim of giving exposure to a diversity of voices and of supporting independent publishers. I spy books missed by my radar previously, including the autobiography of Rob Halford from Judas Priest. The older I have got, the more I have been drawn to heavy metal and hard rock and, with all the other old men, I imagine that their mosh pits are now potentially brutal, but also quite civilized. All of the pent-up rage and injustices of life are crushed by this mighty sweaty chaos, but should someone be in jeopardy, order is found to retrieve them and then the chaos starts again.

I am to be the first and last live event of 2021 at Truman Books. As the audience file into the shop, I drink tea, eat Oreos and chat about genocide with a criminologist. The bishop of Leeds comes to collect me. I haven't been collected by bishops from enough bookshops during this tour, which I think must be an oversight by the General Synod.

Before I leave, I rudely demand that Amanda pays me, and today's currency is one paperback copy of Rob Halford's *Confess*. To make up for my insolence, I buy a copy of my book – the first time I have bought a copy of my own book, at least at full price. I have sometimes bought them second-hand. The worst thing about buying your own book second-hand is finding an inscription or dedication that you knew you put a bit of thought into when you met Alice/Hector/The Randalls in 2009/2010/2011 in Lewes/Pinner/Droitwich. An author once told me the worst experience he had in finding a second-hand copy of one of his novels in a charity shop was that he opened it and discovered it was the copy he had given his mum and dad, and the spine was still unbroken. I bet it was quiet around the Christmas table that year.

I finish the night drinking red wine with the bishop and we talk of many things, including how to avoid saying the wrong thing to the Archbishop of Canterbury about Dostoyevsky. I am not sure when I will be able to use this information, but I am hopeful that the day will come.

Dozily, I read the first few pages of *Confess* in bed. Halford speedily moves on from childhood pollution and soot-grey sheets hanging on the clothes line to the afternoon when he found a dildo hidden in a drawer in the youth club, and where that led. Should I be reading of such things in a bishop's palace? It feels more suitable for the bed of a deanery.

Next day is Remembrance Sunday, and the pub at Leeds station is busy with suited ex-soldiers pinned with campaign medals, drinking towards the 11 a.m. silence. On the train home, I'm pleased to see that Rob Halford uses the word 'mither' – a word I don't think he ever squeezed into the lyrics of a Judas Priest song. It reminds me that I should use it more often, and 'ginnel' too.

I make a note.

CHAPTER 8

Black Holes Drowned Out by the Bells of God

Chippenham to London

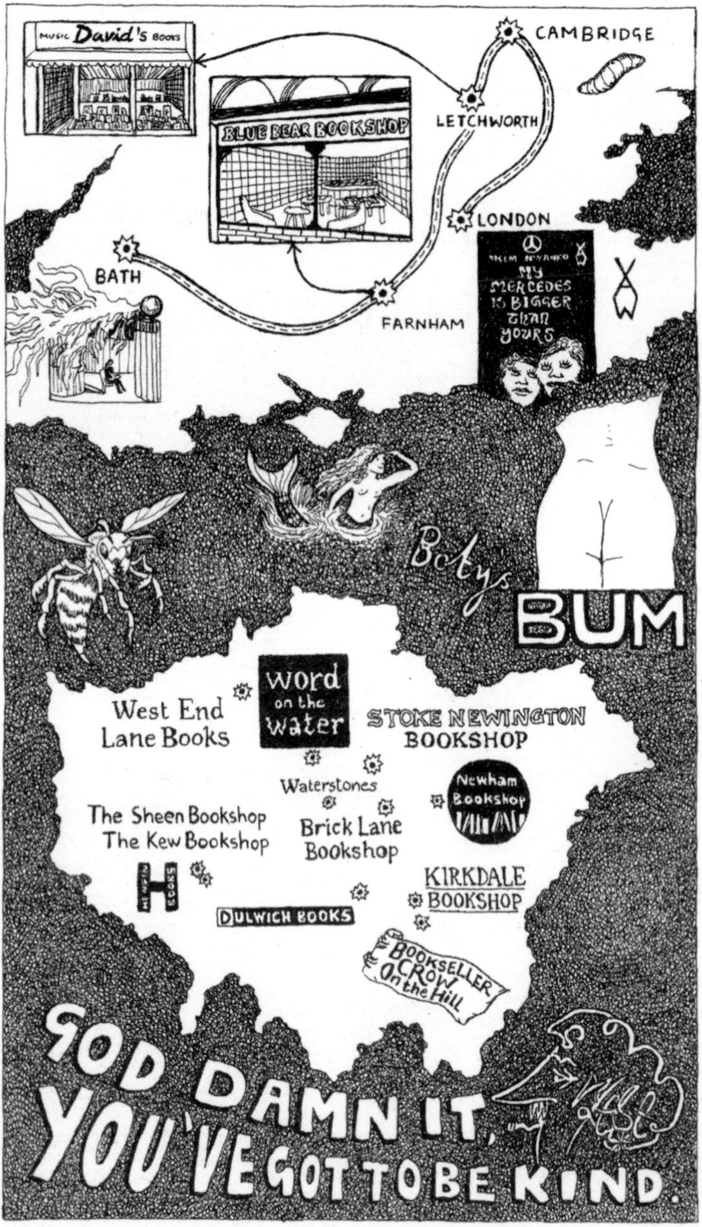
MUSIC David's BOOKS
BLUE BEAR BOOKSHOP
CAMBRIDGE
LETCHWORTH
LONDON
BATH
FARNHAM
MY MERCEDES IS BIGGER THAN YOURS
Betys
BUM
word on the water
West End Lane Books
STOKE NEWINGTON BOOKSHOP
Waterstones
Newham Bookshop
The Sheen Bookshop
The Kew Bookshop
Brick Lane Bookshop
KIRKDALE BOOKSHOP
DULWICH BOOKS
BOOKSELLER CROW On the Hill
GOD DAMN IT, YOU'VE GOT TO BE KIND.

There is nothing to mither about on Monday, as my journey to tonight's bookshop involves a diversion to my favourite barber's and beauty parlour, Chippenham's Hepcats. It is run by Wil Hodgson, who is a barber, but also a comedian and a social historian. I sometimes trade books for beard trims and Jack Chick cartoons.

A recent swap included some photography-book oddities that I had previously put on display during the *Bad Book Club* shows. They included *Yoga for Men*, which is entirely devoid of photos of men in the Lotus Pose, just scantily clad women. In the seedy 1970s this is what yoga for men was. There was also *Men on Men: Their Secret Ways*, which was predominantly photos of men who had forgotten their swimming trunks, casually fishing in the Mediterranean.

In return, Wil gave me three Jack Chick pocket books and a haircut. Chick's little gospel cartoon books are known as Chick tracts and, if you were lucky, you used to find fundamentalists giving them out at railway stations. Titles have included *This Was Your Life* – 'Everything you have said or done will be played back at judgment. Will your name be in the Book of Life?'; *Charlie's Ants* – 'Through Charlie's ants, young readers learn that God became man to die for us'; and *Evil Eyes* – 'What do you get when you mix Catholic superstition with voodoo? Santeria! But there is a way out...'

Chick tracts fit neatly in the palm of your hand, but they would get lost in a bookcase. I keep mine safely in an unused promotional sick-bag that was given away with the film *Mark of the Devil*.

Daniel Clowes, the author of great comic books such as *Ghost World* and *Like a Velvet Glove Cast in Iron*, has said of Jack Chick, 'As a comics aficionado you don't really think of those as being part of the official canon of effective comics... one day I sort of changed my mind on that. I thought, "These are really compelling and interesting and I'd rather read these than pretty much anything else published in 1985."'[1]

I am short on time to fit in a Chippenham haircut and a Bath Spa book talk, so I rush across Chippenham to get towards my date with the hot towels, but still breathlessly stop off in the Dorothy House hospice shop and debate about buying the autobiography of the 1960s club comedian Charlie Williams, *Ee – I've Had Some Laughs*. I decide the £9 price tag is too high. It will be another decision that I later regret.

As a cultural archivist, Wil's trim includes conversation about the rich history of the New English Library skinhead paperback series written by Richard Allen, which include *Suedehead*, *Top Gear Skin* and *Knuckle Girls*. Richard Allen was one of James Moffat's many pen names. Rather than being an English youth writing from experience, Moffatt was a middle-aged Canadian who turned his hand to writing many pulpy exploitation novels on youth cultures. He was also Trudi Maxwell, author of *Diary of a Female Wrestler*, the story of a twenty-one-year-old virgin who goes into the particularly seedy world of wrestling to support her mother.

And he wrote as Etienne Aubin for *Dracula and the Virgins of the Undead* and, under his own name, he wrote the adaptation of the film flop, *Queen Kong*.

As part of Wil's active archive, his aftershave cabinet includes a history of manly smells from the early 1970s onwards. The most remarkable bottle of aftershave that I have seen in his museum was adorned with a label showing Christopher Lee in full cape, surrounded by kneeling naked women. It was clearly one of Boots's under-the-counter top-shelf smells. It made me wish I was clean-shaven, just to smell so spicily vampiric.

Bath

> His own E.S.P. experiments during space travel produced results 'far exceeding anything expected,' he asserted, but scientifically, they were only 'moderately significant'.
>
> The *New York Times* on Apollo 14's Edgar Mitchell[2]

I arrive in Bath just in time for the Oxfam bookshop. I look in the glass cabinet and find an expensive volume that must be mine, *An Index of Possibilities: Energy and Power*. It was originally intended as a UK version of Stuart Brand's Whole Earth Catalog and includes pieces on Apollo astronaut Edgar Mitchell's fascination with ESP and a terrific cartoon of Kurt Vonnegut (which sealed the deal) – so that was another £30 out of my pocket and in the till shortly before closing.

Tonight I am at Topping's. The bookshop has recently moved premises and is now in The Friends' Meeting House.

The Quakers of Bath had a lot of friends, looking at the size of it. It is now the largest independent bookshop in the UK.

I browse the shop and build up another pile of other people's books to reference during the talk, including Salena Godden's *Mrs Death Misses Death* and Janna Levin's *Black Hole Blues*. The bookshop move is so recent that the shelves are still being populated and reorganized, and it seems that quite a few of the titles I am after fall under the category of 'Now hang on a minute – I know I have seen that somewhere, but we are only just beginning to sort out the zoology section; it might still be in those boxes over there.'

There is an extra excitement with this uncertainty and all these stacks of books still seeking a home. In one of them I spy a James Baldwin biography that I have not seen before, *Living in Fire* by Bill V. Mullen, and place it on my pile of probable purchases. A life well lived always requires more James Baldwin.

The shop is very close to the Abbey and we discover that tonight is bell-practice night, perfectly coinciding with my talk. It is an intriguing cacophony to battle with, and sometimes the bell successfully knocks my thoughts off their path. Is this the Church trying to drown out science through campanology? If only it were, that would be good publicity.

The door into the shop is solidly wooden and ancient in appearance and lies directly behind me as I am delivering the talk. In a tradition somewhere between farce and the Old Dark House, the bell-ringing is occasionally disturbed by an echoey knock on oak and I, as Karloffian butler, open the door and declare, 'You'd better come in, it is a dark and stormy night', with the latecomers seeing an audience staring at them like a Satanic mass with nibbles.

I take what's left of the hospitality wine – half a bottle – and my new James Baldwin book and make the late train.

Being a Monday, the late train is library-quiet. With my bottle of wine I am the only rowdy element, but even when the bottle is finished, I try to turn my pages as quietly as possible.

Farnham

On the train to Farnham a woman is humming one of those tunes that you hear in a horror movie, a tune that mixes childish innocence with murderous insanity – the one accompanying the sweetly smiling middle-aged lady sitting in the chair by the still-moving rocking horse, before the camera pans back and it is revealed that she is surrounded by a number of battered bodies and has apparently bludgeoned everyone to death. She interrupts her humming to make a call to her friend. She needs to warn her that she is wearing lurid leggings, as they were a Bikram yoga necessity. Then it is back to the humming.

Walking straight from the station, as if by magic, I collide with the Oxfam bookshop. They are now materializing wherever I go. It is beautifully laid out and spacious, and I am early, so there is plenty of time to search. There are many books here that are on the cusp, but they don't tip me over the edge. I eye up a J. G. Ballard short-story collection that I am sure I have in some form or other, and a book on the Sufi way by Idries Shah. I must be sleeping well, because my mind has enough energy to deny me and, in what is a rare occurrence, I am leaving a bookshop empty-handed.

But then... Ah... hang on. Just as I reach the door I see a spine. It's Janet Frame's *An Angel at My Table*, and then another Janet Frame and then: two Borges; one Jean Rhys (which I think I have already, and I know I have already read, but I like this other cover); *Luckenbooth* by Jenni Fagan; Marilynne

Robinson's *Housekeeping*; Monique Roffey's *The Mermaid of Black Conch*; and a couple more besides. So that's my holiday reading sorted, I argue to myself. The fact that I have no holiday in the foreseeable future has nothing to do with it.

The Blue Bear Bookshop is only a few doors further down. This really is a bookshop that exists in a dream. It is bookshop as artwork. It is a bookshop ready for the director to say, 'Action!' *Vanity Fair*'s set-dresser would not have been able to create such a magical space, even if Annie Leibovitz had demanded it.

It is so alluring it's almost as if it could have been devilishly conjured up by a witch out of candy, so that she could stuff the bibliophiles in her oven. It is a space made to bathe in books, and it is a space in which to fall in love with books. The shelves are high, illuminated by a chandelier, and there is a central table where I can enjoy my peanut-and-banana cake and drink tea.

There is only one copy of each book and they are all sealed – something that was introduced during the pandemic. The shop is also dog-friendly. It is called the Blue Bear Bookshop after Walter Moers's *The 13½ Lives of Captain Bluebear.* Sylvia and Nils, who created the shop, have an autistic son. It seemed impossible to get him interested in reading. Then he was given Moers's book and devoured it. From that point onwards, his book-devouring didn't stop.

There is a vast David Hockney book in one corner of the shop, the size of a hockey goal and with a price tag of £3,000. As people arrive for my talk, some wander over to examine it, coffee in hand. This is rightly perceived as being a more dangerous area than the splash zone around a disembowelled llama, and the customers are politely asked to be very, *very* careful.

I talk at length, and there are many questions and I feel wonderfully relaxed – something that is suddenly shattered when I see that the later evening train timetable is not as populated with trains as I might have hoped, and suddenly I need to spring out of the bookshop and dash to platform one.

I drink alcoholic ginger beer and read of mermaids all the way home.

Letchworth

Letchworth was the world's first Garden City. I imagine it as a landscape of crafts and creativity that sprang forth from the mind of William Morris – a past image of the future as it was meant to be. I also imagine that it can't possibly look like the garden idyll that was intended.

It was once home to a writer of the most lurid works of horror fiction. For those who found James Herbert too genteel, with his castrations and rat-gnawing fatalities, there was Shaun Hutson. His work has been described as 'splatterpunk' and became part of the 1980s horror generation's coming-of-age, along with *Fangoria* magazine's celebrations of gory decapitations and eye-gougings, and with all those movies where sex-hungry teens went to holiday camp to be eviscerated. Hutson's aim was to gross out his audience, to go further than any other author in stimulating your gag reflex. *Assassin* is high amongst his masterworks in this realm. You may wish to skip the rest of this paragraph.

Have you jumped ahead? I've warned you… Okay, I will continue.

Assassin includes a sequence where a zombie is being fellated and eventually ejaculates maggots. This was something that Hutson imagined and put to paper whilst seated in the idyll of a Garden City.

I hope you skipped the last couple of lines. If you did, don't look back now.

I realize I am now on the final third of the tour, approaching the eightieth bookshop. On usual tours, this is where I enter my disenchanted phase, where I confront my self-critical mind that says, 'What sort of ludicrous idea did you have? What was the bloody point of all this hullabaloo?' At times like these I have called on friends like the musicians Grace Petrie and Laura Kidd to join me on the road. Their presence gives me someone else to speak to in the dressing room rather than just myself and helps me to settle the mania and paranoia.

However, something different seems to have happened on this tour. The comfort of all these magical independent bookshops, and the committed booksellers within, have kept the negative voice, if not at totally at bay, then often preoccupied. When that negative voice creeps over to have a word, I can say, 'Not now, I'm browsing' or 'I'm in the middle of this highly entertaining conversation.'

The shows themselves have often become a direct rebuttal of that negative voice. I have tried to focus on creating talks that have an air of celebration, and that has encouraged the voices within that excite me rather than inhibit me.

Arriving at Letchworth, it does indeed look how I imagined it would look, not how I dreamt it might. It looks like the perfect location for a 1980s sitcom about marital bliss and annoying neighbours.

I am won over by David's Bookshop the moment I walk in. It is not quite labyrinthine, but it has enough corners to find yourself facing the unexpected – and then very probably buying it. David's sells both new and second-hand books, and behind the counter is a display of 1950s and 1960s Pan paperbacks: an exhibition of the finest cover art. Many will be coming home with me by the end of the day.

Julia, a school librarian of note, brings me a jar of Letchworth honey and I have leisurely conversations and sign a pile of books. David's Bookshop involves the longest browse of the tour so far. On the first floor I finally go book-blind and have to stop.

I look at the pile so far. My first debate is exactly how many of the Pan books I must have, but I am also distracted by the Heinemann African Writers Series. In yet another confrontation with my ignorance, they were a series I knew nothing about, despite the publisher releasing more than 300 titles. The series began after Heinemann published China Achebe's groundbreaking *Things Fall Apart*.

The series ran from 1961 to 2003. David's Bookshop has at least thirty titles on display, and I am allowed into the back room to see even more of this series, as well as further Pan titles. It is my Wonka golden-ticket moment. From the African Writers Series I pluck out *We Killed Mangy Dog and Other Mozambique Stories* by Luis Bernado Honwana, *My Mercedes is Bigger than Yours* by Nkem Nwankwo and John Munonye's *A Dancer of Fortune*. I was immediately fascinated by the back-cover blurb of Munonye's novel – 'Ayasko dances to advertise patent medicines. Whenever he goes to work for a new pharmacist he brings vast new business.'

The Pan books include a mixture of science fiction, two early publications of Robert Heinlein, a teenage dystopia called *Only Lovers Left Alive* and a novel about extraterrestrial giant wasps, kitchen-sink dramas *Cathy Come Home* and Nell Dunn's *Poor Cow*, a little bit of beatnik *Young Adam* by Alexander Trocchi and a couple of Kerouacs, two smidgens of cannibalism, *The Last Cannibals* and *Cannibals and Human Sacrifice*, plus Lady Cynthia Asquith's *The Second Ghost Book* and *Exploring the Occult*.

I leave the copy of Nell Dunn's *Talking to Women* as I want someone else to find it. It is a book I love, but rather than buy it to pass it on, I leave it so that someone else will find it for themselves. It is a superb collection of interviews, including one with Pauline Boty, a once-overlooked artist who, hopefully, is not so overlooked now. She died tragically young after a cancerous tumour was discovered during a prenatal examination. Not wanting to harm the foetus, she rejected chemotherapy and died a few months after giving birth, aged twenty-eight years. Her daughter died aged twenty-nine, after taking an overdose. I knew nothing of Boty until I visited Wolverhampton, where there was a retrospective of her work in 2013, and then I became a little obsessed with her. She said, 'Lots of women are intellectually more clever than men. But it's difficult for men to accept the idea... They just find it slightly embarrassing that you're not doing the right thing.'

Cambridge

Cambridge can be more confusing than Birmingham. It is clearly designed to be navigated by only the finest theoretical mathematicians.

One of the sweariest car journeys I have experienced was while returning from a family holiday in Norfolk. My dad found himself trapped in Cambridge's one-way system while our dog repeatedly vomited all over the back seat. We never went to Norfolk again. Next time we might never escape, and the dog might never stop vomiting.

I couldn't find a Cambridge bookshop that was interested in selling books at my Cambridge Junction gig, so my publisher has come along. I psych myself up for the stage by reading the back blurbs of the Pan titles I bought in Letchworth:

> 'Smashing, looting, killing, loving – the teenagers take over all Britain.'
>
> 'She's a charmer – but she's a Cannibal.'
>
> 'Fighting, drinking, scorning convention, making wild love – the antics of America's young beats in their mad search for kicks.'
>
> 'I was disgusted. I was nauseated. I was saddened. But I was not bored.'

Afterwards there is the now-traditional jog trot to the station for the late train. Then the Pan books carry me all the way to King's Cross:

> 'Men and women roasted alive. Limbs cut off, cooked and eaten in front of their suffering victim.'
>
> 'Cruel humiliation and the kinkiest ever way of gaining a bitter revenge.'

I wonder if I shall ever read the pages beyond the cover or if it is best to let the blurb create a rip-roaring tableau in my mind, exactly as the promotional stills of horror movies in the books of my childhood let me create a whole film in my head.

Back at my home station, I find myself walking behind a lurching and inebriated woman at exactly the wrong distance – just far enough away that if I speed up to overtake I worry that she would think I was pursuing her. Anxious not to create a sense of threat, I force myself into a dawdle until she is in the far distance, which, due to her roundabout way of moving forward, takes some considerable time.

Finally home, I dream of cannibals and giant wasps.

London: Friday

Before the 100-bookshop idea had fully formed in my head, I originally considered doing simply a weekend of crossing London and talking in twelve bookshops – a different chapter in each bookshop. From that grew the 100-bookshop event idea, across the UK, and the London extravaganza shrank a little. But I am still doing eleven events from Friday to Sunday. I am a victim of my own optimism, another by-product of my manic moments. I am briefly given a vision of magnificent success and then reality is a damnable failure. In my dream, people would follow me from shop to shop and the shows would end up like a Ken Kesey escapade, with a magic bus and party streamers.

Of course the truth of it is that London is very busy, and many people have much better things to do than traipse about after yet another person who has written a book; after all, their neighbours, Polly and Shaun, have written books, and then there's Uncle Bob's epic novel about the Dutch War of Revolt, and the man who came to fix their solar panels said he had just published the third in his quartet of dystopian tales set on the edge of a mythical-event horizon.

To make it even more downbeat, the prologue to the eleven-event weekend jamboree is a Covid booster jab, so I spend much of the forty-eight hours hyper-alert to hints of temporary decline, as my body peps up my resilience to spiky proteins and the little robots that I am told will start controlling my mind as they hatch Machiavellian plans in my bloodstream.

I start at Brick Lane Bookshop, a place with a history of counter-culture and protest. Today it also has shortbread biscuits. It opened back in the 1970s as part of Tower Hamlets Art Project, as an act of protest. The owner, Denise Jones, says that the promoted misconception was that there were no bookshops in Tower Hamlets because there was no demand: people in the East End did not read. She proved how wrong this was – like the snotty belief that miners did not read Dickens, when we know that it was actually Churchill they weren't so keen on.

It was comforting for some to believe that books were not something the proles were attracted to. Sadly, I still see a myth of happy ignorance about inquisitive and enquiring minds. When I was involved in library campaigns I would often be told that libraries were a middle-class luxury, despite all the evidence I saw to the contrary as I travelled. This can seem to be a country that encourages disdain for the bookish and the intrigued. It wants you to surrender, to sink to the lowest common denominator, but I always find energetic resistance to this easy route.

I place myself in a convenient corner of the shop, aiming to create as little obstruction as possible, attempting once again to flatten myself into a two-dimensional cardboard cutout. Denise encourages some visitors to enquire about my book, and I attempt some travelling sideshow spiel about the universe. They nod and smile, ask questions and leave empty-handed. I sign a few pre-orders and chat to Pip, who had encouraged me to put the shop on the route.

I worry that I have let down the shop, and I worry that they worry they have let me down. I worry.

Before I leave, Alan Gilbey enters. I knew him on the comedy circuit in the 1990s, and his performance years go back to being a teen in the punk/post-punk poet era. Like Denise, he was part of the activism that cocked a snook at the notion that the East End wasn't ready for books, poetry or art. To prove that he likes books, he even goes so far as buying mine. Back in the 1990s the first book he recommended to me was *Roadside America*, a gazetteer of the roadside attractions that could be stumbled upon as you traversed the less-populated parts of North America.

Small towns in the US, it seems, build strange edifices to lure people to their diners, motels and bars. You can't die until you have seen the peach-shaped water tower in Gaffney, South Carolina; the world's largest Longaberger picnic basket in Newark, Ohio; or Carhenge, the used-car re-creation of Stonehenge in Alliance, Nebraska.

I leave Finchley Road station and trust my memory to lead me to West End Lane Books. It turns out that my muscle-memory has turned to fat and I find myself at a dry cleaner's instead. My phone has a flat battery and so, terrifyingly, I must return to the 1990s and attempt to use my rusty geographical ingenuity and interact with other people.

I swear my way up Finchley Road. The Friday pavements are too busy with slow people, and I am impatient and infuriated by my incompetence. Fortunately the memory of where the shop is comes flooding back, the moment I see it. This has all the usefulness of déjà vu.

This evening's event is full and has a special guest. Halfway through my talk, a man opens the door, shouts gibberish passionately and aggressively and then runs away. We discuss what he meant, but fail to translate. The non-sporty crowd believes it might be something football-related, but we flounder like anthropologists on an alien moon.

My book zooms through the tills tonight, greatly aided by

Karyl, who decides that at least twelve of her friends will be getting my book for Christmas, and with the same dedication about her excellence written in each one: *Thank you, Karyl, you ensured a sell-out.*

I am staying tonight in my past. I am sleeping in the flat in Peckham where I lived with my pal Ed, who now owns it. Ed is a strange one. He only buys as many books as he is going to read in a month. The flat still has about 100 books that I left there in 2002. To help keep the place neat and tidy, on each visit I take a couple back with me. This weekend I'll take back a Spike Milligan biography and a 1960s Pelican special on the dispossessed.

We used to have a corduroy sofa, which was quite a talking point. It was ruined when we put up an Australian back-packer who insisted on sitting on it in only a T-shirt and no pants. Our corduroy was cursed by his testicles.

London: Saturday

Saturday morning starts at 9.30 a.m. in the Kirkdale Bookshop in Sydenham, a mix of old and new, and with many highly desirable items. There is a lovely hardback copy of Beckett's *No's Knife* in the locked cabinet of special things, but it may be too early for that level of existential anxiety and expenditure.

Ed gives me a lift to Bookseller Crow in Crystal Palace, to save time. He has only just learnt to drive and repeatedly apologizes for his slow and careful driving, but I have always preferred the tortoise to the boy racer. I am quick to panic and slow to calm. Soon he no longer needs to apologize because our time-saving journey by car is hindered by frozen traffic, and we spend an hour enjoying the theatre of people swearing inside their cars as they fear the sofa of their choice will be sold out by the time they reach the warehouse. Will there be any corduroy left for anyone?

Bookseller Crow is, fortunately, busy with both Christmas shoppers and with people after my book. They include Vanessa, who always brings her dachshund to events, and Ben.

Ben Moor, a notable writer and performer, always insists on his books being signed: 'To Ben, You are my greatest inspiration.' His belief is that after his death, as his book collection is explored, people will gasp at the enormous number of authors he inspired, and he will become even more of a cultural icon in death than he was in life.

Ben's own work includes sweet and thrilling monologues mixing scientific theory, philosophical conundrums and highly inventive puns. They have been described as cures for all forms of disillusionment and have been published in his *More Trees to Climb* and *Who Here's Lost?*: 'At home – a card on the mat: "we tried to deliver your place in a queue." Tomorrow I'll have to go to a building and wait.'

He is a romantic who beautifully captures love and its fragility: 'I looked at her with my lone eye as wide as a butterfly net, just like the first day. She returned my look then, a slow smile like swelling strings. This was the moment we would remember, this was our summit of happiness,' says the narrator of Coelacanth.

Ben used to organize a festival of toast after Christmas. All you had to bring to the party was something that would go well with toast, and he provided the rest. He is also a pioneer of Frisbee tree-golf.

I lurch west to Kew Bookshop for my first proper talk of the day. Changing trains at Clapham Junction, I join the rugby crowd on the way to Twickenham. I wonder if they would instinctively know what the man bellowed through the doorway in the bookshop last night? I try to remember the noise that came out of him, but my mind has mislaid it overnight, so I don't bother to ask. The gibberish will remain gibberish.

The small parade of shops by the station is leafy and amber, as if ready for the photoshoot for the cover of a romance novel about a divorced doctor and a recently widowed florist getting to know who they really are. There are bakeries and health-food shops and a better way of life.

It is a dinky little bookshop and it will be almost impossible for me not to be in someone's way, but I work out the optimal corner for talking from and the curious people gather. Wives are drawn in, while some husbands seem to have less interest. Alex, who saved me from insanity in Birmingham, or at least forestalled it, happens to be nearby and has gathered his friends. It is all winningly informal.

As I am standing by the children's bookshelf I make way for a young browser every now and again and they look at me quizzically. 'Why is this man here, in front of the *Horrid Henrys*? Is talking in a bookshop an actual job?'

Then I walk leisurely to the sister shop, Sheen Bookshop. I am early enough to loiter on the high street. There used to be a bookshop that specialized in books about comedy, called The Lighter Side, but it is long gone now. Such specialists, if they exist at all, often find themselves surviving only in the virtual world.

A detour to the Mind shop leads to a Pan edition of *Saturday Night and Sunday Morning*. I cannot risk it getting into the hands of someone who does not show it full respect. Once the dam is broken by this purchase, I realize I need Martin Gardner's *The Ambidextrous Universe*, *The Faber Book of Madness* and John Williams's *Into the Badlands*, a journey the author made around the US meeting authors of crime fiction, plus John M. East's biography of Max Miller, *The Cheeky Chappie*. I also buy a book about The Cure – *A Visual Documentary* – because I like remembering when I had hair that had the same possibilities for follicle chaos as Robert Smith.

There is a small gathering in the Sheen Bookshop, which includes a vocal dog. I take the barks as encouragement. I am also able to help someone who is looking for David Baddiel's *Jews Don't Count* and, having found the book they were looking for, my assistance is rewarded by them staying for the rest of the talk and buying my book too. A couple remark that they have only seen me onstage in arenas previously, and have enjoyed seeing me standing in front of the more low-key environment of the cookery section.

I read the Cure book on the train to Waterstones in Piccadilly and discover that Robert Smith's eyes have been cut out from the photos – for the purposes of collage, revenge or so that they could be kept in a purse for reference, whenever a happy goth needed to remember how to apply their eyeshadow.

Foolishly I had imagined 'the heart of London's busy West End' would be a busy place to do a Saturday-night talk, but it seems 'the heart of London's busy West End' is so busy with other things to do that it is the smallest audience of any of the evening gigs. There are faces I know in the audience: regulars who altruistically thought, 'If we don't turn up, no one will.' They were right.

The audience includes someone who once gave me a Kurt Vonnegut doll holding a placard reminding us all: 'Goddammit, you've got to be kind.' Now this cuddly Vonnegut stands on my desk, reminding me of this every day, in case frustration looks like it is about to spill into social media.

On the train to Peckham, I am engulfed by a nauseous wave of failure. In a bid to boost my flagging ego, I remind myself that tomorrow's gig at The Wanstead Tap sold out many months ago. Success is lightly held; failure – perceived or real – has a vice-like grip.

As I fall asleep, I wonder if someone in Sheen has Robert Smith's eyes still following them around the room.

London: Sunday

Sunday starts with stomach cramps. In all the scurrying about, I have not spent enough time in health-food shops and have mainly gorged on pizzas instead. Too much dough for middle-aged digestion. The most convenient food is often the most inconvenient the next day.

I decide to walk to Dulwich Books; after all, Peckham is only just round the corner from East Dulwich, so Dulwich must only be a swan's glide away.

It is a little further than that. I get brisker as I realize the distance still to cover, and I am helped by those out for their jog or throwing sticks for their dog. I catch snatches of conversations, and the main thing I gather is that a lot of people are having an extension to their kitchen, but can't work out what rustic tiles are most suitable for a city suburb. These are the quandaries. I am in a world halfway between Shirley Hughes and a lifestyle pull-out from a Sunday newspaper.

A dog catches a ball in its mouth and the owner is so elated by its athleticism that he congratulates it at length. Should he ever have a child who learns to ride a bike, I fear he will have no superlatives left. The dog looks vaguely embarrassed by the whole affair. 'I'm a dog, that's what I do.'

Having skipped breakfast, I enjoy a cup of tea and some biscuits at Dulwich Books, and it is lovely and friendly and very Sunday. I think most national traits usually crumble under scrutiny, even if others drape themselves in nylon flags to try and make you believe in them, but the independent bookshop and the ambition of those in them is of an Englishness that I wish to believe in, although maybe it is just a bookishness. One day, Bookish will be an acceptable nationality for your passport. It is not about where you are born; it's about which books you are living in.

I talk to some children dressed as astronauts who are going to the zoo, and we debate which animals they are most looking forward to seeing and eventually decide that it is *definitely* the tigers. I wonder whether to tell them about when I watched a tiger tear the skin off a rabbit on an early-morning visit to the zoo, but I bet they've heard all those stories before, so I keep quiet.

Stoke Newington is not a natural geographical double-up with West Dulwich and it takes three trains to get there. On one of the trains I start to obsess about the book that someone across the way from me is reading. Why do I care? But I so often do. I know it is in the Oxford Classics series, but I don't recognize the painting on the cover. Maybe it's a Turner, but the title is too small to make out.

I don't know why discovering what a stranger is reading, and whether it is something I know and admire, gives me a little dopamine hit, but it does. It is highly unlikely that, on discovering what it was, I would then break the ice and attempt a literary conversation, but I like imagining the conversation that I will never have.

I was once reading a book of David Foster Wallace essays on a late-night train. A stranger started talking of his admiration for Wallace and then asked me if I had read *Infinite Jest*. Sure I had. I'd read *Infinite Jest*. Well, I had read forty pages of *Infinite Jest*, then I got distracted, but I kept that quiet. I had the full intention to return to *Infinite Jest*, and I've got at least ninety pages through it since that train journey.

When I said I had read it, the stranger's enthusiasm erupted. He'd never met anyone else who had read it all before. I kept it quiet that I hadn't yet. It was too late. I go red as I remember this.

What did I think of this scene and that scene, and the bit with the car boot, its relationship to the *Odyssey*, the satire of subsidized time...?

And then my feeble 'Yeah... yeah... oh yeah... mmm, I did find that affecting... from the nature of structure... in a postmodern meta-dissemination of structural... integrity... er, unreliable narrator... something-something.' Why couldn't I simply say, 'My mind makes odd decisions for me, and three minutes ago it made the wrong choice. I have not read *Infinite Jest* – would you like to talk about *The Great Gatsby* instead... or Shaun Hutson's *Slugs*'?

We've not stayed in contact.

Stoke Newington Bookshop is a big enough space for me to drift among the shelves and not look conspicuously like an author waiting for someone to buy his book.

There's a regular drift of people coming through the door. My friend Stewart Lee pops in with his daughter. He has a strong psychogeographical knowledge of the area, which is not always useful if you need directions in a hurry. It is never as simple as: turn right at the high street and left at the lights; there will always be the need for some historically accurate anecdote about a William Blake vision that happened 'just where that pub stands now'; or at that crossroad an almost unknown prog band invented a sound that had never been heard by human ears, but then dropped it down an open drain, causing both death and mutation in a rare breed of Victorian sewer rat – a rat homicide that was initially blamed on Michael Horovitz or one of the other *Children of Albion* poets. You'll always be late, but better informed, if you use Stewart as your guide.

Retired librarian Richard comes into the shop and tells me that it wasn't him who gave the old lady the disc of *Fifty Shades of Grey* with marmalade on it, although the story is true.*

We are looking at a new biography of Nico, and Richard tells me about when he worked at a record company. One day he walked into the office and saw Nico reading a novel and laughing uproariously. When he asked what she was reading, she beamed – '*Bleak House*!' – and returned to chuckling away. Imagine the hilarity she would have found in *The Old Curiosity Shop*. As Oscar Wilde wrote, 'One must have a heart of stone to read the death of little Nell without laughing.'

Stewart shares another story about Nico and his late producer, David Johnson. He tells it better than I do, so ask him next time you see him.

In Stoke Newington you are never more than fifteen minutes away from a Nico anecdote. We have further conversation about free jazz and Norse gods, but I need to leave and go and stand on the roof of a narrowboat and meet Ben Moor again. I did tell you he was my greatest inspiration, didn't I?

Word on the Water is moored just north of King's Cross, and is also known as the London Bookbarge, run by Paddy and his

* You'll have no idea about this reference to *Fifty Shades of Grey*. If you did read that footnote, you know what it is about. If you didn't, you're not reading this.

daughter. There is no pressure for me to push my book too hard while I recite from the roof, as Paddy hasn't got any of them.

I step delicately onto the roof of this floating bookshop – an inelegant entrance. I conquer my vague embarrassment at standing in the open air as passers-by pass by and decide I will commit to at least two poems, on top of the stories about space exploration and encounters with Neolithic stone circles. Some people walking by stop to look, some keep moving while looking, and some people don't look at all and keep moving. No one heckles, though. A victory.

I buy an Oliver Sacks book I didn't know existed, *Everything in Its Place: First Love and Last Tales*. His humanity illuminated everything he wrote.

I am ending the day at The Wanstead Tap, in a railway arch of fine booze and red-velvet curtains: my favourite railway arch to perform in. This event is hosted with Newham Bookshop, one of the great pugnacious and tenacious independent bookshops. Owner Vivian Archer has won numerous awards for being a superlative bookseller, and deserves every one. The poet Benjamin Zephaniah describes the shop as both local and international: 'This bookshop has helped the local people pass exams, fall in love, meet authors, become authors, get work experience, get life experience, learn to read, understand Britain, understand the world, understand themselves, and engage in political struggles to liberate themselves and show solidarity with others.'[3] Now that is an impressive roster of achievement. Author Attica Locke calls it the 'smartest, chicest, and most daring bookshop in London'.[4] Vivian is a truly loved bookseller.

This combination of railway arch and award-winning bookshop gives me all the motivation I need to end the weekend with excessive amounts of showing off.

Afterwards I sit on the edge of the stage and sign and

drink wine and stay just the right side of slurring. Any further inebriation and my editor would have to be called in to clean up the mess. I wonder if I should employ my editor Mike to travel around with me everywhere, to interject when I become extraneous and tangential beyond comprehension. The job is open to offers. He's read this now. I wonder if this paragraph will survive.

What is clear from the weekend is that I am not the kind of author who is suitable for the bright lights of London's busy West End. That's the signing destination for the Vegas Strip big-hitter authors, like Richard Osman and Marian Keyes. I'm still a bit Atlantic City, dilapidated but louche and under the railroad track.

After the event I am still full of vim, or at least a reasonable amount of vim, considering that I have now visited eighty-five bookshops. Home is only thirty-five miles away, but in case of collapse, I have sorted a budget hotel. I end the night eating crisps and Milky Ways on a budget-hotel bed as if I were an Aldi Nero, but not a Lidl Caligula. No horses allowed here.

CHAPTER 9

Hurricanes at the Benighted Inn

Malvern to Malton

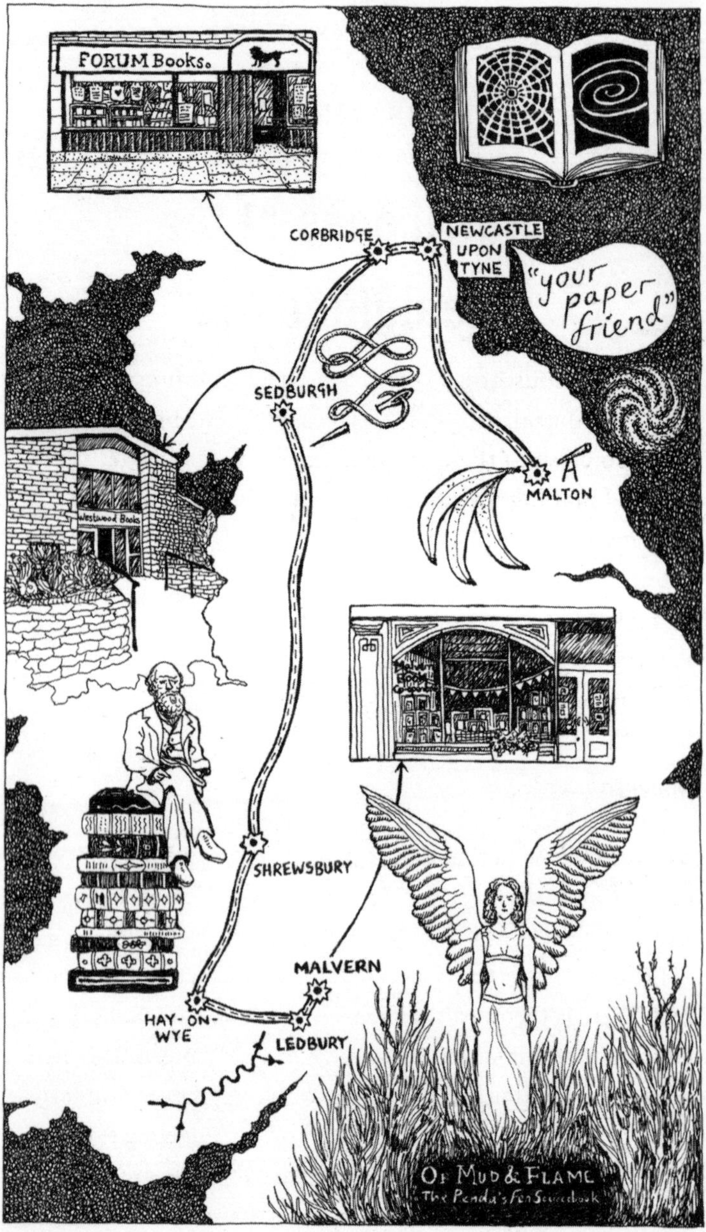
FORUM Books
Westwood Books
CORBRIDGE
NEWCASTLE UPON TYNE
"your paper friend"
SEDBURGH
MALTON
SHREWSBURY
MALVERN
HAY-ON-WYE
LEDBURY
OF MUD & FLAME
The Penda's Fen Sourcebook

The last fifteen days of the tour will take me on a circuitous route from Malvern to Hungerford, via Edinburgh and Hull. I like to try and break myself as I get so close to the end. When I plan a challenge, I have a habit of making the last laps the most demanding. I imagine that my energy will be having an Indian summer, but I am often wrong.

If there is any wheel I wish to be broken on, it is a wheel made of bookshops – death by 1,000 tiny paper-cuts from all the books I left behind.

Malvern

Malvern seems fictional even as you walk through it. It is too calm, too pretty. It grips the side of the hills in a way that inland English towns so rarely do.

Malvern also has a deep cultural footprint embedded in me. There is the music of Elgar; it was where C. S. Lewis was educated; and it was the inspiration for Lantern, the setting of Jamie McKelvie's 2007 comic book *Suburban Glamour*, a story of teenage boredom dispelled by a changeling revelation. Many of us may feel like changelings when we are teenagers, but this book suggested that some are more changelings than others. This was my first Jamie McKelvie book. Since then he has gone on to draw critically acclaimed works such as the *Phonogram* series and *The Wicked & the Divine*, as well as many Marvel comics.

Malvern is also the resting place of Annie Darwin, Charles and Emma Darwin's beloved daughter, who came to Malvern for hydrotherapy, but tragically died aged just ten years old. Darwin's great-great-grandson, Randal Keynes, found a box containing mementoes of Annie, and from that grew a brilliant book that dealt with Darwin's science, fatherhood and how Darwin and Emma survived the loss of Annie.

Annie's Box was the first book that I read about Darwin, and it inflamed my imagination about him and his work, and led to me reading much more by and about him. It was the perfect book with which to start the Darwin adventure, as the scientific story is wrapped up in a very human story.

The letters back and forth between Charles and his wife, Emma, are particularly affecting. He was with Annie during her treatment in Malvern while Emma looked after the rest of the family in Kent. He wrote of Annie's death, 'She went to her final sleep most tranquilly, most sweetly at twelve o' clock today. Our poor dear, dear child has had a very short life but I trust happy … we must be more and more to each other, my dear wife.'

It is a book that I return to frequently, and its impact increases with my age. Annie is buried in Great Malvern Priory churchyard, and as well as the name and dates of her birth and death, the gravestone says merely 'A Dear and Good Child'.

My final Malvern connection is *Penda's Fen*, a remarkable, hallucinatory television play by David Rudkin, which follows a teenage boy as his connections to his sexuality, nationality and identity unravel and mutate. Aired originally on the BBC in 1974, it would eventually be repeated on Channel 4 and slowly built a reputation as a great visionary work, celebrated by that haunted generation who were a little too young to have seen it first time around. The play includes phantasmic visions of Elgar, demons squatting on chests, as well as beautifully lit discussions at dusk on the nature of good, evil and god, filmed in the fields surrounding the town. Nearly fifty years on, its relevance remains in an England where a furious patriotism has been reinvigorated in the culture wars. Strange Attractor, a small press whose books I am perpetually drawn to, published *Of Mud & Flame*, a collection of essays on the play, with titles like 'Making Space for the Shadows: Penda's Fen', 'Katabasis', 'Tradition and Legacy', 'And In the Soil There be Mirrors: Penda's Fen and Folk Horror' and 'Gnostic Anarcho-Punk Anti-Pastoral Visions'. These titles have either definitely sold that book to you or have made you certain you won't be buying it.

I walk up the hill, surrounded by the ghosts swinging off all these cultural branches.

On entering Malvern Book Cooperative, I experience it first through the mist of my spectacle fog, which has grown more intense with the wintering air. The fog clears as the smell of warm cake rises.

The shop is carefully curated and, as ever, I spy a book I have not seen before, despite eighty-five bookshop visits in the last few weeks. It is *Out of the Darkness: Greenham Voices 1981–2000* by Kate Kerrow and Rebecca Mordan. My grumpy grandmother lived near Greenham Common in the early 1980s. Born in 1890, she was very much of a different time. She was far more supportive of nuclear destruction than of feminist protest. The vision of womanhood that she saw protesting at the perimeter fence, with their dungarees, knotted hair and attitude, appalled her. She complained that they would come and shit in her garden, and she had plans to get out her shotgun and shoot them in the bottom. The only thing I ever saw shit in her garden was her whippet. Fortunately she never shot that, either.

I am shocked to discover that none of the workers in the bookshop know of *Penda's Fen*. I had been certain that *Penda's Fen* would be the cultural bedrock of the town. I presumed *Of Mud & Flame* – the one book written about the play – would be piled high on a prominent table display.

I am told that regular customer Lee, who should be popping in soon, will know all about it. He does and volunteers happily to lend his DVD to the bookshop team. I feel that I must organize a screening at the local picture house. The next time I come to Malvern I hope to see everyone I met in the shop out on the hilltop, silhouetted like the figures following Death in the denouement of *The Seventh Seal*, re-enacting the concluding scenes of *Penda's Fen*.

Before I leave, I ask to use the bookshop loo. For once there is no apology for the smallness, pokiness and number of cardboard cutouts of comedians who had a ghostwritten autobiography out last year, cluttering this smallest room. The only clutter is a toboggan, just in case you die in the loo and, as in *Citizen Kane*, whisper 'Rosebud' as you go.

Ledbury

Ledbury is famed for its many timbered buildings, and this evening I will be inhabiting one of them. I am told that the building has hosted book talks since Caxton made the literary festival a possibility.

I totter over the cobbles, getting the boxes of books from Ledbury Books and Maps to the Old Grammar School on Church Lane. Bookshop owner Lindsay began her career as the book-production controller in a small scientific publishing company, after studying biology and geography. She has now run the bookshop for more than a decade. She dislikes people who use her to browse so that they know what they need to get from Amazon. Sometimes they'll even ring up to check the details of the book they have seen, to make sure they get the right thing from the online retailer. Fortunately, this happens only rarely.

Ledbury is also home to a renowned poetry festival, so I decide I can risk only one poem at the talk, in case my charlatanism is found out by such a poetry-literate crowd. The most frequent compliment I get for my poems is 'I don't like poetry at all, but I enjoyed yours', so I am still a poetry impostor, but in a good way.

I eat my second piece of home-made cake of the day. It is ginger, so it's packed with health benefits as well as syrup. I talk about the physicist Richard Feynman and his experiments to try and discover why spaghetti breaks into three or four pieces when snapped, rather than just two pieces. I find it easier to explain his pasta experiments than his interpretation of quantum behaviour.

After the talk I meet someone who was actually lectured by Feynman, and an elderly woman who tells me that she thought she would not enjoy the evening at all, but has actually had a nice time. This is a very English compliment: 'I was expecting this to be awful and it wasn't.'

I also meet Lucie McKnight Hardy, whose novel *Water Shall Refuse Them* was sent to me by a friend who insisted that I would adore it, and he was quite right. It is the story of a sixteen-year-old girl and her family who move to the Welsh borders after the accidental drowning of her sister, hoping that the rural seclusion will aid the grieving process. As you and I know, more often than not, rural seclusion in such circumstances can only bring forth ghosts or demons, or a farmer with an axe and a grudge. It is a story that surrounds you in darkness, even if you are reading it in the park on a sunny day. It's set in the heatwave of 1976, and even the sunshine becomes ominous.

I have her latest book too, *Dead Relatives*, a short-story collection that I haven't begun yet, as I have been warned that the stories are overwhelmingly ominous and the haunting will seep deeply into my skin and create monstrous shadow-puppets in all directions. I decided that arriving in new and strange towns on winter evenings after dark on a daily basis wouldn't be the right time to dive in and that I will wait until I am touring Australia to read it, in the hope that the sunshine will bleach out the ghosts: 'Cook brings the cleaver down on the neck – chop! – and the head comes off easily, like slicing through blancmange'.

Like most (although perhaps not all) authors who commit gruesome acts on the page, Lucie seems quiet and kind and fails even to attempt to murder me at any point in the evening. Another reminder to commit your crimes through art, as it pays better and avoids incarceration.

Hay-on-Wye

There are many too many books in Hay-On-Wye. It's hard to experience that victorious gazelle-hunt sensation when you are surrounded by so many, as it dampens the sense of victory. Mind you, if I found Ernest Thesiger's *Practically True*...

With twelve touring days still to go, I am determined to remain bookshop-frugal for now. The frugality is quickly cracked when I see a book of interviews with Francis Bacon by David Sylvester. I've got this book already, but it is a slightly different edition. This one might have up to fourteen pages that are not quite the same. The book made it into David Bowie's Top 100 books, a list that greatly excited many of us when it was republished after his death. Unsurprisingly, the list of books has now become a book itself.

The list consisted of such gems as Arthur C. Danto's *Beyond the Brillo Box*, Elaine Pagels's *The Gnostic Gospels* and *Mr Wilson's Cabinet of Wonder* by Lawrence Weschler, the story of a museum that includes 'a microminiature sculpture of Pope John Paul II, painstakingly carved from a human hair and mounted inside the eye of a needle'. I hastily tracked down these books to add to the collection. It also led me to D. E. Harding's *On Having No Head*: 'The best day of my life – my rebirth day so to speak – was when I found I had no head.'

Yet another reading project, though it might be too late for this to lead to me inventing a series of taboo-breaking identities and sharing a flat in Berlin with Iggy Pop.

It gets worse in the Cinema Bookshop, Hay's largest bookshop. I buy a hotchpotch of titles, including something postmodern recommended by Kathy Acker that is highly likely to remain unread, and the lovely little *Cassell's Pocket Dictionary of Mythology*, which fits neatly in palm or pocket.

My favourite find is Anthony Storey's biography of Stanley Baker, because I knew nothing of its existence and I love Baker's granite presence in movies. He comes across as a striking figure, powerfully commanding attention in any room he entered. Storey was commissioned to write the book by Baker, not long after Baker's cancer diagnosis. The actor took charge of their meetings and did not take kindly to the notion of disease weakening him. Storey himself is the brother of David Storey, author of the bruising rugby novel *This Sporting Life*.

I am here for the Hay Festival Winter Weekend, a mini version of the vast summer festival that woos over former American presidents and Nobel Prize-winners to a field that becomes a Barnumesque Big Top celebration of books. Book festivals sometimes have authors' dinners, and you can find yourself eating beetroot salad with bêtes noires who turn out to be charming, and professional charmers who turn out to be bêtes noires.

Such is the crammed schedule at these festivals that I have often joined such dinners halfway through, when wine and gin have loosened egos, attitudes and tongues, and I have sat wide-eyed, occasionally sharing glances with the organizers, who are clearly enjoying the melodrama while also wondering when it will be best to suggest to the elderly newsreader that it may be time to go up the wooden hill to Bedfordshire. I have just such a dinner in my diary for after my event this evening.

Tonight's dinner will include the stand-up classicist Natalie Haynes. Her books and shows about the classical world are inspiring a whole new generation to investigate gorgon tales and Trojan horses with more excitement about the classical world than there's been since Ray Harryhausen first bent wire and plasticine to make sword-fighting skeletons for *Jason and the Argonauts*. Hallie Rubenhold will also be there. She is the author of *The Five*, a study of the women murdered by Jack the Ripper. *The Five* shows how it is the stories of the victims and the lives they led that provide the real lessons of history. There will also be a TV historian who I am wary of, as he seems to be going through a phase of 'I'm mad as hell and I'm not going to take it any more' conspiracy-caterwauling on a low-budget news channel. Midlife crises used to be about getting a tattoo and a silly car; now it seems they can come with a transmogrification into the sort of TV broadcaster that Alan Moore would write about when creating stories of a dystopian fascist future.

I am interviewed by Natalie, who always knows exactly where to take a conversation, and then I sign books for a marine biologist and a family of four. I have now seen so many faces at the signing tables over the last three weeks that I am certain I have met previously everyone who approaches.

We go to the authors' meal and, cunningly and selfishly, I manage to get a corner seat, where I can retreat from the general hubbub into pea risotto and can merely eavesdrop on any prophesying from the historian.

My wife is aware that I might be having dinner with the conspiracy theorist and keeps sending texts: *'Try not to sit next to him'*; *'Breathe frequently'*; *'Make sure you don't punch him.'*

I don't punch people, and I am usually intrigued enough to listen to beliefs that seem wonky to me. Arguing back, though, is usually a waste of time. Few people enter such discussion with any interest in breathing in new information; they simply want to breathe out their opinions with increasing ferocity – sometimes for free, sometimes for money.

I talk briefly with the historian about the astronomer Tycho Brahe, whom he mentioned in his talk. I am surprised he was unaware that Brahe owned an elk that he got drunk, which led to the elk falling downstairs and dying.

Making sure that my mouth was always full, to avoid having to say much, led to a bad night's sleep. My stomach howled as it attempted to digest too many breadsticks and a crème brûlée.

The next morning anxiety exacerbates my stomach cramps, as Hay is some distance from the nearest station and I imagine an uncomfortable journey where I have to suddenly insist that the driver pulls into some cow parsley for me to evacuate my agony. I'm at the pharmacy as it opens and pop a pill that promises to pull me together. I bet this never bothered Stanley Baker. I bet he could eat five crème brûlées and then do 100 press-ups on top of a moving train.

Shrewsbury

I don't see the red weather warnings on the TV news before I leave Hay. And I make it to Hereford without having a cow-parsley diversion, and the psychosomatic cramps calm.

The first event of this new day is at the Shrewsbury Festival of Literature, run by Susan from Pengwern Books, which is a homely bookshop where customers are greeted like friendly neighbours. It is a few steps from its former home, St Alkmund's Church, which offered sanctuary to Susan when she had nowhere else to set up her bookshop – it was the church warden's idea. Stories like this could lead to my conversion. If I am ever going to see the light, it will be in a bookshop. In fact I frequently see the light in bookshops, just not *that* light.

Susan, a former nurse, has grit and tenacity. She was not brought up with much wealth, but the things the family treasured were books, plenty of books.

Charles Darwin was born in Shrewsbury in 1809 and the town makes the most of its association with him, so I started the event with some stories about his life, his writing and the importance of pigeons. One reader of *On the Origin of Species* suggested that Darwin should really focus on the pigeon elements of the book, as there was a big pigeon-fanciers' market at the time – probably more than the market for one that undermined the religious philosophy of what it was to be a living thing on the Earth. The reviewer Whitwell Elwin was sure that if Darwin wrote a short book on pigeons, it would soon be on every table in the land – 'Everybody's interested in pigeons' – rather than Darwin's current book, which was 'a wild & foolish piece of imagination'. Elwin is the biological-history equivalent of the man who didn't sign The Beatles because guitar bands were on the way out.*

Today I had the perfect audience, who not only asked interesting questions that made me think, but also bought two, three and sometimes four books at once. On the way back to the station, I pay my respects to the statue of Charles Darwin outside the public library.

It is getting cold and windy, and it has reached that time on Friday when station platforms are filled with people confused by travel, trains and, from the look of the puddles of hot chocolate, how to hold a hot cup. Changing trains at Crewe, there are the first brooding warnings of the destructive weather. Delays are announced and updated with increasing frequency.

Sedbergh

The wind and horizontal rain pick up as I arrive at Oxenholme Lake District station. I am collected and driven to Westwood Books in Sedbergh. The trees are still standing by the side of the road, but this will change.

* This was Dick Rowe, head of A&R (Singles) at Decca Records, according to Brian Epstein's autobiography, although Rowe contested that.

Sedbergh is England's official book town, as Wigtown is for Scotland and Hay is for Wales. It doesn't have as many bookshops, but plenty of shops include books on their stock-list, and they have a book bus shelter too. Westwood Books is the centrepiece of this bookish town. Arriving at the back entrance, I hurry through an alley of science fiction and then a vale of biography, before finding myself in front of a wall of instructional embroidery books.

I walk straight into the seated area with bag and rucksack, seeing the audience already there, and I just start talking. This takes everyone by surprise, including me, as I had planned to go to the loo when I first got there. I will consider this event a prostate test that I successfully passed.

As I am in front of the very well-stocked embroidery section, I start off telling the story of Ernest Thesiger's *Adventures in Embroidery* and how he hoped to set up a disabled soldiers' embroidery industry after the First World War. After visiting wounded men in hospitals, he wrote that he was 'struck with the interest which invalids took in needlework and the skill they evinced in working their own rather crude designs. I offered to supply them with something a little more decorative in the way of patterns; but while they were still in hospital found that they were not easily interested in anything apart from their own artistic efforts.' The top brass were not keen on Thesiger's efforts to give wounded soldiers purpose and employment through embroidery, as they felt it was not a manly enough pursuit for warriors.

Afterwards, with the storm raging outside and nowhere to go but to a dark inn, I am allowed time to browse. Paul and Heather, who own Westwood Books, kindly give me a copy of Shelley's works of poetry and prose from 1864. I have a nice, slightly later nineteenth-century edition of collected Shelley works at home, but this copy has something different about it. They have given me this because it was awarded to Charles Darwin's son, George, after his first year at Trinity College. It is a very thoughtful gift.

Westwood's former owner specialized in antiquarian science books and there are some intriguing titles by scientists, both revered and forgotten, in one corner. I buy a nice hardback first edition of Martin Gardner's *In the Name of Science*, later republished as *Fads and Fallacies in the Name of Science*. Gardner was a hugely inspirational figure, especially for the mathematically minded, and a frequent writer on pseudoscience and anti-science. *In the Name of Science* covers many areas, including UFOs, Atlantis, 'Food Faddists' and 'Eccentric Sexual Theories'.

I also pick up two hardback works of the renowned anthropologist Margaret Mead; *Leaves from the Golden Bough* 'culled by Lady Frazer' and illustrated by H. M. Brock; J. G. Frazer's *Psyche's Task*; and *Wolf Child and Human Child* by Arnold Gesell, because I just don't have enough books about children brought up by wolves (even after this, the tally is only four). I make a mental note that in future I must make sure this is the last bookshop I visit before going home. There is so much more I want, but which my spine questions.

On the journey back to Oxenholme we discover that it is the sort of dark and stormy night that can leave people benighted in an Old Dark House, the sort where Ernest Thesiger would offer you a potato as well as a pyromaniac relative. 'They were all godless here. They used to bring their women here – brazen, lolling creatures in silks and satins. They filled the house with laughter and sin.'

On our first attempt to get to the inn where I am staying we drive for twenty minutes and then find a large tree blocking our path. Paul reverses and takes another road. After twenty minutes we find this route is also blocked by a fallen tree. The third route is circuitous, but turns out to be the Goldilocks road and we make it through, although this one passable route will not be passable by the morning, as I will discover.

The pub stands alone.

The room is cold.

The wind howls.

I like it.

All those ghostly stories from childhood that I read mean I can find the romanticism in some of the shabbier hotels (so long as the sheets are clean). However, I have decided that I won't use the kettle. It looks large enough to fit pants and socks in it, and I think whatever I brewed would end up with another psychosomatic aftertaste, at the very least.

After looking at my radiator questioningly, I go into the bar with my new pile of books and order a Guinness and a whisky to generate the heat to get me through the night. I leaf fondly through the collected works of Shelley, and think of the wretched night by Lake Geneva when Mary Shelley dreamt up Frankenstein. I pity any of the wild wolf children of the Lake District who are trapped in this weather.

I order another whisky and turn to Gardner's essays on orgone energy and psychoanalyst Wilhelm Reich's 'orgone energy accumulator blanket' for the bed-bound. I could do with one of those in my hotel room – not for the orgone energy, but for the warmth. I sleep fitfully, listening to panes rattle and imagining Ernest Thesiger's face at the window.

When I return to the bar for breakfast, the server is telling another lone traveller that it is hell out there. Everything is impassable. Being trapped here is our destiny. She says she had to walk across the fields to get to work and she did not like it. She is quite jolly for someone who got tangled in barbed wire on her commute.

She seems more troubled by my breakfast order. I start with Frosties, which is fine. But then I order beans and mushrooms, with toast on the side. Apparently that is a first. Never has such an eccentric breakfast been ordered in Oxenholme. There are still some places where if you do not order the full English – which includes the head of a pig, with poached eggs in the eye sockets – then you are viewed with suspicion as the word spreads and you are crossing the market square later.

I hear rumours that train travel may be rare today, as oaks and elms lie strewn along the tracks, so I leave early for the nearby station. Halfway down the hill I see a group of locals contemplating last night's Goldilocks route. Now it is blocked by a large tree that stretches across it, branches splaying in all directions. They look at me, with my wheelie suitcase, rucksack and large carrier bag of books, and wish me luck. At least they have a show now. I weave through, clamber over and crouch under the fallen tree, and eventually find myself on the other side without a scratch. Locals from the other side are approaching, holding hand-saws, their breath sighing through their teeth. I have three bookshops today and I am both determined and powerless – an impotent cocktail.

At 9.30 a.m. I manage to get the 8.22 to Carlisle, which is a good start. Carlisle is where it all ends. Trains are going no further north or east. The storm was even worse up here and the system has shut down. On platform three we stare at the cancellations like a magic-eye picture, hoping that if we look for long enough the pixels will transform from 'cancelled' to '5-minute delay'. I resort to my only possible course of action: pointlessly tweeting things about the journey not going very well.

Helen, who owns all three of the bookshops I am meant to be going to today, decides it will be best if she just comes and collects me in her car, if the roads are passable. I wait and I dawdle.

I have been to Carlisle a few times over the years and I haven't really managed to get a handle on it. I've found that, walking through the streets, there can be a harshness and it rarely takes long to stumble upon angry and unhappy faces. Men are pushing pushchairs unhappily. The whole of Carlisle seems to be hungover. I pop into the Oxfam bookshop again, but still no copy of *Ronnie and the Catechism.*

Helen arrives in a small red Fiat that is an apt rebuttal to all the great big boxy cars that seem to dominate the roads. We take the scenic route closest to Hadrian's Wall and I see the Sycamore Gap Tree – a striking tree in the landscape.

The sycamore has survived last night's gales as it has survived much throughout history. The rolling scenery that creates the dip in which the sycamore grows was created by meltwater flowing under ice-sheets. Such a dramatic tree and its attachment to Hadrian's Wall have, unsurprisingly, inspired a murder mystery. *Sycamore Gap* is the second DCI Ryan mystery by L. J. Ross – 'In the early hours of the summer solstice, the skeleton of a young woman is found inside the Roman Wall at Sycamore Gap. She has lain undiscovered for ten years and it is Ryan's job to piece together her past...'

Sycamore Gap was also a location in the film *Robin Hood: Prince of Thieves*. With the usual duplicity of film geography,

Kevin Costner cons you into believing that Cumbria is far closer to Dover than it is.

The road is strewn with bark and branch debris, but the fallen trees have the good manners to block only one side of the road at any one time, so we spend the journey slaloming elegantly.

Corbridge

Forum Books in Corbridge is housed in a former church. The preservation order on it means that the pulpit must remain, so this is where authors magisterially sign copies of their books. Beneath the pulpit is a font big enough for full baptismal immersion or for hiding a corpse. Local author Ann Cleeves, who created the hugely successful Vera Stanhope crime-thriller series, wrote an exclusive short story for Forum Books utilizing the font for just such murderous purposes.

Some pews have also been repurposed as shelf space, and it strikes me that this is a place to worship books. Knowing that I am already weighed down with books, Helen gives me a slim collection of short stories by Saki, *Christmas with Dull People*.

It is increasingly looking like tonight's main event at The Bound in Whitley Bay will be cancelled. The streets are covered in broken glass, the top of the sea-front clock has been blown off, and Helen is worried about inviting people out on such a potentially treacherous night. Her house is without electricity and, although her children found a first night without light and iPads a novelty, she is not sure how they will take to a second.

My greatest disappointment is not meeting up with Dr Kathryn Mannix, who was going to join the audience and then accompany my wine-drinking. She is an author I admire a great deal for her compassion, eloquence and intelligence. Her most recent book is called *Listen: How to Find the Words for Tender Conversations*. Her writing reminds me of something my friend Helen Crimmins said when she had cancer: 'After you have asked me how I am, you don't have to say anything else.'

Kathryn is a retired palliative-care doctor who strives for us to better understand and deal with death and trauma. Being impatient and grumpy, I like to spend time in the company of those who can be patient and kind.

Newcastle

We drive on to Newcastle's Biscuit Factory, an independent art gallery, where Helen has a bookshop concession.

I spot a Patti Smith book I didn't know existed, *Woolgathering*, and Helen kindly gives me that too. She tells me that one of her youngest customers calls books 'your paper friend'. That is how she sees the wonderment of the relationship with a good book – that personal feeling as you are enthralled and ask, 'But how did the author know to write this book for me?'

Now I have something to read for my night off in Newcastle, which has been forced upon me by a hurricane. I decide it is not a good idea for a solitary middle-aged man to go roaming alone on Saturday night in Newcastle. I am too timid for that sort of thing. I never got the hang of Saturday night, even when I was young. I've always been more of a Tuesday-night person.

I pop to Marks & Spencer at the railway station. The security guard looks like he's been busy already, trying to prevent thieves making off with the calamari and red-pepper hummus. An inebriated man is shirty when told to leave because he has no mask. If it's kicking off near the M&S take-home tapas, then I am definitely making the right decision. I retire to the hotel with my dips, Sauvignon blanc and Patti Smith.

I was also given a luxury box of chocolates by an optician in Corbridge who was unable to attend the signing, so I languorously indulge myself with soft centres as I read about Patti Smith rescuing fleeting thoughts as she found her way to becoming an artist. Outside, I can hear Saturday night gaining momentum. There will be squid-rings and tzatziki flying across the streets by now.

Malton

It is a short trip from Newcastle to Kemps Books in Malton. I think about bananas and cruelty on my journey. Malton is not far from Castle Howard, which, in popular imagination, is where Evelyn Waugh's Brideshead of *Brideshead Revisited* is set. The comedian Russell Kane, an Evelyn Waugh enthusiast, told me he could think of no other author who showed so few glimpses of humanity in his own life yet was able to write characters with such humanity. Sometimes we are able to write on the page what we cannot be in the world.

Auberon Waugh tells the story of his father, Evelyn, getting hold of some rare bananas during the Second World War. He gathered all his children together and sat at the head of the table with these prized fruit, and a jug of cream and some sugar. Then he proceeded to peel each banana, lavish them in cream and sugar, and eat each one himself before dismissing the children. I am sure there is some kind of life lesson in that, but don't ask me what.

Malton is known as 'the food capital of Yorkshire' and yet I find myself eating a Pot Noodle in the middle of the afternoon.

To be fair, the local supermarket has a very wide range of Pot Noodles – possibly far wider than you might find in Ripon, Halifax or Farsley. My mistake was to forget once again that rural English towns keep strict hours. I waited until 2.30 p.m. to start strolling around the town to find a restaurant, only to be told at every door that 'The kitchen is closed, I'm afraid'. In England any suggestion of a hotel meal after 2.30 could only come from the mind of a lunatic – the kind of person who orders beans and mushrooms, with toast on the side, for their breakfast. Best to starve such freethinkers out of town. As well as a Pot Noodle, I spread Dairylea triangles on some Ritz Crackers and eat them with salted peanuts and a tub of tasteless cherry tomatoes, to give myself some health points. I would have loved a banana too, but there were none to be had.

Malton feels like a proper tour day, frittering away time in a closed town in a hotel room that has an uncertain smell created by budget carpet-cleanser and a dehydrated toilet air-freshener. I think that it is what robot sweat would smell like.

Fortunately I have Kemps Books to look around, and I find myself in conversation with someone there about the work of the artist Laura Knight, as we both find ourselves staring at the recently published book of her work, *A Panoramic View*. Shortly afterwards I am asked if I can help advise on books in the nature section. I suggest Susan Ogilvy's *Nests*, but they are more interested in walks than habitats, so I point towards Nan Shepherd's *The Living Mountain* and they start reading. My bookseller cloaking device is almost complete. My identity is becoming hazy, and soon I will forget I was ever an author or a performer.

There are many beautiful books of art and nature in Kemps. The one they love selling most is *The Lost Words* by

Robert Macfarlane and Jackie Morris. The descriptions of living things are delicious: magpies 'Gossip, Bicker, Yak and Snicker All Day Long!', while the silver birch reminds us to 'Rest your head now, silver-seeker; Close your eyes and cease your searches.'

It is an unusually big book, one that I would swear at for being such an uneasy fit on any bookshelf, but all is forgiven because of its beauty.

Malton was not too storm-tossed, but it is now lightly dusted with snow. The pavement looks like icing sprinkled on a Victoria sponge cake – exactly the sort of sponge cake that Malton kept from me, as I was too late for treats.

Even light snow worries me. I possess very slippery feet. I've always had them. I have a knack of losing grip, both physically and metaphorically. I don't know why, but my tread is made for slapstick, as if my shoe leather was banana skin; but, being Bambi-legged, I do not fall.

The hall in Malton is draped in bunting. I consider using it to explain string theory, but I don't understand string theory, so I don't try. Instead I talk about astronomy, and photons travelling across a galaxy. This is my ninety-third talk in under two months, and my inner monologue is overcrowded with argumentative voices trying to undermine me and shout me down for being repetitive or boring.

After the talk I am warned that the pubs of Malton might all be closed, as it is nearly 10 p.m. I know the bar in my hotel closed at 5 p.m., though everyone there had got drunk enough to sing Johnny Cash's 'Ring of Fire' by 4 p.m. They had managed to pack the night into the day.

The one light on, in the street that I walk down, is fortunately another hotel with a bar that is still open. There is no country-and-western singalong here. It is quiet and genteel.

The bar is furnished with the type of books that get bought by the boxload – books to decorate rather than to be read. I check the spines, in case there is any wonder hiding there. In a little daydream I imagine finding Ernest Thesiger's *Practically True*, but it's all biographies of the sort of military men who frowned on Thesiger's embroidery ambitions for injured men.

Fortunately I have small books in both my coat pockets to keep me company. On one side there is the palm-sized dictionary of mythology from Hay, and on the other is Ursula K. Le Guin's *The Carrier Bag Theory of Fiction* that I picked up in Glasgow. It had been hiding behind a face-mask for more than a month now.

I drink red wine and read of Minotaurs, then I turn to Le Guin: 'We've heard it, we've all heard all about all the sticks and spears and swords, the things to bash and poke and hit with, the long, hard things, but we have not heard about the thing to put things in, the container for the thing contained. That is a new story. That is news.'

CHAPTER 10

Important Lessons from a Porpoise

Edinburgh to Hull

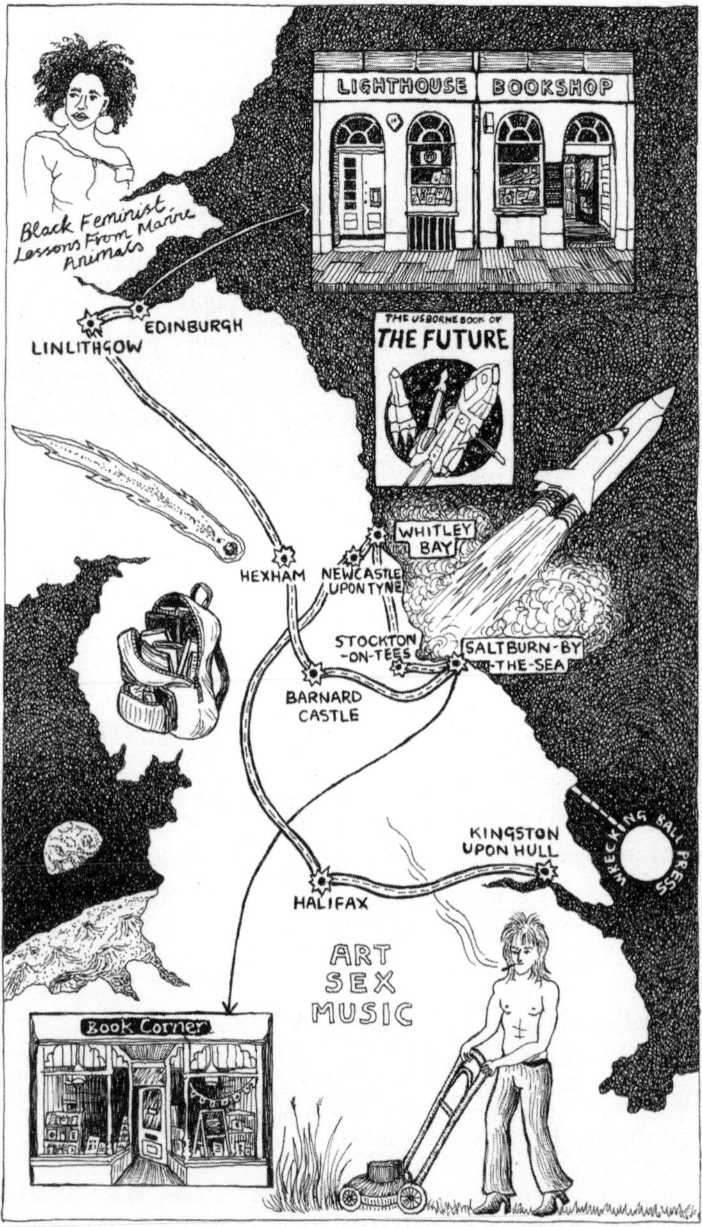

LIGHTHOUSE BOOKSHOP
Black Feminist Lessons From Marine Animals
EDINBURGH
LINLITHGOW
THE USBORNE BOOK OF THE FUTURE
WHITLEY BAY
HEXHAM
NEWCASTLE UPON TYNE
STOCKTON -ON-TEES
SALTBURN-BY-THE-SEA
BARNARD CASTLE
KINGSTON UPON HULL
WRECKING BALL PRESS
HALIFAX
ART SEX MUSIC
Book Corner

I am never particularly gregarious in the morning, but in hotels there is always a danger that other breakfasters might be. Today in Malton I learn much about another diner's problems with his family, his problems with other people's families, his hopes, his nightmares, his wife. I fear it would be hypocritical to request silence from a stranger when I talk at speed to strangers for a living.

I make up a fictional life when he asks me what I do. I know his interest is minimal, so my answer is of little importance.

You have to be careful when lying about your life. Follow-up questions can catch you out: 'Aha! Got you. I knew you weren't the Lord Mayor of Guernsey.' My friend Michael once decided to tell his barber that he worked for the council, rather than admit that he was a comedian. He was worried that the barber might regale him with his own jokes and he wasn't in the mood. Unfortunately the barber was very, very interested in his fictional job. The barber asked him so many questions about working for the waste-management department of Lewisham council that Michael cracked and admitted he was a comic. The barber was furious, and suddenly and severely trimmed his eyebrows. When my friend protested that he had been happy with his eyebrows, he was brusquely informed, 'They looked a mess.'*

* He has put together a book of his stupid decisions and life, called *Strawberries for Pigs*. His name is Michael Legge.

Malton is still closed when I leave, but I hope that the train lines to Edinburgh may be open now. By the time I get to York, that hope is gone again. We all change at Newcastle. I step back while others elbow and shove.

Fortunately I have a book by Sarah Bakewell about Montaigne in my rucksack, so I get lost in that – 'Not everyone can have the benefit of being insane, but anyone can make life easier for themselves by turning down the beam of their reason slightly.' This book and Sarah's *At the Existentialist Café* are high on my 'most-repeated reading' list. I own four copies of *At the Existentialist Café*, including the audiobook, just in case. It is always good to have it near at hand. If I see Sarah's name on the book-jacket blurb of someone else's book – on Jim Holt's *Why Does the World Exist?*, for instance – then the likelihood of me buying it quadruples.

She is the polar opposite of Deepak Chopra. If I see his effusive praise on a book jacket, I will usually back away. As yet, I have not found a book that has been recommended by both Chopra and Bakewell, and should such a thing ever happen, I presume the book will be caught in a vortex created by a clash of matter and antimatter and it will hover between the shop shelf and my hand.

People on platform four are now using their coffin-sized suitcases as weapons, so I remain static and read: 'For Montaigne, human failings are not merely bearable; they are almost a cause for celebration.'

Edinburgh

To see Edinburgh is always life-affirming. There are so many bookshops. Glasgow and Edinburgh have always seemed smarter to me than the average city. I imagine they have fist-fights over Dadaism, Diderot and David Hume.

During one visit to Edinburgh I discovered that Hume can be the philosophical spur for exotic dancing. At a storytelling night during the Fringe, audience members wrote down one-line true stories to be read out in between the acts. One of them concerned a topless dance performed on top of Hume's tomb at Old Calton Cemetery. Sarah, the host, read it out as the winning anecdote, and then I was invited onstage to tell my story. I was meant to be the headliner, but my anecdote seemed like a pale tale compared to the enigmatic one-line story we had just heard.

I wanted to know how this strange turn of events had come about. It could be up there with the story of the eminent philosopher A. J. Ayer intervening between supermodel Naomi Campbell and heavyweight boxer Mike Tyson at a party held by the underwear designer Fernando Sanchez.*

The author came up onstage and explained that she had had to finance her degree by working as a topless dancer. Striking up a conversation in the club one night, a customer explained that he was fascinated by Hume's system of empiricism and also liked looking at breasts. He wondered if she might help him combine the two, if he paid her well. She found this an intriguing proposition. They both went to Hume's tomb, had a drink, then she danced and they said their goodbyes and never saw each other again. It is one of the stranger tales from the annals of eroticism and empirical thinking, and is also a

* Tyson said to Ayer, 'Do you know who the f**k I am? I'm the heavyweight champion of the world.' The philosopher then told the then twenty-one-year-old champion: 'And I am the former Wykeham Professor of Logic. We are both pre-eminent in our field. I suggest we talk about this like rational men.'

story of remarkable levels of trust on her part. It is a tale full of ethical quandary and moral confusion. Sometimes things can seem splendid *and* terrible.

Edinburgh probably represents my highest per-day rate of book purchases of any city I have visited. I won't list my favourite purchases, but rather the one I most regret leaving behind. Usborne books for children were enormously popular for my generation, in particular their books on monsters, UFO's* and ghosts. *Usborne World of the Future* was published in 1979. By the year 2000 it was highly collectable; it now sells for hundreds of pounds. Back in 2008 it was in the glass cabinet of the Oxfam bookshop on Nicolson Street in Edinburgh. I desperately wanted to read its predictions about farming in the sea, wristwatch communication devices – 'the risto' – and the 2020 first Olympics on the Moon with the fourteen-metre lunar high jump, but I couldn't persuade myself to part with the £40 it was going for.

At the time of writing, the cheapest copy I can find online is £300. The one thing that *Usborne World of the Future* failed to predict was quite how much *Usborne World of the Future* would be worth in the future.

I can always read Arthur C. Clarke's *July 20, 2019* instead – a look at how the world would be fifty years after Neil Armstrong stood on the Moon. You can normally pick it up for under a tenner. Clarke goes beyond robotics and space exploration and explores the future of sexual relationships. The chapter 'A Night in the Bedroom' begins with a personal ad from *The Village Voice* from the past future of 2019,

* I know some of you thought: 'UFO's – the fool, it should be UFOs', but much to the disgust of punctuation pedants, the original cover had the pointless apostrophe. My pal Dallas was greatly disappointed when this error was corrected for the recent reprint.

from a 'married white female' seeking a well-endowed man for '3 month intimate companionship', as her husband is six months pregnant. She is okay with drug-enhanced orgasm, but would prefer someone with an original penis rather than an implant: 'send photo and vaccination certificate to PO Box 2238'.

The Portobello Bookshop is a wide and bright space, staffed by young and enthusiastic readers with many recommendations. I cannot believe anyone would be able to leave empty-handed.

Imogen recommends *The Breaks* by Julietta Singh, 'an earnest reflection on how to "mother at the end of the world" which proposes a route through the human disasters of climate catastrophe, capitalism and colonialism and towards a hopeful, collaborative future'. Gavin is compelled by Jackie Kay's biography of Bessie Smith; Helena fell for Maria Stepanova's 'poetic memoir', *In Memory of Memory*; and Kira recommends *Hood Feminism: Notes from the Women White Feminists Forgot* by Mikki Kendall, as it represents 'the feminism that we should all be striving towards'.

The shelves have both the mainstream and the specialist, from independent presses and local authors. It is the kind of space that enables readers to feel as cool as we all know we really are, whatever jibes we may have put up with in our life, for our bookwormery.

I receive a tote bag of treats from the shop, and a parcel of books from an audience member who found the many podcasts that I presented with Josie Long useful in lockdown. I really do have too many books and I should advise people to stop giving me more unsolicited books, but if I tell them that, then they'll stop giving me unsolicited books, and that would never do.

The next morning I have a date at another Edinburgh bookshop, before my trip to Linlithgow.

The Lighthouse Bookshop describes itself as 'a queer-owned and woman led independent community bookshop'. I love visiting shops like this as they remind me to fight against being a tedious middle-aged man grumbling about 'young people nowadays', 'what is it with safe spaces?' and interminably whingeing about not understanding what non-binary means. As you become the older generation, it is very easy to fool yourself that you are still really the younger generation and that anything you don't understand about people under thirty is their fault, not yours.

The shop used to be called Word Power. It was always stocked with fascinating fanzines, newspapers and manifestos, though it could be a little slow when ordering books. I ordered a book by the anarchist historian Howard Zinn there during the Edinburgh Fringe in 2008 and it arrived just before I departed from the Edinburgh Fringe in 2009, but it was worth the wait. How often we hurry to use a company because it promises 'next-day delivery', but then we don't actually read what turns up twenty-four hours on until months later. Next Year Delivery worked perfectly for me.

Mairi runs Lighthouse Books now, and the shelves around me are distracting. I have the usual small pile picked off the shelves to recommend during my talk, including Laura Bates's *Men Who Hate Women* and Liv Strömquist's *Fruit of Knowledge: The Vulva vs the Patriarchy*, a book I happened to buy on my last trip to Edinburgh – 'From Adam and Eve to pussy hats, people have praised, pathologized and politicized vulvas, vaginas, clitorises, and menses… Liv Strömquist calls out how (since time immemorial) genitalia-obsessed men have stigmatized women's bodies.'

After my talk, Mairi gives me a book I've never heard of, *Undrowned: Black Feminist Lessons from Marine Mammals* by Alexis Pauline Gumbs. A younger me would probably have looked at this title and immediately sought to mock it. I am glad I am less of that person now. Mockery is a secure blanket to suck on when you feel uncertain or confronted by culture or theories that are unfamiliar. I start to read it on the train to Linlithgow and it is beautiful and accessible and, as all good writing should, adds to my vocabulary and visible spectrum. The book aims to produce 'not a specific agenda but an unfolding space for wonder and questioning'.

Gumbs's study of marine mammals led to her pondering their use of echolocation: 'I had to focus not on what I could see and discern, but instead on where I was in relationship to the structures and environments that surround me...' It is a book full of love, too. Asking who the book is for, she emphatically declares that it is for *you*: 'Everyone who knows that a world where queer black feminine folks are living their most abundant, expressed, and loving lives is a world where everyone is free.'

Linlithgow

I arrive too late to browse in Linlithgow's Far From the Madding Crowd bookshop and go straight to my venue, the biggest church yet: St Michael's. It is the size of a cathedral. I'm finally allowed into a pulpit, but am warned not to talk too fast, as my words will bounce around amongst the columns and will be gobbled up by gargoyles. There is a designated man in a pew who will hold up a sign saying 'Slow Down' if my pace gets too fast for the architecture and for comprehension.

Sally from Far From the Madding Crowd gives me a Tupperware box containing delicious baked goods. She introduces me at a pace that brings the warning sign into view. I take a deep breath and aim to halve my usual speaking speed. I think I succeed. The vicar in me comes to the fore, and I notice how my turn of phrase about the wonders of the universe elevates itself to sermonizing, with a few heavenly gesticulations.

I don't like talking too slowly, as it gives the negative thoughts in my head more time to interject. When I am in full flow, the ideas trip over each other and, as they fall, they create new thoughts. I feel lost without my chaos. I think this is why I experience an attack of anxiety during the first forty minutes. I don't think it is being in the house of God; although I feel out of sorts inwardly, I think the cold sweat is barely noticeable in the transept light.

Signing books, I am given a copy of a new Hammer fanzine, *Claret*. It is impressively illustrated with sketches of Christopher Lee, Joanna Lumley and Roy Kinnear and has essays on all of Hammer's Dracula movies, including *The Legend of the 7 Golden Vampires*, in which Hammer attempted to boost their flagging franchise by introducing a martial-arts element. I read about *Dracula A.D. 72* on the way back to Edinburgh, and its dynamite duff dialogue: 'You're talking about black mass and that sort of jazz, right?' 'Yes, that sort of jazz.'

Hexham

Nine days to go. I am beginning to regret buying so many books back in Sedbergh. Since then, most of my additions have been small, but the weight of paper builds. It will be death by a thousand pocket books. It is just a three-hour trip today – from Edinburgh Waverley to Hexham.

Hexham was home to my brother-in-law's mother and her incontinent dog. She insisted that it was only incontinent at Christmas, which happened to be the only time of year we ever saw that dog.

I'm met at Hexham station by Peter, a north-east England gig promoter and former UK editor of the Marx Brothers fanzine, *The Freedonia Gazette*. On the way up the hill to Cogito Books he tells me about Sandy Powell, a great old variety act who performed an enchantingly chaotic 'ventriloquism gone wrong' routine, and who was on the bill in the 1920s with the Marx Brothers in London when their comedy was still new and misunderstood.

Cogito Books is situated down a cobbled side-street in Hexham. It was the North of England Bookshop of the Year in 2021. During the lockdowns it kept up communicating with its customers and delivered their books. Claire, who owns Cogito, said they splashed through fords and trundled along farm tracks to make deliveries, often late into the night. The lockdown reasserted in her the belief that traditional bookselling is still in demand.

It is a quiet Wednesday signing. By chance, someone comes in to buy my book for her daughter, quite unaware that I was going to be there. Whether she wants to or not, she is forced to meet me and have her book signed. I do not insist that she has a selfie taken with me. I am also able to play the bookseller again, as a woman mulls over philosophy books for her teenagers. I tell her that Julian Baggini's *The Pig That Wants to Be Eaten* is a wise choice.

In the evening I give a talk in Hexham's Queen's Hall. At the signing afterwards, an audience member shows me a thin shard of the Winchcombe meteorite. You know that you are attracting the right type of audience when they bring meteorite samples to your talks. The conversation leads to a book that will help me comb fields for cosmic detritus, Jon Larsen's *On the Trail of Stardust: The Guide to Finding Micrometeorites: Tools, Techniques, and Identification.*

Barnard Castle

Darlington is one of my favourite stations. It is far from ornate, but it has so many bricks. I started obsessing about tall station walls outside Euston one day, and Darlington station has an impressively tall wall. I can fall into a reverie thinking about all the hands that laid those bricks. I think they remind me of the wall that I used to imagine would be at the end of the universe.

My first event is at McNab's, a bookshop that mixes old and new. It is possibly the most homely-feeling bookshop yet, with sofas and soft chairs. I feel like I should deliver the talk while toasting a crumpet. Fortunately there is a café next door, which delivers tea and cinnamon buns to the audience and the browsers. I have an armchair that makes me look like a grandfather reminiscing on scrumping for apples, or a cult leader about to give instructions on reaching the mothership.

McNab's glass cabinet of treasures includes Don Wilson's *Our Mysterious Spaceship Moon*: 'here you will find the Soviet Artificial Moon Theory in its entirety…' Even though my copy at home is a little tatty, I decide I won't splash out £30 for a slightly more pristine copy. Someone will be overjoyed to find it in the cabinet another day and I shouldn't steal that moment from them.

I nearly leave without any books at all, but that seems an insult to such a warm and hospitable shop, so I buy a copy of William Sargant's *Battle for the Mind*, as I am getting very low on brainwashing books, and Michel Faber's *Under the Skin*.

I have now reached the point (on this tour? in my life?) where an afternoon nap is not out of the question. I lie under the covers in my pub bedroom and allow an afternoon repeat of *Poirot* to lull me to sleep. I have read that twenty minutes is the optimum nap, and that any more means it is like having to wake up and start the whole day again. I am not a morning person, so I don't fancy going through it twice. Fortunately my sleep coincides with the filler bit of Poirot's investigation, and I wake up in time to find out that the murderer killed the dentist to cover up his bigotry.

Gig number ninety-eight is at Barnard Castle's theatre, The Witham. It is sold out, so I take the gig very seriously and buy a tub of performance-enhancing mango cubes from the Co-op. They are close to the food in pill form that I would have learnt more about if I had got my hands on that *Usborne World of the Future*.

The mango works. The whole show is performed on a mango high. I spray words like a wood-chipper. No one would believe that the man they are watching is the sort of man who has a nap during afternoon repeats of *Poirot*.

McNab's come to sell books in the foyer and we are left with only two copies by the end. Unfortunately I notice a charity bookshelf behind the signing table. Discoveries in such places are usually rare, and I couldn't resist Charity Blackstock's *The Woman in the Woods* from the Great Pan series. It has an ominous cover of a painting of a man carrying a woman's body through a dusky autumn wood with the tagline: 'He thought he had got away with it – now each tortured moment brought discovery closer.' What a great author name too: Charity Blackstock. Unsurprisingly, such a wonderfully vivid name is a nom de plume. Charity Blackstock was actually Ursula Torday. *The Woman in the Woods*, originally published as *Miss Fenny*, was nominated for an Edgar Award. Ursula/Charity also won the Romantic Novel of the Year award, writing as Paula Allardyce, for *Witches' Sabbath* in 1961.

Just a few books away is *Dead Men Don't Ski* by Patricia Moyes, another murder mystery with an irresistible and, I believe, irrefutably accurate title, up there with *Dead Men Don't Yodel*, *Dead Men Don't Do the Rumba* and *Dead Men Don't Query the Bill at Pizza Hut*.

Saltburn

Saltburn is in monochrome when I arrive. It is the end of the line. It has the perfect bleakness of an out-of-season holiday destination. I see a Victorian bow window looking out towards the pier and the waves. I want to be sitting in it, writing a labyrinthine novel that will never be completed.

I walk down to the sea. The dog walkers are buttoned up tightly, but there are plenty of them. It is invitingly forbidding. I recite a little *Get Carter* as the waves crash: 'You know, I'd almost forgotten what your eyes looked like. Still the same. Pissholes in the snow.'

I've started reading Ted Lewis's *Jack's Return Home*, although my Pan copy from 1971 is simply called *Carter*. The cover is a promotional shot of Michael Caine as Carter, holding a shotgun on the grey slag beach that will soon be his graveyard. On the back, for thrill-seekers and those lured by pulpy exploitation, there's a naked Geraldine Moffat being handled by an enraged Caine.

I make my way back up the steps from the beach to Book Corner. This is another shop that's smaller than *The Bookseller*'s advised minimum size. The *Guardian* described Book Corner as 'as lovely as Saltburn'. Its carved wooden window is inviting and, for strangers to the town, coming across it is a delightful surprise, situated as it is at the end of a thin row of shops. Jenna's stock is comprehensive, especially given the limited space. She runs a local reading group that she put online during the pandemic, and decided to focus on books from independent publishers as she knew they might be struggling too.

Despite its size, I still manage to find two books I need to buy: Brett Anderson's second volume of his autobiography and *In Search of the Lost Chord: 1967 and the Hippie Idea* by Danny Goldberg.

I also have enough spare time to visit the charity shop, which has an irresistible offer of £2 on all hardbacks, so I buy Douglas Adams's essay collection *The Salmon of Doubt*, Michiko Kakutani's *Ex Libris* and *Adrian Mole: The Wilderness Years* – and these take the tipping point to tottering. I have been away for nine days and I have returned to peak hobo-hoarder. Book Corner has no plumbing, so I go to use the public conveniences by the station. It is a cramped convenience and I discover that I am now too broad with books to fit through the door. I am a Mr Creosote engorged by books, rather than by pâté and frogs' legs in a bucket. Now, on top of spine and knee damage, it seems that a future lies ahead racked by bladder-damage issues, also brought on by book obsession.

Stockton

Just north of Stockton is a Brave New World, or at least some of the industrial landscape that inspired Aldous Huxley. The ICI works built by Sir Alfred Mond influenced Huxley's imagination – an 'ordered universe in the midst of the larger world of planless incoherence'. The powerful Controller of one of Huxley's world states is even given the name Mustapha Mond. Sadly, no local entertainment entrepreneur has yet managed to create the dystopian rollercoaster theme park, Brave New World World.

Drake the Bookshop in Stockton is my 100th bookshop event. This is where it could have finished, but that would have been too lazy. It's a neat new shop in a recently developed area of Stockton, run by two former teachers, Mel and Richard. Journeying through the Lake District, they stopped off in a bookshop café and said to each other, 'This is the sort of thing we could do.' Their son eventually challenged them, 'Well, are you going to do it? You've done nothing but talk about it.' And so they did.

The shop is neatly divided into two halves: one side adult books, the other children's books. A regular pops in to apologize that he will not be able to attend this evening's event, but asks whether he could buy two copies from me now. He enquires if it would be an inconvenience to me, and then we talk about the future of space exploration and our shared dreams of Mars. Mel tells me that it is very typical of this regular to go out of his way to visit and buy books if he is unable to attend an event. He is very happy that Stockton has a good independent bookshop and is determined to support it.

This evening's event is in the ARC Arts Centre, and I am on in Screen 2. I played there before, and it was possibly a mistaken booking. It was Valentine's Day and my show had been marketed as a romantic night of loving punchlines. I was actually touring a show about Charles Darwin and natural selection. Fortunately, evolutionary biology can be adapted into romance, and I made sure to focus on the behaviour of the bonobo ape and then I ended the show by telling the audience some stories about orchid pollination. Hopefully they left that evening feeling fuzzily warm towards their partners.

My hotel skirts on the edge of being dubious, but there is a bolt on the door, so all is fine. I realize that I have run out of space for all the books I have so far, so I pop the *Adrian Mole* and an anthology of short stories from writers across the world where the Gideon Bible would usually go.

Then the zip shuts... just.

Whitley Bay

I am kindly given a lift to Whitley Bay by Dan, who runs the Kielder Observatory. I will take any opportunity to avoid hauling my library on and off public transport. I am more book than human now.

I make it to Whitley Bay a week late. The streets are now clear of shattered glass. The Bound bookshop is already busy with browsers perusing every genre. I hope to be asked for some help at the anthropology or gender-studies section, but obviously I look less like a bookseller today and more like a lost old man. I am placed in the window to sign my books. A dad with toddlers comes in and I sign his book for them. He has hopes of hothousing them towards the Nobel Prize in Physics.

Mystery-crime writer Ann Cleeves is in browsing with friends. She also cut the ribbon when The Bound opened in

2021. Ann encouraged Helen to open the bookshop here and other local authors frequently support the shop, as it has been a while since Whitley Bay had its own bookshop.

My ups and downs are moving faster now and I slump for a while in the stockroom, which, conveniently, is full of sugary pastries and an open tin of Christmas chocolates: 101 shops in, and I never tire of hearing people in bookshops talking about their books of the year. What is perhaps surprising is that it is rare that the same book is mentioned twice. There comes a glint in the eye with each recommendation, the hope that the brief synopsis and description of the emotional reaction will catapult you into the world they have just been immersed in. Then there is the excitement that comes from finding out that you have read it too, and the momentum of delight speeds up. As I wipe doughnut sugar from my lips, we are ecstatic over *Mrs Death Misses Death* and I am convinced that I should read Patricia Lockwood's *No One is Talking About This* and hopeful that I have convinced someone else to read Kerri ni Dochartaigh's *Thin Places*.

Newcastle

It is a short Metro ride from Whitley Bay back to the centre of Newcastle. I am doing an afternoon show at The Stand, perhaps my favourite comedy club in England. It is situated in a large basement room. At the edge are green-and-white tiles that look like they might have once festooned an Edwardian butcher's. I wonder if the space was once a big meat fridge, with corpses dangling where comics now spill out jokes.

On one visit, most of the front row were tattooed and pierced goths. I recited one of my poems that was about the passing of time and, as I reached the conclusion, I could hear the gentle clanging of nose-jewellery as the goths wept. I don't know why I wasn't a goth, as I am very fond of their attitude to life. I once went to a goth club in Edinburgh with a friend, but he wasn't allowed in because he was wearing slippers.

Helen from Forum Books has come to sell my book, which is an interesting challenge as credit-card readers can be obstreperous when underground. She nobly battles with technology not made for the underworld.

Feeling weak and rundown, I make a cold fizzy Lemsip and wonder what sort of show I am capable of. I am very good at erasing the more wearing moments of my ridiculous endeavours, and by the end of this tour I will remember almost all of it as a high old time. Writing this, I had to be reminded by my friend Johnny that I hit at least two points on the tour when I thought I was on the cusp of insanity, but that was wiped away as soon as I made it to the final shop, so you won't have to deal with any of that whining. It is the time in between that gets you, when the negative voices start burbling, but the cracks were always sealed again when I was in the company of booksellers.

Suitably high on Lemsip, I am blessed by a technical hitch when I get to the stage. Fuses blow and I am in darkness and unamplified. I realize that I need to create something out of the unexpected. I am ignited.

I am blessed again with an audience that speak honestly and passionately. We talk of Asperger's, melancholy, mathematics and 'finding your crowd'. I am glad that I am strange enough to be able to encourage other people to voice how strange they feel too.

As I knew I would be finished by 6 p.m., I have decided to travel to Halifax tonight for tomorrow's lunchtime signing.

I thought the train would be quiet and I could retreat into a book. *Wrong!*

I get whiplash again, leaving the company of a kind, thoughtful and happy audience and head out onto rainy, hectic, half-drunk streets. My unease and sense of menace are increased by my fogged-up glasses, so potential threats begin to blur. It is wet and slippery, and the streets are full of people bursting with adrenaline for the night ahead, and a few who have peaked too soon. Two men are being hurled out of the pub, their gesticulation as wild and drunken as their legs.

I make it to platform four. The train is packed with people on the way back from a wild time. I'm guessing there has been some form of sport involved.

I decide the vestibule is the safest place again. Two slightly boozed-up women, still sober but losing their potential for balance, decide on the vestibule too. Every now and again they whisper to each other, and my paranoid mind fears that they are talking about the peculiar mountain goat-man surrounded by carrier bags, with his nose pointed firmly towards his book. 'What even is a Salmon of Doubt?'

Halifax is predominantly quiet, with splashes of drunk choirs and occasional screaming. A few people have fallen out and some are making up, but I just keep my head down and follow the lines to the budget hotel. I am elated when I put the 'Do Not Disturb' sign on my door and fall into bed. Safe again.

I have half a bottle of red, a packet of pistachio cookies and solitude. I spread out my books and read five random pages from each one. Short of focus, I decide not to focus and read erratically, bouncing in and out of books until, exhausted by other people's ideas, I fall asleep with a book across my face.

Halifax

There are only six bookshops left now, and my spine is still holding up in a functional line. People have started to tell me that I must be looking forward to putting my feet up, but that is not how I work. I like to run myself ragged, imagine collapse and then, the moment the finishing line is in sight, I see the potential chasm of terrible boredom looming and work out a new route to busy chaos. Putting my feet up is what happens when I am placed in my wicker coffin.

Eddie Izzard once commented that she found it necessary to work so hard because she knew how lazy she is. She runs all those marathons, learns all those languages, goes on all those tours because she is lazy. She once told me that it was a bad thing for creativity to have an airing cupboard. She had come to my old Peckham flat to play the 1970s board game *Escape from Colditz*, which she played with great competitiveness and won. On seeing that my flat had a small airing cupboard, she voiced suspicion that such a luxury would remove my hunger. Damp towels create epics and operas. There would be no *Ulysses* if James Joyce could have dried himself without frustration.

How right this is, I do not know, but it is true that I only really started making headway in my career when I moved to a basement flat with no heating rail. It eventually flooded with sewage, and not long afterwards I wrote my first book. The flat was now sodden enough for creativity.

The Book Corner is in Piece Hall, a beautiful structure originally built for trading cloth. It is an expansive open-air square, a suitable place for a modern-day Socrates to seat himself. On the right day it is uncannily Mediterranean. At the entrance, a security guard with an apologetic look says that he needs to check my bags. There are a lot of bags. The Book Corner is a long, narrow shop, sister shop to Hebden Bridge's The Book Case, which I visited merely weeks ago, though it also seems an age ago. It was autumn then, and now the season is 'Locking', if you use Kurt Vonnegut's six-season calendar. Autumn is September and October, while November and December are 'Locking', 'when nature shuts everything down'. The two-month season is followed by 'Unlocking', when nature lets life in again, then spring, then summer.

I leave my bags at the shop and stroll around the underpasses, side-streets and edges of the nearby council estates. It is a cold, bright day. I am in one of those moods where even the underpasses are attractive to me. It is an adventure to walk towards the light and then see what sort of blocks of flats are under the sky.

I wander to the Dean Clough gallery, where they have an exhibition by an artist called Alan Gummerson. I knew nothing of his work, but I like what I see – it reminds me of Robert Rauschenberg and Louise Bourgeois (but no giant spiders). I am the only person there, apart from the two women at the reception desk, who are talking about what makes a cyborg. 'Once you've put metal jewellery through your earlobe, you are a cyborg.'

On the journey back, I see a small Oxfam. Of course there are books I need – an anthology of W. B. Yeats (another one), a book on Auschwitz and a memoir of Alice Herz-Sommer who, until she died in 2014, was the oldest survivor of the Holocaust. Her story begins with her memories of Franz Kafka. He brought some wilting flowers to her mother and apologized for them being in too many colours, but he just couldn't decide.

I have some prior knowledge of these three books, but not of *Invisible Residents*. This a non-fiction work about the invisible beings that live under the sea, which may be responsible for phenomena such as UFOs and the Bermuda Triangle.

At forty-nine pence per book, these titles cannot be left on the shelf. They seem so cheap that I overpay, which leads to much confusion and the offer of a free bag, which I reject. My rucksack now has books of so many different sizes in it, and they are so jammed in, that it is resembling an ill-thought-out early work of Cubism – as if Georges Braque designed this season's Mountain Warehouse range.

I only have a rucksack for the security man to check this time, and books pop out like a Cerberus-headed jack-in-the-box. I am still early.

Sarah gives me a cup of tea and a copy of their current bestseller, *The Gallows Pole* by Benjamin Myers, which she thinks I would like. It is hard to be discreet in such a narrow shop, so I lean awkwardly near the table with my books on it and try to advertise my presence as little as possible. Sarah was right: *The Gallows Pole* is very much my thing.

It is a casual signing, with time for conversation. I am happy to hear from a young lad that he reads books very methodically and has made specific space in his diary to read mine.

On the train to Hull, I listen to a man lengthily explain to his girlfriend that he was not flirting with 'that woman' – they just used to go to school together. Eventually they both resort to a noisy silence.

While rummaging through my rucksack, I find a book that I have no memory of – have I been sleep-browsing? Simon Finch's *Golden Voyager* is a decadent romp 'through every cavern of depravity of the ancient world' and mixes 'the degradation of a pleasure slave' with 'the agony of the galleys'. The book falls open on page 72, where Vesuvio is nearing 'his second explosion'. I remember now that I got the book from a railway-station charity bookshelf, but I can't remember which one. It is a mark of collapse and exhaustion if I cannot recall where a book is from.

Hull

Hull, the end of the line, buffeted by the North Sea wind, is another city that is dismissed by many.

The narration inside my head when I passed the Humber Bridge and approached the end of the line at Hull used to be Philip Larkin: 'Here', with its 'cut-price crowd', 'tattoo-shops' and 'grim head-scarfed wives'. Larkin would occasionally be interrupted by my friend Marian. Born and brought up in Hull, she would remind me of the city's tourist slogan – 'It's never dull in Hull', delivered with a nonchalant fatalism.

That soundtrack changed in 2018, when I read Cosey Fanni Tutti's *Art Sex Music*. She lived in a Hull that would have been too tough for a poltroon like me, but I was safe with her as a guide on the page. She writes of wastegrounds and the gangs and parties with cake that ended up in destruction, even when everyone was under ten. When an older girl beat her up at school, her dad told her to go round to her house with a pair of garden shears. He watched from a distance to make sure she did what she was told. When the door opened, she punched the girl 'and screamed at her that if she ever touched me again I'd be back and have her with the garden shears. That's Hull for you.'

Cosey is self-effacing and iconic. Mick Ronson, Bowie's glam accomplice, was too. He was the Hull girls' pin-up when

Cosey was growing up. Long before he was a Spider from Mars, he was the topless man who cut the municipal grass – an Adonis with a lawnmower.

Stevie Smith was born here, and the Humber does indeed seem to be a river that is not for waving in. Over the river is Barton-upon-Humber, where I regularly used to play the Ropewalk Art Centre, the longest Grade 2-listed building in England, where they made the rope for hangmen's nooses.

I arrive in Hull on Sunday afternoon, hungry and with five minutes to spare before the vast supermarket closes. I have no idea if there will be time to get food any other way tonight. I enter the Sunday panic. The store is too vast to navigate, so I impulsively grab what I see.

I return to the hotel with a small cheese-and-onion quiche, tomatoes, Dairylea triangles, 'Japan's favourite noodle pot', some digestives and a packet of pumpkin seeds – all the major food groups.

I am talking at Wrecking Ball Press, originally just a publisher, although it now has a large shop, café and performance space. Wrecking Ball Press publishes of one of my favourite authors, Barney Farmer. He writes some of the darkest comic strips in *Viz*, such as George Bestial and The Drunken Bakers. His comic work is the *Beano*, but as if written by Samuel Beckett and Charles Bukowski. His first poetic novel, *Drunken Baker*, is an unsung classic – a portrayal of a harsh reality with a rhyme scheme. 'What is it if you see a run-over black cat? Lucky or unlucky?' I pick up a copy of his latest, *Park by the River*: more isolation and mounting alienation.

I am onstage with a chair and a radiator. One audience member comments that the radiator seems to be an inanimate double-act partner. Add a pineapple and it might look like I was an adventurous juggler about to burn his fingers in an ill-thought-out routine.

The audience seem quiet, and I am unsure how they are receiving the talk, but I know from experience that this can happen in Hull, and it turns out everything is fine.

It's near the end of the run, event number 104, and I take a risk and agree to go to the pub afterwards. I have been pretty careful about Covid, but maybe I am getting blasé about the pandemic as the year comes to an end. I stop at three pints. I am offered more, but there are still four bookshops to go, and then back to gigs in London.

My hotel window has a good view of a large car park that glistens in the rain and has only one solitary vehicle, right in the middle of it. I contemplate that car's story as I eat my pumpkin seeds. Desolate night-time car parks are almost up there with big walls, in terms of things that I increasingly delight in as I get older. A British touring performer has to be adaptable when it comes to finding beauty and moments of transcendence.

CHAPTER 11

From the End of the Line to the Girl Guides' Hall

Hull to Hungerford

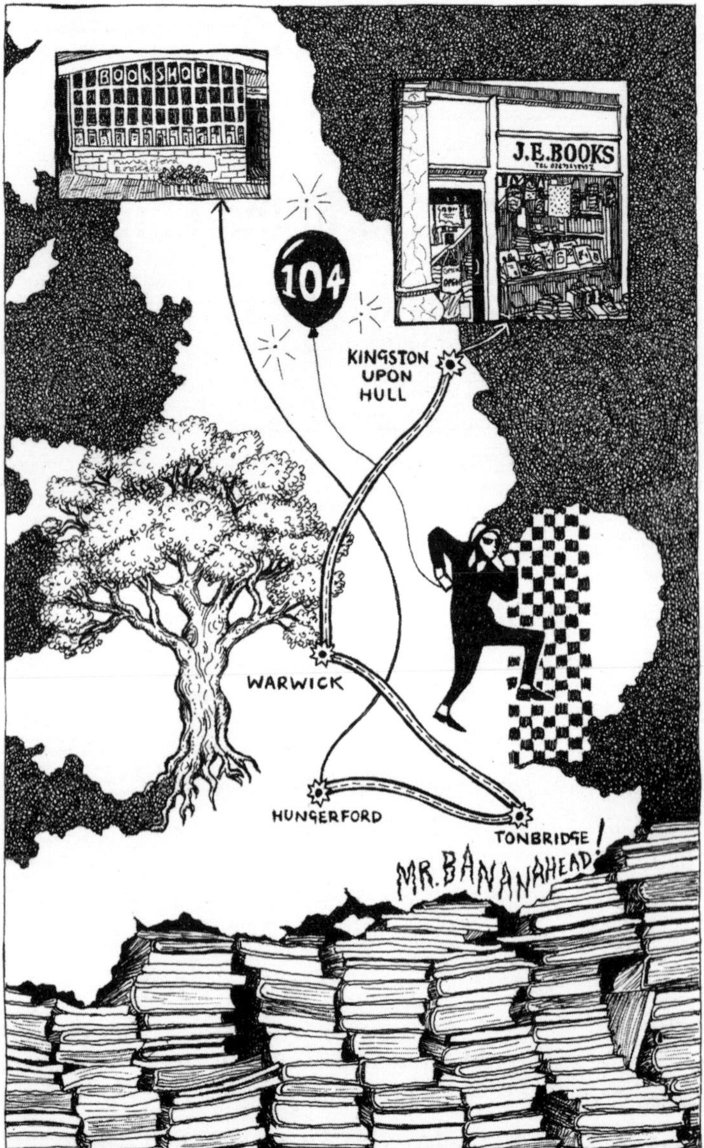
BOOKSHOP
J.E.BOOKS
104
KINGSTON UPON HULL
WARWICK
HUNGERFORD
TONBRIDGE
MR. BANANAHEAD!

The size of the shop has never been of any concern to me on this tour, and Hull's J. E. Books is probably the second-smallest bookshop, after Cardiff's Shelf Life (and that has moved to bigger premises since I was there). Julie is cheery and thoughtful and the perfect person to meet when you are tired on a Monday morning. She has worked in a bookmaker's, the Civil Service and has taught English literature at the University of Hull. Her PhD was about love in the novels of Jeanette Winterson.

The shop is in Hepworth Arcade, where you'll also find Beasley's Clothing, Fanthorpe's HiFi and Dinsdale's Joke Shop: 'We Sell Laughter – Keep Smiling!' The high streets have become increasingly dominated by chains and many city centres have become boringly homogeneous, but this is definitely Hull and I adore it.

Julie has set up a table and chair outside her shop, with a cushion and a hot-water bottle in case I get a cold bottom. There is also a bottle of disinfectant gel and a box of chocolates. This is living.

For a term-time Monday-morning signing, it gets very busy. A couple have popped over from Sheffield with Dean Wilson Film Club badges on their overcoats. A historian of Hull turns up to catalogue the event. There are so many friendly people turning up that we run out of books.

It is clear that Julie is very popular and that a lot of effort has been put in. Throughout the tour it has been a pleasure to see the affection that local people have for their booksellers. Julie's happiness that I have turned up increases my happiness, too. It is the most joyful Monday morning that I can remember in a long time, and it is the final Monday of the 100-bookshop tour.

After eating two soft-centres and disinfecting my hands, the time before my train leaves is tight, but I still speed-browse Julia's wonderful book piles. No room for judgement, so I dig straight in – I need an early 1950s *Penguin Guide to Devon* so that I can monitor the changes in Ilfracombe and Saunton Sands; David Foster Wallace's *The Last Interview*, which will be finished long before *Infinite Jest* is begun again; and Paul Feyerabend's *Against Method*, which I will read until confused – that shouldn't take long.

Almost out of the door, I see a Richard Allen skinhead book, *Skinhead Escapes*, the further adventures of Joe Hawkins and his dubious pals: 'Billy shrugged and settled back against the Cortina's upholstery. At twenty-one he was beyond reach of the do-gooder society's leniency. Beyond the screaming newspapers' leniency. Beyond all leniency!' I may well exchange this for another haircut and beard trim with Wil at Hepcats when I am next in Chippenham, as long as he doesn't get confused between my haircut preference and the book title.

I enjoy the Humber Bridge as I eat more chocolates and sink into a nostalgic world of juvenile delinquency and crime. This is the last of my longer journeys of the tour.

At home, I unpack the books of the last twelve days and it is a pile more than three feet tall.

Warwick

I have three days and three nights of the tour left. These are short jaunts and each day has only one bookshop. I planned them in my head as the safety bookshops – bookshops to ensure I made the 100, if Covid and other plague inconveniences got in the way – but mainly these are bookshops I just couldn't say no to.

Exhaustion has departed now. It hangs over me only when it can be a threat, when it can create the anxiety of failure. Now that I am near the end, I start to wonder if I could have fitted in more bookshops – whether every day with only one bookshop was a lazy day. I have already started to wonder if I can do an eighty-bookshop tour for this book. Maybe you bought this after seeing a wild-eyed and terrifying vision of me in Liskeard or Kirkcaldy.

Warwick is dark and mainly closed when I arrive, and I am reminded of the story from EC Comics' *The Vault of Horror*, *Midnight Mess*, where the murderous man gets his just deserts in a restaurant full of vampires. The square that is home to Warwick Books is effervescent with Christmas lights. Today is the first day that I really start to notice that people are preparing to be festive.

The bookshop is run by Mog and her wife, Pauline, and everyone behind and around the counter has books to recommend to me. I am travelling light and am only gone for seventy-two hours, so there are fewer spinal restrictions when it comes to weighing myself down with books all over again.

The recommendations are the perfect tag-match, with each recommended novel or anthology leading straight on to another necessary and beautiful book. It starts with *A*

Ghost in the Throat by Doireann Ní Ghríofa. Despite the many awards it has won, today is the first time it comes into my field of vision. 'This is a female text and it is a tiny miracle that it even exists, as it does in this moment, lifted to another consciousness by the ordinary wonder of type,' the author asserts.

The paperback edition has four pages of effusive reviews from lauded authors and publications. How I missed the book, I have no idea, save for the fact that we all know there are simply too many magnificent books to keep up to date with. Just as I have come across many titles that are new to me on this journey, so I have also frequently recommended books that I love to booksellers who have never heard of them before. It is this sharing of love that creates so many layers of delight in the shops: 'Oh, if you liked that book, you simply must read this one.' Then there is the suspense after we have taken the risk of declaring love. Will the reader return and apologetically admit that the book 'didn't really do it for me'?

I go to buy a copy of Whitney Chadwick's *The Militant Muse*, which tells the stories of Leonora Carrington, Lee Miller, Dora Maar and more, but I am kindly told that my money is not needed here. I am also given a copy of Delphine de Vigan's novel, *Gratitude*. It is a translation from French, but Pauline is French and she tells me it is excellently done. Will it 'do it for me'?

I fall in love with it the moment I start reading. It is a story of losing language, but also of finding ways to express thanks. It is about what we owe and what we can give back. It is brief and perfect. Another reminder that reading is fuel for empathy, that reading is the best way of trying to walk through other people's minds.

There's not enough space in the shop for my talk, so we are going to some hidden hedged gardens in Hill Close. There's Prosecco, grapes, cheese cubes and cheese straws. *It's a party!*

Meeting people like Mog and Pauline reminds me of how almost instantaneously fond I am of people who work in bookshops. Like librarians, bat-carers, art-gallery volunteers and Quakers, I feel I can trust them instantly.

I am surrounded by paintings of gardens, so I use this as the spur to talk about nature, chimpanzees and the psychological advantages of looking at acorns and oak trees. I overrun (with permission) and then take questions, which include 'Do you meditate?' No. I can't shut this grey matter up. And 'Who would win in a fight – Alan Moore or Morrissey?' Alan Moore would both refuse to fight and at the same time mentally crush Morrissey, so he would be left untouched, but utterly vanquished on the canvas.

At the signing I meet Steven, to whom I sold books when I became the Blooming Buzzing Bookshop online during lock-down. He has presents for me – two books by the artist Hunt Emerson. *You Are Maggie Thatcher* is a 'dole-playing game', co-created by Pat Mills, in which, as the title suggests, you take the role of the Iron Lady and make decisions, much like Steve Jackson's *Fighting Fantasy* role-playing books, but involving manipulating the unemployment figures and privatizing the police force.

The second book is *Lives of the Great Occultists*, a series of comic strips about Jung, Yeats and Austin Osman Spare, taken from the back of the *Fortean Times* magazine. I am very happy with both books.

Tonight I am staying with Horace, bass player with The Specials, one of my favourite bands of all time. Their debut album was the first album I bought with my pocket money.

Horace wrote a book entitled *Ska'd for Life*, which tells the story of The Specials from the initial days up to their first split. It goes from the early and effusive days, supporting The Clash – the commotion, the mania, the international tours – to the eventual falling apart, when every day in the studio felt like a funeral: all that in five years.

Tonbridge

The next morning Horace drops me at Leamington Spa. He is off to unveil a plaque on the studio where the band recorded their masterpiece single, 'Ghost Town', at a time when the band was undergoing demolition from multiple angles. In *Ska'd for Life* Horace writes, 'The whole thing was not a pleasant memory, but the finished result made up for it. It's my favourite Specials song.'

As the train leaves Leamington Spa, John Betjeman waves at me for the last time on this tour. I haven't seen him since Chorleywood:

Beside her the lonely crochet
Lay patiently and unstirred,
But the fingers that would have work'd it
Were dead as the spoken word.

Betjeman's 'Death in Leamington' reminds me of sitting with my father and listening to *Betjeman's Banana Blush*, his poetry put to music, which elevates even further the melancholy nostalgia of his work. I listen to 'A Child Ill', the final piece, most often now. A father worries over his poorly child and remembers watching his own father die. He asks his god to keep this light alight and not take him too.

For many years I have had a morbid habit of thinking of the artefacts that will bring someone back into my mind after they have gone. It is like nostalgia in the present – that moment when you are experiencing something delightful, such as watching your child build a great big sandcastle on a flawless beach, and you feel a nostalgic joy even as it is happening before you. Some days I open a book that I bought with my dad at a book fair, or I hear or read a poem we once heard together, and I think of how these things will bring him back when he is gone, their weight continually increasing.

Even without that morbid poignancy, I am fascinated by how works of poetry and prose change for me over time. Some work becomes more potent and visible with experience, and other work thins and crumbles and can eventually be put in the box of donations. I reread *Slaughterhouse Five*, *The Stranger* and *Wide Sargasso Sea* every few years and each time they become new novels to me. On each revisit, the adolescent soldiers walking through the snow become more tragic, Meursault more noble and guiltless, and Rochester more despicable than before.

I am passing through Sevenoaks on my way to Tonbridge. There are many bookshops that I wish I had the time to visit. One day I hope I will make it to every independent bookshop that will have me. High on my list would be Sevenoaks Bookshop. In 2021 it was named UK Independent Bookshop of the Year, but I don't have time this year and I feel annoyed and ashamed. It seems that the greater the number of bookshops I have managed to reach, the greater the sense of failure that there are those I have not reached.

I look through the Sevenoaks Bookshop window ruefully and with a sense of guilt. They might not have wanted me anyway.

Sash, my radio producer of thirteen years, picks me up from the station so that I can say hello to her fish, her tortoise and her daughter. For no reason we can ascertain, her daughter always calls me Mr Bananahead and then cackles wildly. Is it because my head peels in the sun?

Tonight I am playing my first and last oast-house of the tour for Tonbridge's Mr Books, owned and run by Phil. Mr Books is ramshackle in exactly the way I like a bookshop to be: dishevelled, but still ordered. It has the perfect touch of chaos to surprise you.

I pick up a *Doctor Who Annual* from 1976. It is not in great condition and has marginalia, but it is in such a state that I must buy it. A pristine copy of the *Doctor Who Annual* is not nearly as good as one that has 'Tracy is a silly little nitwit' written at the top of a page, alongside a doodle that I presume represents that nitwit, Tracy.

I also pick up the *Psychics Directory*, the equivalent of the Thomson Local Directory for those who like to tap the shoulders of ghosts. It is forty years old, so I presume many of the clairvoyants have long since left the earthly plain, but that is no reason to think they are no longer working. Looking through the county-by-county breakdown, I see that both Kent and Essex are blessed with a prodigious number of mediums, including Manouka (clairvoyance and Tarot), Kiera (astrology, crystal, Tarot, sand and I Ching, among others) and Fred Clark ('Churches served anywhere').

I also decide that *Precious Remedies Against Satan's Devices* is irresistible. It's a reprint of a book first published in 1652, so I am not sure whether the remedies are still effective against the contemporary Satan, but maybe I'll find out at the Oast Theatre. Phil also gives me a copy of a play by his son Jack Holden (which will go on to be nominated for an Olivier Award) and the memoirs of a mentalist, Frederick Marion.

Phil has many friends. He seems to know everyone in the Oast Theatre bar. Questions from the audience include how to counter arguments about the Earth being flat, and my beliefs about the existence of telepathy, which I do not think I answered satisfactorily (and yes, I did the joke that you are imagining in your head right now).

At the signing, Norma, in her eighties, tells me that she did not want to come to the event. Of all the people who have come over to tell me they were more than reluctant to attend my talk in the last two months, Norma gives the longest and most detailed explanation for her reluctance and why she thought the talk would be rubbish. Fortunately, just when I think there will be no change of tack, she asks if she can buy a book and, furthermore, she doesn't burn it – at least not while I am still there.

The tortoise and the daughter are asleep by the time I get back to Sash's, but the fish are still swimming and debating David Foster Wallace's lecture 'This is Water'. At least that's what I think they are doing, because they go quiet when I come in and swoop for the sunken galleon.

Hungerford

I can see the finishing tape and feel it wrapping itself around my waist.

A dachshund has been added to the Sevenoaks menagerie. These dogs are impossible to look at without feeling a surge of energy and hearing, 'Schnitzel von Krumm / with a very low tum... Muffin McLay / like a bundle of hay'.[1] I have a similar connection when I see a cat in a hat.

On the way to Hungerford I have a spare hour at Reading station, so there's time for one last trip to its Oxfam bookshop. I nearly buy a couple of Slavoj Žižek books, but then I remember that there are still twelve of his books on a shelf that I haven't got round to reading yet, and the argument is wearing thin that if I build up the weight of an author enough, eventually that will propel me into their books.

John, who I last met on my visit to Winchester, has popped by to meet me at Hungerford station with some gifts, but his daughter is about to give birth, so he won't be staying for the final show. He gives me a hard-wearing filtered face-mask with inbuilt technology that should greatly reduce the steaming-up of my glasses. He knows that I have had problems browsing at speed since winter came. There is also a brown-paper package tied up with string, which contains some of his favourites: in this instance, the dark comic-book tales of John Tucker. They are disturbed little nightmares and I like them.

I am staying in the loveliest hotel of the tour and spend a quiet half an hour contemplating the beams in my room, eating complimentary chocolates and then colliding with the beams that I have been contemplating just moments before.

Emma and Alex run the Hungerford Bookshop, which is enormous when compared with J. E. Books, but of average size really. It is densely packed with browsers. We are playing in a local hall, though, and are kept waiting by the Girl Guides, who have tonight's venue for longer than expected. Then we work together to turn what had been a hall showcasing extreme knot-making into a theatre.

After asking permission, I overrun by thirty minutes, and only one young couple walk out, and it seems the rest of the babysitters in Hungerford earn overtime. Foolishly I have mentioned that there is a typo on page 310, so during the signing I am repeatedly asked to correct this typo by hand.

I am well reviewed by *Newbury Today*: 'The performer was in great form... the audience revelled in linguistic detours.' I think *Linguistic Detours* will be the title of the next show I do, or maybe of my first poetry anthology.

And that is that: it ends, not with a bang, but with a complimentary chocolate. We have a wrap-party in the pub – two glasses of Sauvignon blanc and a packet of luxury crisps. Before I leave, Emma gives me a copy of Sosuke Natsukawa's *The Cat Who Saved Books* and Robert Macfarlane's *The Gifts of Reading*.

I have travelled 8,000 miles in the last two months, done 111 events and been to 104 independent bookshops. With some ideas that I have, I curse myself when they become a reality, but this one I don't. It was a good idea – before, during and after.

I worried it would be a flop, but I never ended up with one of those stories of disaster where only two people turned up: one to get out of the rain, and the other under the misapprehension that I was Len Deighton. In a world where mainstream media is often dominated by a few names, the tour reminded me of what I always knew: it is beautiful to grow something among the grassroots.

Would I do it again? You bet I would. Maybe I've just done it again now, before you bought this book?

My new idea is to try and fit events in eighty bookshops into sixteen days. Have I just done that? How do I look? Did you ask me to help you choose something from the Paddington Bear section?

Afterword

Today, I finished writing my book. Today, I am back where it almost began. The final sentence was typed in a marquee in a pub car park in Laugharne. It's six months since the last festival.

There'll be no blackberries now. I was last here in Vonnegut's season of 'Locking', and now I stroll along Dylan's birthday walk during the 'Unlocking'. The rich blossoms tell me there are plenty of berries to come.

I am about to interview Lauren John Joseph about their first novel, *At Certain Points We Touch*. It is a beautiful story of a dead lover remembered. It is filled with literary references. It is a book that is a library, and a book that is an art gallery, as well as all else that it is. We begin by talking about Jackie Collins's *Rock Star*. I think Lauren, like me, is drawn to the highbrow and the lowbrow, but is less interested in what lies between.

I have spent the weekend making shows and watching shows. I punched a melon again, this time in a church.

In that same church, a few hours before, I watched the poet Hollie McNish read her poems about being a teenager, about motherhood and about fingering. There are few churches that will have heard quite so much about fingering, or will have had a melon punched quite so hard under the illumination of a stained-glass window.

The physical effects of the tour finally kicked in a month or so after it all ended, though really they are the physical effects of how I have lived my life for the last thirty years. Now I have occipital neuralgia, which I imagine has been preparing itself since the day I swore at the ground, the sky and the lamp posts in Birmingham. It consists of sharp pains and headaches – the reward for bibliomaniacs who lade themselves like packhorses.

Despite this, I was unable to resist Jeff's bookstall, set up outside the church. Jeff even brought a box of books especially chosen for me, to see which wriggling worms would hook me. I searched the shelves first and picked out a Folio edition of *The Ghost Stories of M. R. James*, with a foreword by the great television writer Nigel Kneale: 'In his real world his closet companions were a cat and her kittens.' In the other, '… terrible bodies began to break out of the trunk, and it was seen that these were covered with greyish hair'. The book also contains a home-made bookmark, an illustration of The Ash Tree that appears to have been cut out of a Sunday supplement.

Then there was *Beckett at Sixty*, a 1967 celebration of his work by many who admired him. And I needed yet another *Encyclopedia of Ghosts and Spirits*, which includes tales of Ralph Richardson's wife spying a Native American ghost in the south of France, and of a beheaded spirit in a farmhouse in Rickmansworth. I also needed a Patricia Highsmith, *The Two Faces of January*, and a self-published guide to higher consciousness, which begins with a Supertramp lyric and ends with Johnny Nash's 'I Can See Clearly Now'.

And then I started to dig into the box:

A collection of British screenplays, which included *Odd Man Out*, perhaps my favourite James Mason movie.

The Technique of Persuasion, a guide to political and commercial persuasion, which at one point is illustrated by an advert highlighting the problems of pig-food supplies.

The Theory of Laughter by V. K. Krishna Menon.

B. Traven's *The Creation of the Sun and The Moon*, an illustrated edition of a Mexican myth of cosmology.

The Necessary Angel by Wallace Stevens – essays on reality and imagination in poetry.

Yesterday's Tomorrows by W. H. G. Armytage, a historical survey of future societies as imagined in literature. Its section titles, such as 'The Barchester of 1980: Early Clerical Science Fiction' and 'Alice: Madonna of the Moderns', captured me.

Another book that stood out was *Thirty Years of Arkham House* 'prepared by' August Derleth: a bibliography of the publishing house that published, among others, Lord Dunsany, Ray Bradbury, Colin Wilson and H. P. Lovecraft. Within you could find the stories behind the publication of such books as 'Beyond the Wall of Sleep', *Fearful Pleasures*, *The Curse of Big* and *Strayers from Sheol.* There was a bookmark – a notelet from a Trust House hotel on which the reader catalogued the books they had and the books they had yet to find.

My final purchase was *A Happier Sex Life*, a heavily illustrated sex manual by Dr Sha Kokken. Don't worry, there is no flesh within; just over 420 photographs of a wooden artist's mannikin in every sexual position imaginable. This is my final gazelle of this safari.

As you can see, the excesses of the book tour and the pain it caused have not cured me of my obsession. I walk up the hill and feel the sharp pain in my occipital nerves, but I am also gleeful – ready to spread out my latest purchases on a table as I drink tea and eat Welsh cakes.

Since I finished the tour, I have often been asked for a favourite bookshop. I am not being diplomatic when I refuse to offer an answer. There is something to savour, discover and enjoy in all of them. Apart from there being slightly less home-made cake than I had imagined, most of my presuppositions came true. I love the company of curious people.

Every bookseller I met was in love with books. What became even more apparent to me was the need for individuality on the high street. No bookshop had exactly the same books on display as another, and no bookshop had the same recommendations to make.

When I began the tour, it was just a passion project, but the more I travelled, the more I wanted to celebrate everything I saw and every conversation I had. I am obviously biased, but in no other shops have I experienced the same delight and passion in what the sellers are doing as I witnessed in all the bookshops I visited.

I am a bibliomaniac.

There is no cure and I am not seeking one.

I will keep falling into books, and I will keep advancing out of them with a jubilant head full of other people and other stories, new skies and strange creatures, and new main courses with asparagus tips and mushrooms, slathered with cream sauce and served with a glass of Schluck.

Notes

Chapter 1

1. blogs.lse.ac.uk/equityDiversityInclusion/2018/05/section-28-three-decades-on-the-legacy-of-a-homophobic-law-through-the-lse-librarys-collections/

Chapter 2

1. lesliesguidinghistory.webs.com/guiding-fiction
2. *Roadside Picnic*, Gollancz SF Masterworks imprint, 2007, Afterword, p.195

Chapter 3

1. Joe Dunthorne, 'At night I would be woken by the screech of stolen cars', *Guardian*, 16 May 2019, www.theguardian.com/books/2019/mar/16/joe-dunthorne-made-in-swansea
2. See Rhian E. Jones, 'Do Miners Read Dickens?', *Tribune* magazine, 16 January 2019, tribunemag.co.uk/2019/01/do-miners-read-dickens
3. Serena Livingstone-Stanley, *Through Darkest Pondelayo*, Chatto & Windus, 1936, p.113
4. Julian Cope, *The Modern Antiquarian*, Thorsons, 1998, p.291

Chapter 4

1. www.cherrygallery.com/journal-posts/henry-kane-woodcut
2. Bertrand Russell, *Wisdom of the West*, Crescent, 1959

3. From the preface of *The Philosophy of Heidegger* by Michael Watts, Cambridge University Press, 2011
4. Mark Fisher, *The Weird and The Eerie*, Repeater Books, 2016, p.13
5. *Fortean Times*, 412, December 2021

Chapter 5

1. Susan Cooper, *Dreams and Wishes: Essays on Writing for Children*, Prentice Hall, 1996
2. fivebooks.com/best-books/london-iain-sinclair/
3. Iain Sinclair, 'Pulped Fictions', *Guardian*, 12 March 2005, www.theguardian.com/film/2005/mar/12/books.featuresreviews

Chapter 6

1. David Seabrook, 'All the Devils Are Here', *Granta*, 15 January 2018
2. Suzannah Ramsdale, '*Insatiable* by Daisy Buchanan' review, *Evening Standard*, 12 February 2021, www.standard.co.uk/culture/books/insatiable-daisy-buchanan-review-b918363.html

Chapter 7

1. D. J. Taylor, 'Entertaining the masses', *New Statesman*, 18 June 2017, www.newstatesman.com/culture/2017/06/entertaining-masses-uses-literacy-60-years
2. Daniel Sheridan, 'Incredible opening weekend success for new Farsley shop', *Yorkshire Evening Post*, 21 June 2021, www.yorkshireeveningpost.co.uk/news/people/incredible-opening-weekend-success-for-new-farsley-shop-truman-books-as-customers-queue-down-street-3281267

Chapter 8

1. Sam Thielman, 'Remembering Jack Chick', *Guardian*, 25 October 2016, www.theguardian.com/books/2016/oct/25/jack-chick-christian-comic-cartoonist-death
2. 'Astronaut Tells of E.S.P. Tests', *New York Times*, 22 June 1971, www.nytimes.com/1971/06/22/archives/astronaut-tells-of-e-s-p-tests.html
3. Newham Bookshop, 'Celebrating 35 years: words of support from our friends', www.newhambooks.co.uk/2014/35years.php
4. Ibid.

Chapter 11

1. From Lynley Dodd, *Hairy Maclary from Donaldson's Dairy*, Mallinson Rendel Publishers, 1983

Thank You...

Let me start the 'thank you' page – I think it is meant to be called the 'acknowledgments' page but it is more than an acknowledgement – with a thank you to the family I married into.

To my in-laws, Peter and Susan, who have always been so generous and have never publicly shown any horror that their daughter married an obsessional fool. Peter has always been ready to offer me lifts to and from some of the more obscurely positioned villages in England, and there has always been a glass of wine when we have returned and frequently a conversation about *Steptoe and Son*, a favourite of both of us.

Susan has not only made me amazing food, cut my hair and taken us all to the seaside, she also insists on buying everyone a copy of my books when they are published to try to get them on South Devon's bestseller chart. Thank you.

And thank you to my dad, for hothousing me to the point of book obsession.

There are many other people to thank, as always.

Thank you...

To Natalie Kay-Thatcher for her magical work in creating the illustrations that I love and I hope you do too.

To all the booksellers who made me feel so welcome.

A special extra thank you to two booksellers I have known for quite a while and who are massive figures of inspiration as booksellers and book lovers: Jeff Towns and Vivian Archer.

To all the people who turned up to the bookshops and festivals I visited.

To all the people who encouraged and gave advice during the writing of this book, especially Lee Randall, Edward Dyson and Johnny Mains.

To Kirsty Doole for her help organizing the tour.

To James Nightingale and Mike Jones for their editing notes.

To Jamie Knight for helping me understand my mind.

To John Ottaway for giving me a face mask that helped me browse bookshops without steamed glasses.

To Mik and Angela for being such a supportive part of any audience.

To Julia Hamer for being another excellent member of the audience and for all the lifts to gigs and shops.

To Elaine Downs for the whisky and encouragement.

To Trent Burton for being a truly dependable human.

To Richard Osman, Ian Rankin and Natalie Haynes for taking the time to read this in proof, meaning the back cover wasn't blank.

To Carl Cooper for his brilliance both as a purchaser of self-inflating lilos and as a radio producer.

To the authors whose books I read but it was too late to put them in this book, including Sarah Polley, Jocelyn Nicole Johnson, Darryl W. Bullock, Laura Bates and Cookie Mueller.

To Penfriend, aka Laura Kidd, for being a great tour companion – you should check out her music.

To Nick Cave, Warren Ellis, John Carpenter, Lanterns on the Lake, Tindersticks, Michael Nyman, Cat Power and Haiku Salut for being the soundtrack as I wrote.

And a special thank you to the person I have forgotten, because I always forget someone. I was thinking about you all along, I can't believe you slipped my mind, I was very tired when I wrote this. You see, I forgot about this page all together when the proof arrived, so it was all a bit hurried and the fact that it was you in particular that I forgot makes you rather special, I think.

And always thank you to Nicki and Archie for being there for love and adventures.

'Last Night'...

Here is the poem that is in the foreword of the paperback edition of my previous book, *The Importance of Being Interested*. I know some of you may have bought the hardback and might feel short-changed that the paperback had something extra, so I thought I would pop the poem back here. It is about looking at the stars and thinking about our curiosities and our connections.

Last night
A ghost collided with my head
It was the light from something dead
Once
It breathed hydrogen into helium
Created a beacon
Projected its life across the sky
And some of its life hit me in the eye
And expanded my mind

In its size
And in its power
It had been grander than I could ever be

It never knew how grand it was
It never knew the awe inspired
It never experienced its existence
There was nothing it was like to be that star
Only something it was like to marvel at that star
Because
The stars cannot wonder about the stars

And Jupiter too
Is without curiosity

Me?
I am small
And I'm fragile
I'm easily felled
By meteorites
or by microbes

But
I'm pugnacious
Inquiring
Tenacious

I can chew on the quandaries of the cosmos

I've got a skull full of questions
And pictures
And problems too

I don't like my anxiety
But it's also my fire

Much that destroys me
Also creates me

There is something it is like to be me
And it is not always satisfactory

My atoms battle
My molecules revolt

Yet still more than
A solo chemical reaction
Or the single line of an equation

Confused
Confusing
Absurd

But flashes
of inspiration

And out of my ashes
May grow apples

Emergent complexity briefly defeats the void

Index of Bookshops

Index of Books